DESIGN REVIEW

CHALLENGING URBAN AESTHETIC CONTROL

DESIGN REVIEW

CHALLENGING URBAN AESTHETIC CONTROL

———— EDITED BY ————

BRENDA CASE SCHEER & WOLFGANG F. E. PREISER

CHAPMAN & HALL

 An International Thomson Publishing Company

New York • Albany • Bonn • Boston • Cincinnati • Detriot • London • Madrid • Melbourne • Mexico City
Pacific Grove • San Francisco • Singapore • Tokyo • Toronto • Washington

First published in 1994 by
Chapman & Hall
One Penn Plaza
New York, NY 10119

Published in Great Britain by
Chapman & Hall
2–6 Boundary Row
London SE1 8HN

Library of Congress Cataloging-in-Publication Data

Scheer, Brenda Case, 1951–
    Design review : challenging urban aesthetic control / Brenda Case Scheer and Wolfgang F.E. Preiser.
      p. cm.
    Includes bibliographical references and index.
    ISBN 0-412-98351-6 : $69.95. — ISBN 0-412-99161-6 : $36.95
    1. Architectural design—Standards.   2. City planning.   I. Preiser, Wolfgang F. E.   II. Title.
    NA2750.S33   1994
    729—dc20
                                                  94-19274
                                                      CIP

British Cataloging-in-Publication Data available

Please send your order for this or any Chapman & Hall book to **Chapman & Hall, 29 West 35th Street, New York, NY 10001, Attn: Customer Service Department.** You may also call our Order Department at 1-212-244-3336 or fax your purchase order to 1-800-248-4724.

For a complete listing of Chapman & Hall's titles, send your requests to **Chapman & Hall, Dept. BC, One Penn Plaza, New York, NY 10119.**

Contents

III   CRITICAL PERSPECTIVES OF DESIGN REVIEW

Foreword

That the topic of design review is somehow troublesome is probably one thing all readers can agree on. Beyond this, however, I suspect prospects of consensus are dim. Differing opinions on the subject likely range from those desiring control to those desiring freedom. Says one camp: our physical and natural environments are going to hell in a hand basket. Says the other: design review boards are only as good as their members; more often than not their interventions produce mediocre architecture.

As a town planner and architect, I am sympathetic to the full range of sentiment. Perhaps a discussion of these two concepts—control and freedom—and their differences would now be useful. But let me instead suggest that both positions share common ground in their goal of producing good design. And this common goal can allow both freedom and control in design to coexist.

The context for discussion of design review changes when review is coupled with regulation. That is: control and freedom can coexist most effectively when incorporated in regulations that precede the act of design, framing the parameters of a given program, rather than conflicting in judgment exerted on the completed design. Review without regulations, or some clearly articulated intention, is nonsensical, painful at least, and often resulting in banal compromise as holistic conceptions submit to fragmented adjustments. Design regulations reduce the unpredictability of the review so that it substantiates articulated intentions rather than punishing the designer.

My biases are clear from the start: I am among those who believe that, despite all signals to the contrary, the physical structure of our environment can be managed, and that controlling it is the key to the amelioration of numerous problems confronting society today. I believe that design can solve a host of problems, and that the design of the physical environment does influence behavior.

Clearly, this is a perspective that encompasses more than one building at a time and demands that each building understand its place in a larger context—the city. Indeed, anyone proposing physical solutions to urban problems is designing or, as may seem more often the case, destroying the city. It seems difficult enough to distinguish design from destruction these days. The question "What is good design?" spawns another: "Is it possible to suggest criteria for good design?"

Allow me to venture a few that, although referring to architecture and cities, might be applied to other design endeavors as well:

1. Good design is an intentional act that provides an elegant solution to a given problem, hopefully without generating any major new problems of its own.
2. Good design often achieves maximum results from minimum means. It is not a cosmetic addition that can be cut from the budget, it is a process of solution.
3. Good design understands the broader parameters of a problem, beyond those given in a program or superficially evident. For instance,

providing affordable housing is not just a matter of building inexpensively or finding a cheap site, it is also a matter of providing different types of housing and integrating them into the community.

4. Good design is critical of assumption and clichés. Widening roads or building new roads does not necessarily solve the traffic problem. However, reorganizing land use and detailing streets to encourage pedestrians, and thus transit use, might do so.

5. Good design has a healthy respect for history, understanding that some experience transcends time and can be beneficially applicable under new circumstances. There are still relevant good reasons, related to infrastructure efficiency, why eighteenth- and nineteenth-century houses and cites were compact and dense.

This reference to history inspires the question of how good design has been produced in the past. The quick answer is that harmony of form was traditionally generated by a consensus among practitioners, and a palette limited by geography and materials and methods. We all have our own favorite Mediterranean village to illustrate this theory.

A closer examination of specific historic cases, however, shows that drawings and verbal regulation together often played a part in making beautiful places. For those reluctant to look abroad for inspiration, our early American heritage offers precedent for building-design controls. Nicholson's design for Williamsburg, for example, required all the houses on the Duke of Gloucester Street to be built six feet behind the front property line, to be fenced, and to "front alike"[1] (Fig. F-1).

But, one can argue, these were simple rules for simple times. In our day and age, are not design rules just another layer of regulation impeding the design process and precluding the affordability of building? Yes, of course they are, and this is due in part to a structure of governance that did not anticipate the metropolis and has produced fragmented and overlapping jurisdictions. But let us not be fainthearted. Let us indulge in

---

1. John W. Reps, *The making of Urban America,* (Princeton, N.J.: Princeton University Press, 1965), pp. 110–11.

Figure F-1. Williamsburg, Va., was founded with regulations establishing the relationship of buildings and fences to the street.

a clear picture of how things should be in order to attack the situation.

To make a beautiful, functional, and sustainable environment, one must have a master plan conceived in three dimensions, and regulations to guide its implementation in two aspects: public space and building surface; in other words, urban design and architecture. The first is typological, the second elemental. If the regulations are limited in their purview to the effect buildings have on the public realm, as in Williamsburg, then control and freedom can coexist in their common goal for good design.

The implied relationship is that control is exerted in the realm of common good while freedom is pursued in the private realm. That is a simple concept, acceptable in most civilized societies, yet somehow confounded in the built environment today. For example, zoning codes regulating building height in feet rather than in stories result in multiple-floor buildings with low ceilings, thus unintentionally restricting private space, while nonprescriptive setback regulations (establishing a minimum distance rather than a build-to-line) virtually abrogate control of the relationship of building to street, and thus the formation of public space.

The work of my firm has been exploring the range and format of design regulations for master plans of new and existing neighborhoods and towns for over ten years. The fundamental prem-

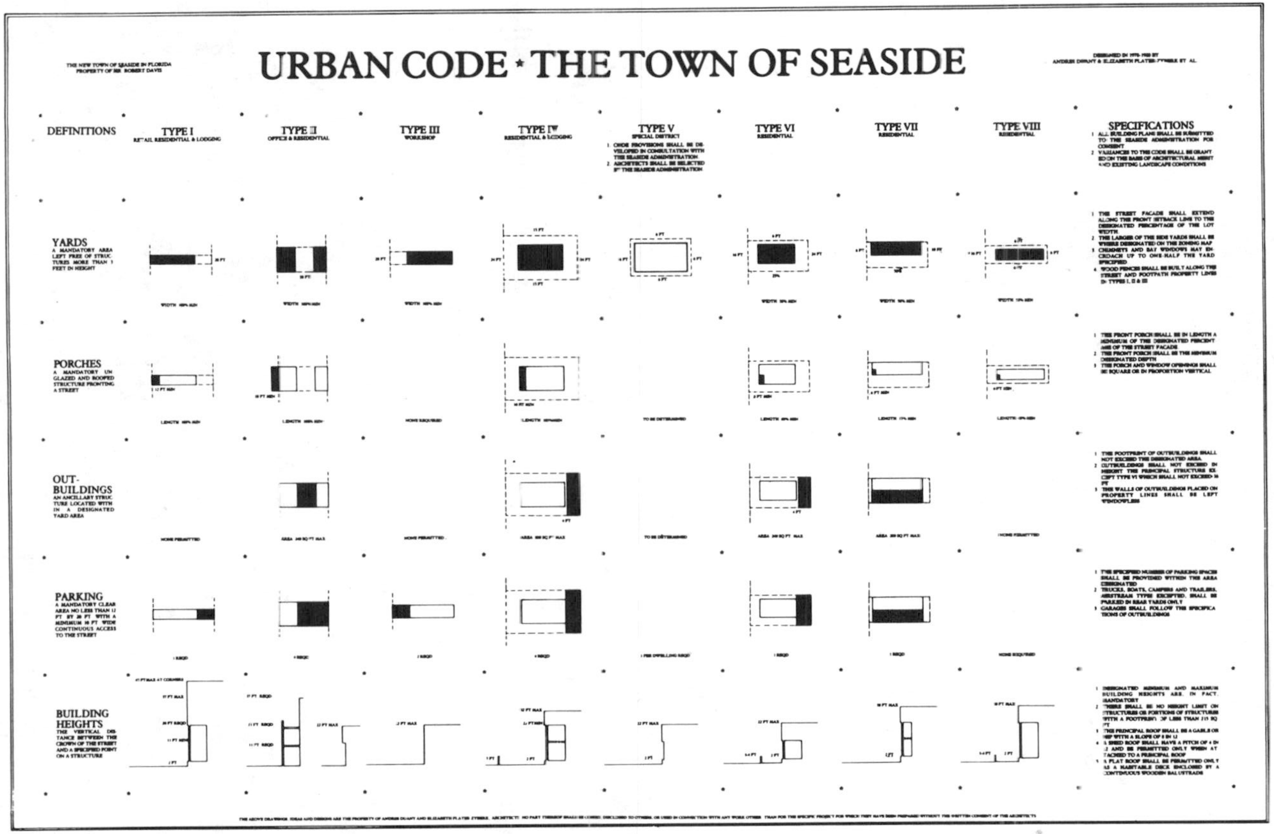

Figure F-2. The Code for Seaside, Fl., regulates private buildings as they affect the public realm.

ZONING CODE

The Seaside Code applies to all privately owned lots. It is a highly distilled document controlling only those aspects of building form which directly affect the public realm.

The Code is graphic rather than written so that the citizen/buyer may understand its provisions without professional assistance and not perceive it as a tiresome obstacle to building.

There are eight building types. Three are for mixed use, three are principally residential and one is for workshops. The Code employs the conventional tools of zoning but with substantial variation. Principal among these are the following:

- Variances are granted on the basis of architectural merit.
- A specified minimum percentage of the lot frontage must be built out in order to maintain the spatial definition of the street.
- Picket fences are mandated for lots with deep front yards for the same reason.
- Porches in residential districts and arcades in commercial districts must be built to a specified percentage of the frontage. This is essential to the southern town as a type, and a positive influence on the social utilization of the street.
- Outbuildings at the rear of lots are encouraged. These create a secondary level of urbanism tied to the footpaths and tend to generate rental apartments dispersed within single family areas. This is intended to prevent the homogeneity of age and income common to modern developments.
- The location of parking within the lots is specified with precision to prevent parking lots from causing discontinuities in the street frontage.
- Minimum and maximum heights of roofs and porches are specified to control the spatial proportion of the public spaces and to determine the degree of formal variation in streets.
- Towers of small footprint (200 sq. ft.) are encouraged everywhere so that even the most landlocked house may reach for a view of the sea.
- Boundaries between zoning types occur at mid-block rather than more conventionally along streets. This allows streets and squares to be perceived as coherent spatial entities with similar building types on all sides.

ise is that a predictable vision of place is the primary goal in town design, and the relationship of individual buildings to the public realm is more important than the style or elemental control of the building. This may seem hard to believe, especially looking at some of the earliest buildings of our best-known coding endeavor—Seaside, Florida—but it's true (Fig. F-2).

The original Seaside code regulated both urban and architectural issues. In subsequent projects, the two arenas have been separated. Seaside's architectural controls were mainly aimed at precluding the worst of 1970s Florida second-home construction, referring to proportions, materials, and methods. And the code prescribes only for private buildings, the urban fabric of the town, not for public monuments. Because the first buildings were stylistically specified, common perception is that the code is stylistically prescriptive. It is not; the Seaside code has room for interpretation, and more recent buildings show that several designers have figured this out.

In subsequent town designs, we have developed the implementation of design with the following tools:

- A master plan based on the principles of compact, mixed-use neighborhood design;
- Specific street and public space designs dimensioned and detailed to encourage pedestrian circulation, illustrated in section;
- Urban codes that establish the allowed building types and their contribution to public space by controlling such aspects as build-to-lines, porches, building heights, location of parking, outbuildings, and fences;
- Architectural codes that direct imagery and character in relation to the geography and history of the place, often limiting materials and methods of construction to those specifically of the region;
- Landscape codes that ensure the compatibility of human planting with the ecosystems of the site, endeavor to enhance degraded natural situations, and support the public-space-making intentions of the master plan.

In all cases the quality of the drawings and the accessible nature of both the drawings and the codes are considered paramount for their ability to elicit admiration and respect and for their effec-

Figure F-3. At Kentlands, the urban regulations require otherwise typical suburban houses to conform to a build-to line, and limit automobile access to private lots from rear alleys.

tiveness in directing implementation (Figs. F-3 through F-6).

A number of neighborhoods are in construction now, testing the method under varying circumstances. Kentlands, a new town in suburban Washington (Fig. F-3), transforms conventional subdivision housing types by their placement in an interconnected street grid of small blocks, and by the relegation of parking to the rear of houses off alleys. And although street dimensions deviate little from suburban public works standards, street design (often terminating vistas with public buildings) and the maintenance of a build-to-line close to the street both spatially define the public realm in a manner outside the contemporary norm.

Windsor, near Vero Beach, Florida in contrast to Kentlands, is more tightly controlled, both urbanistically and architecturally. A limited palette derived from the early Anglo-Hispanic settlements of the Caribbean produces courtyard houses close to narrow streets, with garden walls provid-

Figure F-4.

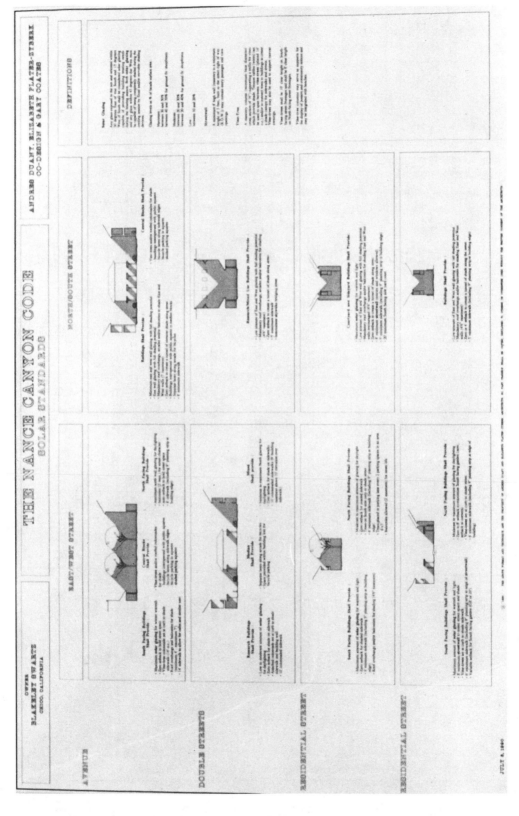

Figure F-5. The Nance Canyon Solar Code specifies shade for public spaces in an arid location that cannot sustain street trees.

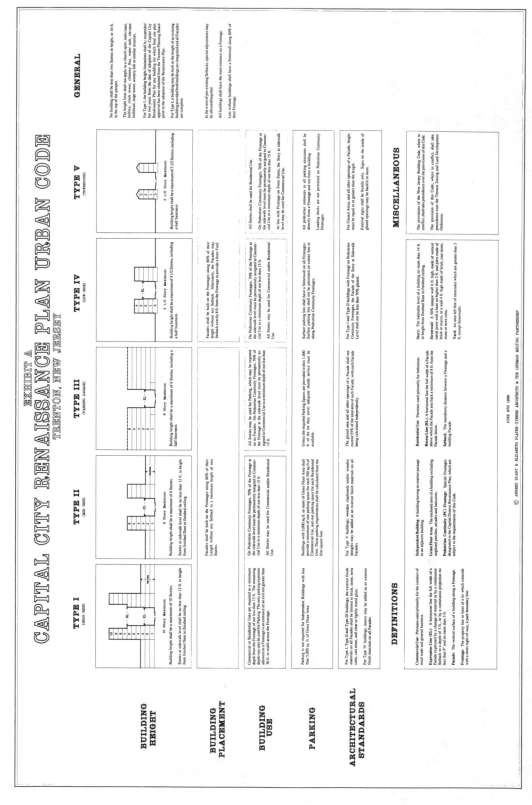

Figure F-6. The Trenton Code's instructions for new buildings reinforce the city's historic street spaces.

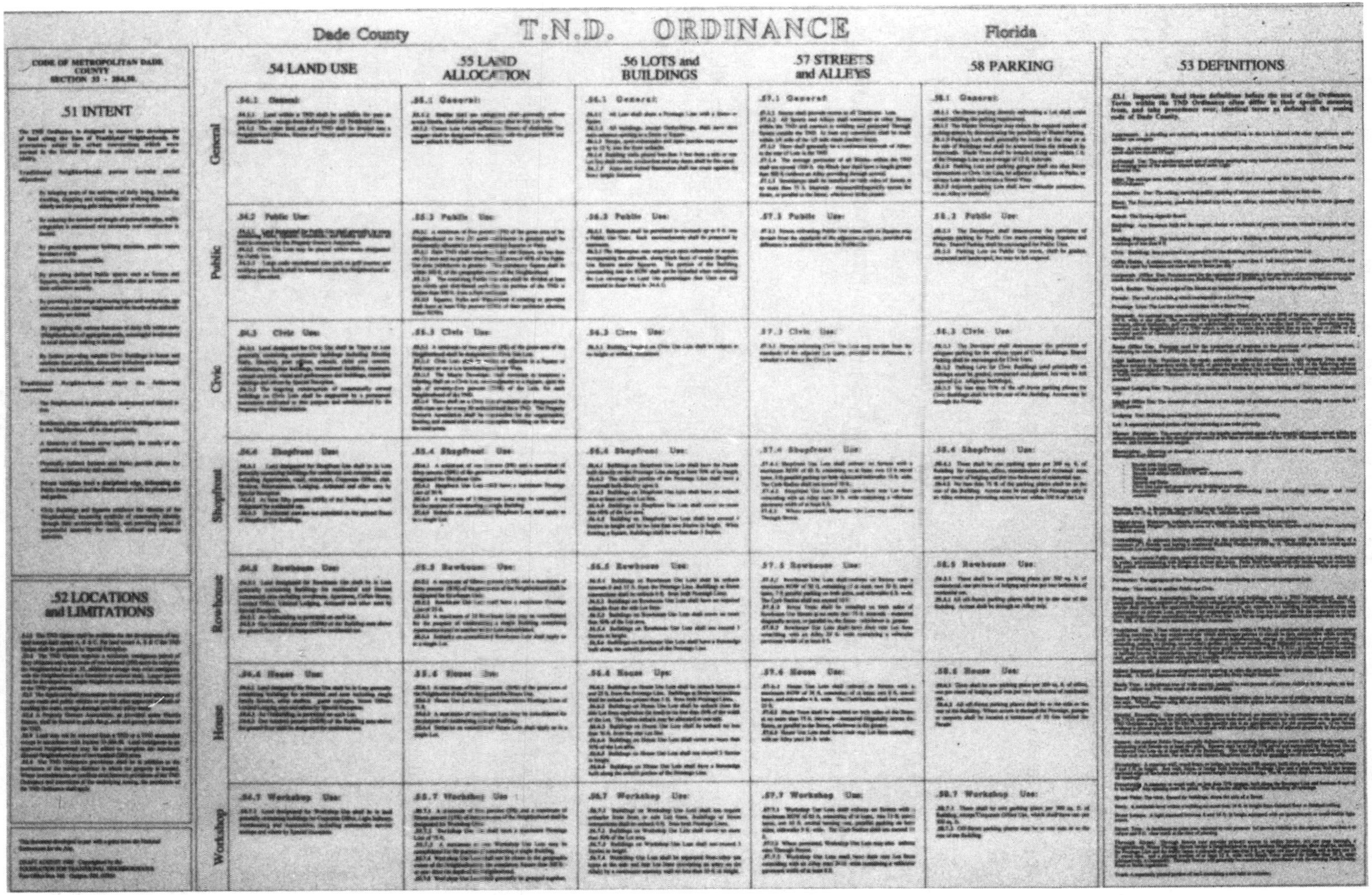

Figure F-7. The Traditional Neighborhood District Code coordinates land use, zoning, street design, and building typology in one ordinance to produce compact, mixed-use, pedestrian-oriented communities.

ing continuity of street edge (Fig. F-4). Other projects, including several in arid locations, have strict environmental design controls mandating neighborhood greens to run north-south, and east-west streets to be narrow and shaded by buildings rather than trees (Fig. F-5).

In existing urban conditions, often perceived to be already overregulated and thus too difficult to redevelop, the codes take on the task of simplifying rules and implementation, while establishing a physically predictable future for the neighborhood. Here, urban design criteria regulating building volume substitute for the abstract formulas of conventional land use and zoning regulations (Fig. F-6). Although these designed and regulated community plans have been generally well received, the American system of fragmented development controls (land use, zoning, public works, and so on), which by default regulate building design, remains entrenched.

The need to reform or at least to provide an alternative to this system led to the invention, several years ago, of the Traditional Neighborhood District Code, which prescribes street space and building type for new development. It is, in effect, an urban design regulation made credible as a zoning ordinance (Fig. F-7). From its basic form the T.N.D. can be tailored to specific local conditions. It is revolutionary in its coordination of land use, zoning, street standards, and building design guidelines in one legal package. This characterization of the T.N.D. might remind readers of another point of likely agreement: the design of buildings is *already* being controlled by zoning ordinances and building codes, and reduced control is unlikely in the near future. If we designers shy away from involving ourselves with the regulation of our work, then we abnegate that control to others, those not visually or aesthetically trained: lawyers, traffic engineers, builders' associations, citizen review boards, and so on. And this brings us back to our fear of the designer losing control over the project.

Let us return to our original agreement that good design is the goal. Then the critical choices to be made are relative to clear and unambiguous intention: are the buildings to be uniform or varied? Are the street spaces to be wide or narrow, episodic or continuous? This is equally applicable whether we are designers seeking the appropriate context for our individual designs or whether we are committed to a social vision of urbanism. Different sizes and styles have appropriate places. Big buildings, big signs, big parking lots are part of the high-speed world of highways. Small buildings and small streets are part of the slow-speed world of the pedestrian. In all options, function, character, and beauty can be found, as long as the intention is appropriately and clearly made. Only thus can we avoid the inefficiency and banality of that lack of commitment that so much of our environment displays today. And through preemptive design regulation, we might even succeed in eschewing the unpredictable process of design review.

In the following pages various aspects and details of design control and review will be discussed, including the legal issues in implementation, and working with communities to create controls. These social, legal, and other issues can be worked out. But in our preoccupation with them, let us not neglect to address the underlying issues that should be the foundation for all these details: the public and professional commitment to design excellence.

Many of us are now aware that public will is key to the making of good cities. But as public support for regulating the environment spreads, a parallel and distressing void seems to be growing in the design professions' willingness to provide the leadership for this groundswell. Practitioners await the initiative of clients, and academics invent theories that remove them ever further from opportunities for engagement.

The condition of our cities demands the activation of our collective professional will. Architects, planners, and landscape architects must come to a common understanding of the importance and role of the public realm, and to a consensus on the intentions of civic design. If we unite in our goal of an environment built by intention, and diminish our public arguments over style to a discourse set within the common context of design excellence, we can be a powerful force in the pursuit of social and cultural change.

Elizabeth Plater-Zyberk
Principal, DPZ Architects, Inc. Miami, FL
Professor, University of Miami

Preface

Design review is not what many people think it is—a panacea to cure the visual aesthetic ills of communities. It has a relatively short history in the United States dating back to about the 1950s. In recent years the use of design review has grown tremendously in communities that hope that it can successfully regulate aesthetic quality. Yet a recent survey of architects found that architects believe design review is a cumbersome, time-consuming tool, ineffective and intrusive in achieving its goals. On the other hand, town planning departments and communities throughout the country seem to embrace the process of design review, as it provides them with an instrumentarium of guidelines, checks and balances that promise to bring order and continuity into what is now perceived to be a chaotic urban landscape. So who is right? The architects, the planners, the policy makers, or—last but not least—the citizens? Are there other countries with successful models of design review that we might follow?

Throughout history there was no formal process of design review, but rather an informal interplay between those who commissioned buildings and urban complexes and the architects/artists/craftsmen who executed them in accordance with the wishes of the sponsors. That cozy relationship between clients/users and those who design and build our buildings does not exist any longer. After all, we are living in an age when decision making is performed by committees and subdele-gation of authority, and therefore, the quality of what results is likely no better than the common denominator of competence of those who participate in the decision making, or regulating, for that matter. This situation is not helped by the fact that we have an ever-increasing specialization of building types, in addition to an ever more complex array of decision makers who meddle in the process of getting buildings done. Thus we have to ask whether design review, as a mechanism for aesthetic improvement, is contributing to even greater differences and chaos in design, or whether it is helping to clarify our vision. That was the question that prompted this book and the International Symposium on Design Review that preceded it. Our goal was to debate practices and critical issues in design review, to define practical approaches as well as theoretical underpinnings. Through case study examples we wanted to share experiences and problems with design review today, so that we could have a better understanding as to where efforts should be concentrated in the future.

INTERNATIONAL SYMPOSIUM ON DESIGN REVIEW

In October 1992 the coeditors of this book convened the International Symposium on Design Review in Cincinnati, which attracted some 120 academicians, practitioners, and public officials from eight countries around the world. They represented an interesting multidisciplinary mix of people ranging from architecture, law, and city planning to historic preservation and landscape architecture. This was the first meeting of its kind to focus on practices and issues in design review. Some of the contributors were very successful in planning new communities, while others were historical preservation consultants or lawyers concerned with the consequences of design review in such cities as Phoenix. The multinational perspective was evident from presentations including countries such as Australia, Germany, Brazil, the United Kingdom, and South Africa. Over the course of two and a half days the pros and cons of various design review mechanisms and guidelines were examined and case studies were presented. The debate that ensued showed that there were more issues than answers and that some critical aspects may never be resolved. One of the greatest benefits of this symposium was the fact that most of the presenters, who had either published or practiced various aspects of design review, were able to meet for the first time. Thus, the symposium afforded them the opportunity to exchange their views in a candid manner. This is also evidenced in the various chapter contributions of this book, which can be seen as a loose-knit matrix covering the topic of design review, thus permitting the reader to get a sense of the difficulty and complexity of the topic at hand.

In preparation for the symposium two surveys were undertaken with the purpose of assessing the experience with design review by architecture practitioners on the one hand, and town planners on the other.

MAJOR ISSUES IN DESIGN REVIEW

The survey of 360 town planning departments (Lightner, 1993) covered a cross section of large, medium-sized, and small communities in the U.S. It not only showed items being reviewed (facades, setbacks, massing, and so on), but also yielded the following major conclusions:

1. *Design Review Guidelines*: There is agreement about the use of certain guidelines, none of which are very profound or constitute what might be thought of as an urban design theory or set of consistent principles. Most of these have to do with hiding or tidying up the most blatant environmental offenses: screening equipment, landscaping parking lots, regularizing signs. Compared to a real urban design idea such as represented by London's Regent Street or Sixtus V's plan for Rome, or even Seaside (distant cousins though they are), these guidelines cannot be said to constitute urban design at all.

2. *Design Context*: Very interesting is the fact that 73 percent of cities with design review use *context* as a principle of good urban design. Here, the ideas that draw greatest agreement actually do begin to suggest a kind of universal idea about good urban design: let new buildings augment the existing pattern wherever possible, let them be quiet and noncontroversial, let them be similar to their neighbors without actually copying them. While planners agree that context is important, they generally limit the meaning of "contextualism" so that it refers to the nearby man-made structures, and not, for example, to other ideas about place such as historic meaning, ecology, or cultural events.

3. *Urban Design*: Design review without an urban design plan is not especially helpful to urban design, per se. Design review, while essentially harmless in its principles of tidying and hiding, does not speak to urban form or design principles such as the importance of streets, major axes, or formal spatial arrangements. In its theme of contextual conformity design review is more influential and perhaps even damaging. But again, it is not concerned with urban design, but a kind of automatic, replicating urban nondesign.

A second survey was undertaken with the purpose of assessing the experience with design review by architecture practitioners. According to the *AIA Memo* (December 1992), the experience of architects with design review is highlighted by the following:

1. *Design Review Results*: Architecture practitioners find that they spend an inordinate amount of time on what they perceive to be

an ineffective process of design review. Major improvements could be made by using better-trained, experienced, and informed design reviewers, and by making the process more objective and less political.

2. *Percentage of Work Undergoing Design Review*: A surprising 54 percent of firms responding indicated that between 50 percent and 100 percent of their projects underwent design review. Thirty percent of the firms indicated that design review *does not* affect the quality of design projects substantially, while less than 23 percent thought design review improved the quality of their projects.

3. *Appropriate Items for Review by Local Government*: Seventy-five percent of the respondents considered the *relationship of projects to public spaces* to be appropriate, followed by relationship to context (58.7 percent).

The coeditors' interest in the topic of design review goes back for a number of years. The Survey of Aesthetic Controls in English Speaking Countries (Preiser and Rohane, 1988) showed a great disparity in the regulation of visual aesthetic concerns, depending on the age, location, and maturity of communities. They ranged from virtually nonexistent visual aesthetic controls in Houston and Amarillo, Texas, to a great number of regulated items in the United Kingdom and its former colonies (which tended to be much more regulated than the United States). Interestingly, in countries like Australia and Canada design review extended way beyond architecture and urban design concerns into such topics as public art, landscaping, and even the color, texture, and materials of building surfaces and finishes. In the United States the aesthetic controls were primarily concerned with building heights, setbacks, signage, and compatibility with predominant uses in a given area. Also, the survey showed the cultural relativity that governs design review, and the varying degrees of willingness of communities to regulate aesthetic quality.

Coeditor Brenda Case Scheer was awarded a Loeb Fellowship at Harvard University in 1989–90, and she served as a design review officer for the City of Boston for the preceding four years. These experiences afforded her time to reflect on issues involved in the use and abuse of design review, and the lessons learned are contained in the introduction to this book. The chapters that follow have been grouped into three major sections: Issues in Design Review, Design Review in Practice, and Critical Perspectives of Design Review.

Acknowledgements

We wish to thank all those who contributed to this project. This project and book was supported in part by a grant from the National Endowment for the Arts, a federal agency. We would also like to express our appreciation for the generous assistance from the Architectural Foundation of Cincinnati, Keren-Or, Inc., the Goethe Institut, Cincinnati, and The Graham Foundation for Advanced Studies in the Fine Arts. The assistance of Hillary Ellison for logistical support in organizing the Symposium is gratefully acknowledged.

Wolfgang F. E. Preiser
University of Cincinnati

REFERENCES

Gordon, D. E. 1992. "Survey: Guiding Light or Backseat Driver?" *AIA Memo*. December p. 28.

Lightner, B. C. 1993. "Survey of Design Review Practices." *Planning Advisory Service Memo*. American Planning Association, January.

Preiser, W. F. E., and K. P. Rohane. 1988, "Survey of Aesthetic Controls in English-Speaking Countries." In *The Visual Quality of the Environment: Theory, Research and Application*, ed. J. L. Nasar. Cambridge, U.K.: Cambridge University Press.

Contributors

David J. Baab, a consultant in urban planning and design, is based in Irvine California, and specializes in preparing design guidelines and engaging in private design review for developers and community associations.

Ellen Beasley is a historic preservation consultant based in Houston. The dual issues of new construction in historic areas and the public review process have been primary interests since the mid-1970s. She has been the recipient of a Rome Prize at the American Academy in Rome and a Loeb Fellowship at the Harvard Graduate School of Design.

Brian W. Blaesser, Esq., is a partner in the Chicago-based law firm of Rudnick & Wolfe, concentrating in the areas of real estate development, land-use law, and litigation. Mr. Blaesser serves as counsel to private clients and local governments around the country on development and discretionary review issues. He is coeditor and author of the book *Land Use and the Constitution* and writes frequently on land-use controls and urban design issues.

John Delafons is a Professor at Reading University, England. From 1982 to 1989 he was Deputy Secretary in the U.K. Department of the Environment, where he was responsible for British Planning and Urban Policy. In 1989–90 he was on a Leverhulme traveling Fellowship and was a Re-search Associate at the Institute for Urban and Regional Development, University of California, Berkeley.

Bernard J. Frieden is Ford Professor of Urban Development at M.I.T., where he is also Associate Dean of Architecture and Planning. His most recent book, written with Lynne Sagalyn, is *Downtown, Inc.: How America Rebuilds Cities,* a study of public-private relations in city development.

Grady Gammage, Jr., is a land-use attorney practicing in Phoenix with Gammage & Burnham. He is an adjunct faculty member at the Colleges of Law and Architecture at Arizona State, and was the first chair of the Phoenix Design Review Standards Committee.

Linda N. Groat is Associate Professor of Architecture at the University of Michigan in Ann Arbor. She is the author of numerous publications on contemporary architectural theory, meaning in architecture, contextualism, and recently on diversity and gender issues in architectural education. She previously taught at the University of Wisconsin-Milwaukee, served as Associate Dean at Michigan, and has lectured widely in both the U.S. and Europe.

Gary Hack is Professor of Urban Design at M.I.T. and a practicing urban designer and planner. He has prepared urban design plans for dozens of cities in the U.S. and abroad, and has written design guidelines for several communities to aid in their design review efforts. He is coauthor of *Site Planning* (third edition) and *Lessons from Urban Experience*.

Michael Hough is a professor at the Faculty of Environmental Studies, York University, and is the founding partner of the landscape architectual firm of Hough Stansbury Woodland in Toronto. He is the author of *Out of Place: Restoring Identity to the Regional Landscape* and *City Form and Natural Process*. He is a fellow and past president of the Canadian Society of Landscape Architects, and a member of the Canadian Institute of Planners and of the American Society of Landscape Architects.

Mark L. Hinshaw is an urban design consultant based in Bellevue, Washington. For eight years, he was the principal urban designer for the City of Bellevue. He has served as the chair of the Urban Design and Preservation Division of the American Planning Association. He is a licensed architect as well as a city planner.

Richard Tseng-yu Lai is Professor of Planning at Arizona State University, where he teaches urban design and planning law. A graduate of Princeton in architecture and of the University of Pennsylvania in city planning, Lai has also taught at the University of Texas at Austin and practiced in Colorado, where he served on the Aspen City Planning Commission. His publications include the book *Law in Urban Design and Planning: The Invisible Web*.

Hayden May, an architect and regional planner, is Professor of Architecture and Dean of the School of Fine Arts at Miami University, Oxford, Ohio. He is a member of the City of Cincinnati Urban Design Review Board.

Harry Moul is a city planner with the City of Santa Fe, New Mexico. He directed the Santa Fe Historic Structure and Townscape Study.

Elizabeth Plater-Zyberk is an architect and town planner who teaches at the University of Miami and practices in partnership with Andres Duany, Miami, FL. Their firm has produced numerous neighborhood and town designs relying on design regulation for implementation. Their work has been widely published, including in the catalog *Towns and Town Making Principles*.

Patrick J. Pouler is an architect practicing in Santa Barbara, California. In addition to completing a masters degree in urban design, he has done postgraduate research in history and theory at the Architectural Association in London and urban design in Rome with Colin Rowe. He has previously taught at the University of Notre Dame and is presently writing a book on the connection between architectural theory and philosophy in *quattrocento* Italy.

Wolfgang F. E. Preiser is a Professor of Architecture at the University of Cincinnati School of Architecture and Interior Design. He has published extensively and carried out design research over the past twenty years, in addition to a consulting practice. His research has focused on post-occupancy evaluation and aesthetic appraisal, as well as guidance systems for the visually impaired. His most recent book is *Professional Practice in Facility Programming*.

John Punter is a Senior Lecturer in the School of Planning Studies at the University of Reading, U.K. He has written extensively on urban aesthetics and design control in the UK, including detailed studies of Reading, Bristol, and London. He is currently researching the design content of British development plans.

Anthony D. Radford is Professor of Architecture at the University of Adelaide, Australia. He holds qualifications in architecture, planning, and computer-aided design and is author or coauthor of several books on design theory and and computer-aided design.

Francis P. Russell is Assistant Director of the Center for Urban Design and an Adjunct Assistant Professor at the College of Design, Architecture, Art, and Planning, University of Cincinnati.

Witold Rybczynski is Professor of Architecture at McGill University, Montreal. He has written on architecture for the *Atlantic,* the *New York Times,* and the *New York Review of Books,* and is the author of several books, including *Home,* the bestseller *The Most Beautiful House in the World,* and most recently, *Looking Around: A Journey Through Architecture.*

Brenda Case Scheer, (formerly Lightner) an architect and urban designer, is Assistant Professor of Urban Planning and Design at the University of Cincinnati College of Design, Architecture, Art and Planning. She was formerly Director of Urban Design at the City of Boston Public Facilities Department, and was a Loeb Fellow in Environmental Studies at Harvard Graduate School of Design.

Allan D. Wallis is Assistant Professor of Public Policy at the Graduate School of Public Affairs, University of Colorado, Denver, where he serves as director of the program in local government. He is also Director of Research for the National Civic League. His publications include the book *Wheel Estate: The Rise and Decline of Mobile Homes.*

DESIGN REVIEW

CHALLENGING URBAN AESTHETIC CONTROL

Introduction:
The Debate on Design Review

Brenda Case Scheer

University of Cincinnati

Design review is a procedure, like zoning, used by cities and towns to control the aesthetics and design of development projects. Although it is a new phenomena, its adoption by local jurisdictions is growing at a rate that compares to the rapid adoption of zoning in the 1930s. I have recently completed a national survey of planning agencies in more than 370 cities and towns on the topic of their design review processes; 83 percent of the towns surveyed had some form of design review. My initial assumption—that aesthetic review was primarily restricted to historic districts and structures—proved to be wrong. Only twelve respondents reserved design review exclusively for historic structures or districts. Therefore, we can conclude that more than 85 percent of the cities and towns in this country have moved into the arena of design review of ordinary, nonhistoric development projects. This widespread use of design review is also new: 60 percent of the respondents with design review have introduced it in the last twelve years, 10 percent in the last two years.

Design review is a difficult and controversial process that needs thoroughgoing, professional criticism before it is introduced on a wide scale. In spite of the astonishing growth in the adoption of design review, it was very difficult to find resources about design review that did not paint it as a rosy picture, a no-lose situation for planners, designers, and citizens alike. Most planners who answered my survey are satisfied with their design review process; the fine-tuning of guidelines was seen as the major improvement to be made, along with giving themselves more autonomy to make design decisions without board interference. Citizens appear in favor, too, as they survey the results of thirty years of McDonald wastelands and trash spec office buildings, and hope that design review will solve the problem. Architects, on the other hand, are curmudgeons of a sort, being somewhat reluctant to throw themselves in with design review fans. Architects who responded to our survey for the AIA consider design review "petty, meddling, and useless" (25 percent), while the largest group said they thought it was a "good concept, but had serious flaws" (50 percent) (Gordon, 1992).

I first became interested in design review while working as a planner in Boston, reviewing and approving storefront and housing projects. Like many planner/architects, I was unhappy with the simpleminded projects being proposed, and like many, I insisted on many changes I felt were more responsive to the context of the city of Boston. As the leader of my staff, I went through a series of developmental phases in my attitude toward the review process. We went from a casual review process, which mitigated the really mediocre and senseless proposals, to a more stringent one, which received criticism for arbitrariness. We wrote guidelines to counter this, but the guidelines were loose, general ones. Review became more formalized, more legitimate. Guidelines hardened and became more objective. Projects submitted were more and more acceptable and similar, responding to the developing sense of what my staff would accept. After several years, I was pleased: my view of the urban landscape became solidified and official. One day, I sat in on a review of a simple housing project. One of the staff reviewers, a recent architecture-school grad, was marking up a set of drawings—drawings that in the early days of mediocrity would have been greeted with pleasure because of their sense of context and originality. He didn't like the porch or the roof detail. The size of the brick was "wrong." A bulb clicked in my head, and the long process of questioning began. It endures today.

Why is this hard look at design review so important? In the end, what does it really matter if we decide to control signs and parking lot landscaping, and require bricks instead of clapboard? Why does it matter if we take the ultimate decisions about the design of buildings away from architects and their clients and put it in the hands of planners, lay persons, and design review boards? Why should anyone but a few primadonna architects care about this regulation of aesthetics in the city? The massive adoption of design review seems like a tidal wave of approval of this method of development control. Why should we not happily lay aside the admittedly flawed way in which cities and buildings have been built in recent years and respond to the new call, indeed a new recognition of the importance of physical design in the environment?

Using the data from the planners' survey and from the architects' survey, I would like to outline the scope of design review, who is doing it, what they hope to get out of it, and the broad areas of controversy that are being defined across this country and abroad.

DEFINITION

Design Review refers to the process by which private and public development proposals receive independent criticism under the sponsorship of the local government unit, whether through informal or formalized processes. It is distinguished from traditional (Euclidean) zoning and subdivision controls in that it deals with urban design,

architecture, or visual impacts. Thus it includes historic preservation review, but not, in my definition, the control exercised by owners' associations or tenant groups, because these are nongovernmental and at least theoretically voluntary. It also does not include review of a project by an owner or owner's agent. Some processes and guidelines are written into the zoning, while some are separate. A few design review processes are advisory, but the vast majority (82 percent) are mandatory and legislated.

Design review also includes, as a subset, processes that use design guidelines. Of cities with design review, well over a quarter have no written guidelines. On the other hand, almost 40 percent have guidelines with "teeth," that is, guidelines that are legally binding, as opposed to recommendations. Guidelines have no prevailing form and there is no model code of any kind that cities use. Most planners assemble their guidelines from several sources or create their own.

Who reviews design? Special design review boards are present in only 36 percent of places with design review, but in most of these the design review board is the most significant influence on the outcome of the design review. In cities without design review boards, planners—with and without design backgrounds—are very likely to be the strongest influence on the outcome of the design review process. Significantly, citizen review is actually rare, occurring in only 17 percent of places with design review, and according to planners it is very weak in influence, although it seems to be particularly controversial from the perspective of both planners and architects. Elected officials are said to participate in about 28 percent of reviews, a surprisingly high percentage, although their design opinions carry little weight compared to design review boards, planners, or zoning commissioners.

AREAS OF CONTROVERSY

Many cities and towns sent me their design guidelines and zoning codes that deal with aesthetic issues. In studying these, one gets a better sense of what planners and their governments are hoping to achieve by instituting design review. Some goals are quite lofty, while others, perhaps not surprisingly, are more economic. Common goals include:

- improving the quality of life
- preserving and enhancing a unique place
- maintaining or upgrading the "vitality" of a place (e.g., commercial viability)
- making a comfortable and safe environment for pedestrians
- improving/protecting property values
- making change more acceptable
- making new development compatible or unified

Two other, less frequently mentioned goals include offering community input to development decisions and creating order. Interestingly, improving the design of buildings or making a beautiful city or urban space are rarely goals.

It is hard to imagine how anyone who cares about the urban environment at all could disagree with most of these goals. Yet it seems that rarely does a planner, a citizen, or, especially, an architect engage in the topic of design review without relating their experiences of woe with a design review process. Is this the result of the raw youthfulness of design review (although design control has a long and colorful history inside and outside this country), or are there are conceptual flaws in the idea, flaws that challenge our fundamental ideas about power, beauty, justice, and freedom?

THE EASY PROBLEMS

A whole set of problems in the design review process relates to the fact that it is a new regulatory system. When most people talk about flaws in design review, they do not mention power, beauty, justice, or freedom. Instead, they seem to be closely attuned to the mechanical difficulties that plague any form of regulation: it takes too much time, the people who review projects are unqualified, it costs too much, connected people get away with anything, it is too political, the presentation requirements are too stringent, the process needs streamlining, there are too many agencies involved. While acknowledging these issues in the following questions, I do not consider them overwhelming arguments against design review. It is not that they are trivial, but rather that reasonably obvious solutions exist for them.

Design review is time-consuming and expensive. Architects considered delay to be the number two

flaw of design review. (The lack of design experience on the part of the reviewers was cited as the primary flaw.) It definitely costs more in professional fees. Of those surveyed, 66 percent estimated the billable hours spent on design review to be between 5 and 25 percent of their time, a percentage that compares to the time spent on the entire preliminary project design. For the client, design review undoubtedly adds to the time and cost of projects. It adds also to the cost of government, which must administer and maintain design review apparatus in the form of additional professional staff, commissions, printed materials, law suits, hearings, and appeals. The additional cost and time factors make the process of design review even more subject to the vagaries of politics: when times are good, government can easily demand design review; when times are bad, clients can no longer afford design review and government is forced to back down or risk losing important construction projects.

Design review is easy to manipulate through persuasion, pretty pictures, and politics. Since the judgment of design is essentially discretionary and inherently difficult, it is easy to use mumbo jumbo design talk to defend decisions that are patently political (pro or con of the proposal) without letting the public become much the wiser. The political tendency is to use aesthetic control for growth control or growth encouragement, or to extract non-design-related amenities in exchange for design approval. Whatever aesthetic purpose design review may have enjoyed becomes completely subordinate to the political agenda in many cases.

Design review is being performed by overworked and inexperienced staff. In the law, the wisest, most experienced minds are called to judge. In design review, the primary reviewer is far more likely to be a junior planner without design background or an unregistered young designer or a politically appointed committee with the common thread of community prestige and power, not design expertise. The staff planners around the country that I have met are tremendously sincere individuals—they study the issues, they work hard to make the right decisions, and they receive very little guidance or reward. They are often overwhelmed by the complexity of design review, which may be the leading cause in their cry for more and better design guidelines—number one reform of design review suggested by planners who review projects.

Design review is not an efficient mechanism for improving the quality of the built environment. Aside from being time-consuming and unpredictable, design review is usually limited to certain areas, uses, or sizes of projects. It is also limited, obviously, to projects undergoing change or being newly built. It is no more effective than zoning in controlling bulk, height, and setbacks (very important elements of urban design), but it is more complicated than zoning and more subject to interpretation and politics.

THE ENDEMIC PROBLEMS

I have separately organized the following sets of issues because they are much more difficult to describe fully and much more difficult to solve than the regulatory issues just mentioned. As it turns out, solving one of them tends to cause problems in another; for example, making design less arbitrary and more objective tends to reduce the flexibility to make discretionary decisions that are a necessary element of aesthetic judgment. I have organized them around the robust topics of power, freedom, justice, and aesthetics.

POWER

The fundamental question in the issue of power is *who*—who will judge, whose tastes will matter, whose interest it is to control the aesthetic quality of building. Many people will support design review because they believe that it gives more community control over the environment, and in many places this is true. But does the design of urban buildings belong with the community (or rather, with their appointed planning representatives) or with those who are design experts involved in solving the whole building problem?

Design review is the only field where lay people are allowed to rule over professionals directly in their area of expertise. It seems odd that we as a society believe that the improvement of the

physical environment can be made by reducing the influence of architects and increasing the influence of planners and lay appointees. As architects, we owe it to ourselves to investigate how this serious turn of events could occur. Are we being punished for the International Style? Are we seen as lackeys of the greedy developer/builder? Have we lost the respect of the public because we no longer even try to defend design excellence in the face of our clients' wishes? Are we elitist, making projects that only we can understand and interpret, without attempting to educate the public or even reach them?

It is certain that architects—even those who approve of design review—are not willing to concede the judgment of design to lay persons. The number one complaint of architects who answered our survey about design review was that the reviewers were not trained professionals with experience in designing buildings. Nearly every architect who cited an exemplary process told us that what made it exemplary was the presence of knowledgeable professionals as reviewers. Even the city agency planners complained about non-professional members of review boards. Yet about 45 percent of all bodies that review project design do not have even one architect on them. Architects whose experience includes being reviewed by other designers are more likely to accept design review, although they may still find it flawed. Several respondents lamented the lay reviewer by making comparisons to the medical world, where lay people are not permitted to interfere with professional judgments.

Design review is grounded in personal—not public—interest. Perhaps if there were a public realm, a sense of public responsibility about the environment that led to design review, it would be a more legitimate process. For now, it is recognizably not so, being more a matter of protecting private property values from "offending" intrusions rather than a genuine public-spirited activity (Scheer, 1992). When neighbors attend design review sessions, their comments, even the fact of their attendance and concern, have more to do with the desire to stop someone from diminishing the view from their deck or to halt the construction of nearby apartment buildings or shopping centers in their backyards. While these are legitimate concerns, they are essentially self-centered, not public-centered. Neighbors seem to realize the inappropriateness of these self-centered concerns, because their rhetoric (as is the developers' rhetoric) is often disguised as protection of the public. Design review is not even effective at controlling the self-centered problems, since the common result of review will be to put a pretty face on a problem. Zoning is a much more powerful and direct tool to address size, layout, and location, but public officials are reluctant to use it. Reducing the size of buildings or denying a permit does not add to the tax base or economic growth, and promoters of large projects tend to wield political influence.

Community aesthetic input seems most legitimate when a public space is involved. Cincinnati's Fountain Square, for instance, is the subject of much public debate about its design, most of it by people who have a special interest, but at least some of which is genuine concern for the symbolic and public role that it has.

FREEDOM

The flip side of power is freedom. Unlike some of our international friends, the spirit of community in this country is heavily tempered by the belief in the rights of the individual. A somewhat related concept is the view that diversity—taken to mean varying perspectives, disagreements, and cultural differences—is a strength for society as a whole because it provides a wealth of criticism and a wealth of ideas; it keeps us on our toes. The constitution protects the individual from the power of the collective government and allows diversity to flourish.

Is design review a violation of the First Amendment right to free speech? The answer rests on two questions: 1) Are architecture and other aspects of the built environment protected as "speech" under the Constitution? 2) Can the government show a legitimate interest that would override the protection afforded to free speech in this case?

Although there has not been a single case adjudicated on the specific issue of architecture and the First Amendment, nearly all legal theorists who have approached the subject of aesthetic legislation (notably Williams, 1977; Poole, 1987; and Costonis, 1982) agree that architecture should be given the protection afforded to most forms of symbolic expression. In what appears to be an interesting contradiction, recent cases have expanded First Amendment protection to cover "commercial speech" such as signs and advertising, while at the same time the courts have overwhelmingly supported the increase in the regulation of design.

Although the language of the First Amendment clearly states that "Congress shall make no law . . . abridging the freedom of speech," there are many examples of laws in the United States that make it clear that freedom of speech is limited. In order to demonstrate that regulations and practices of design review are legitimate limits on First Amendment freedoms, theoretically a jurisdiction would need to define a very powerful public interest that would override the protection of free speech. It seems to be a dubious assertion to claim that the public interest is substantially served by controlling the color of awnings or requiring that the style of new construction is compatible with existing buildings. Even if the test requiring a substantial government interest could be met, this interest would have to be justified on grounds (such as public safety) that are not related to the suppression of an aesthetic message. In other words, it seems clear that laws that have *as their primary purpose* the curtailing of aesthetic styles or the forcing of homogeneity (known in architecture as "contextuality") would encounter First Amendment problems.

Why is it important to concern ourselves with extending First Amendment protection to architectural expression? One of the purposes of the First Amendment is to protect the individual from the tyranny of the majority. Design review/design guidelines can be interpreted as a way of reinforcing a majority-based, cultural bias (i.e., historic, white, European), especially in a threateningly pluralistic architectural and cultural milieu. Architecture is like a beacon, announcing the status, values, and interests of its culture, its creators, and its inhabitants. It could even be argued that the communicative message of architecture is so strong that community leaders, in formulating design controls, are simply trying to control the message. By excluding certain culturally diverse architectural languages or unpopular architectural styles, we literally suppress a minority viewpoint and prevent those with a different, even critical, perspective from speaking. Thus, if you believe that cosmetic imitation of quaint New England village architecture is false and damaging to the authenticity of place, you will have to express that belief without utilizing its clearest language—architecture. And the places where meaningful architecture of this nature can be explored are rapidly vanishing.

Design review rewards ordinary performance and discourages extraordinary performance. This has come to be known as the "Dolby" effect: a review that cuts out the highs and the lows. Although it is frequently cited as a criticism, it is probably less an issue in actual practice, where the excellent, exceptional, and original design proposed is often treated pretty well by design reviewers, especially if it has a famous name attached to it, and especially if the reviewers have design training. A much more severe and insidious problem, however, is related to the *perception* of the Dolby effect, because designers begin to anticipate the range of acceptability of particular reviewers and therefore rarely waste their clients' time proposing something original or exceptional. Of 170 architects who answered our survey, 80 percent felt that their proposals were somewhat or strongly influenced by what they knew to be acceptable to a design reviewer. Some architects told us that they liked design review because it brought them more clients who were impressed with their ability to design projects that were approved quickly. When contemplating the cumulative effects of this tendency, one can only become fearful of the mediocre quality of the future built environment and the dwindling potential for truly exceptional works of architecture in this era.

JUSTICE

Some forms of design review are more "fair" than others; that is, the rules are clearer and more objective, and the procedures are more predictable and consistent. It may seem that we should move this issue to the "solvable" side of the column, chalking it up to the newness of design review and the lack of tested processes and model codes. We must keep in mind, however, that the purpose of design review is not to deliver justice to the players, but to deliver the best environment to the community. Because of the slippery nature of design, a less discretionary system may not be flexible enough to work. Therefore, the explicit and fair process might not be the one that delivers the best environment. What follows is a discussion of the issues associated with justice and protection of the individual in design review, but the foregoing problem must be recalled while we explore these.

Design review is arbitrary and vague. Many areas of the law fall under discretionary ruling; in fact, making orderly discretionary decisions is one of the purposes of the judicial system. A police officer exercises discretion in deciding whether to arrest someone or to let him or her go. When discretion gets out of hand, as it sometimes does with the police, more rules and guidelines are laid down to limit the discretion. Just as there is no way to create a rule for every possible circumstance confronting a police officer, there is no way to formalize every rule about design. Therefore, even the most "objective" design review rests on discretionary judgment. This is not the essential legal objection, however; it is the degree to which these discretionary judgments are made consistent and nonarbitrary. Guidelines help, but many cities don't have them. Even where guidelines exist they may essentially be so vague as to be meaningless, insisting, for example, on "appropriate" scale or "compatible" design. Architects consistently complain of being sabotaged by the unclear language and unclear intentions of design review, which are clarified only in response to a specific proposal.

Design review judgments are not limited. Even though a city or town has guidelines, it is rare that the process of design review is limited to reviewing those items covered by guidelines; rather, the guidelines seem to represent a starting point, after which reviewers are relatively free to critique whatever they like or dislike about a project. There are limits, but these seem to be drawn from a political consensus about how much power the reviewers may exert. In exemplary cases, design reviewers must not only adhere to guidelines explicitly and exclusively, but must also publish "findings" that denote their critique in terms of the guidelines. Unfortunately, the more common pattern is a free-for-all, where the designer can be attacked for any aesthetic or conceptual decision and where no official document records the review criticisms.

Design review lacks due process. Because there are usually no limitations on what is reviewed, the designer is completely at the mercy of the power of the design reviewer. Also, not all projects are subject to the same process, since the process varies from district to district and use to use, and the rules and players are constantly changing. (Only 15 percent of cities have review systems unchanged from ten years ago). In 12 percent of cities with design review, there is no appeal of a review body's decision. Most important, in most places design review is inconsistently applied. There are no provisions for referencing earlier cases or building up case law that would limit the interpretation of guidelines or judgments and help designers and interested citizens defend their positions.

Design review is difficult to protest on aesthetic grounds. Consider the situation of an architect whose building design is severely altered, but not rejected, by the design review body. He or she has two choices: carry out the alterations and get on with the project (a choice the client is likely to support), or mount a time-consuming and expensive battle, possibly losing the client and commission in the process, as well as alienating a design board that he or she must seek approvals from on a regular basis. Thus the very nature of the design review process (use of "negotiated" coercion, discretionary decisions, uneven power balance, client/architect relationship) works against an individual's ability or desire to try fight for aesthetic decisions.

Unless the developer finds it to his or her monetary advantage, cases about design seldom go to court. So, while "takings" suits, which claim monetary loss, are common, First Amendment suits, which claim the right of free expression, are nonexistent. Coupled with the tendency of clients to select architects on the basis of their ability to make it through the review process quickly, this may mean that an architect with thoughtfulness, creativity, and design integrity is at a distinct disadvantage.

AESTHETICS

A design reviewer must sooner or later face up to the difficulty of deciding what is right and what is wrong—in short, making judgments. Some have argued that design review could simply drop the idea of beauty, since it is too slippery to be legal, and focus instead on "shared values" (Costonis, 1987). It is clear that many aesthetic decisions are complicated by moral issues (values). We may share the belief, for example, that mowed lawns are attractive. On the other hand, mowed lawns are not good for the environment because they waste water and provide no shelter for wildlife. Fields of native flowers may not only be better in a moral sense, they may also be more beautiful. Or maybe not. It doesn't help that these decisions are relative: one man's wildflowers are another's weed-infested lawn. Clapboard is fine here, but not there. Sign variety is desired in Times Square but not on Court House Square.

Design review is reluctant to acknowledge that there are no rules to create beauty. Architecture today admits of no reference standards, no abstract principles, no Vitruvius or Alberti or even Le Corbusier to dictate propriety. Principles of good design, for today's architects, are not universal, they are specific to the problem, place-centered, expressive of time and culture. For design review to be consistent, on the other hand, principles must be harder, broader, and applicable across the board. The arbitrariness of design review is a result of the vagueness of the guidelines, and the inconsistency of the reviewers. The solution would seem to be more definite guidelines, more precise rules, judgment tempered by precedent. The tendency to increase the use of objective criteria bears this out. Yet, design excellence is not easily defined by hard and fast principles, beauty is not subject to objective criteria, and judgments are necessarily dependent on the aesthetic response to singular, particular case, not a universal abstraction. A conflict between the increasing objectivity of design review guidelines and the very nature of postmodern architectural thought is inevitable.

Planners do not seem to be morally conflicted at the prospect of making objective criteria, on the other hand. Perhaps it is because that, in the haste to draw up the sign control standards or the contextual controls, the important questions are not being asked. What makes cities well designed or beautiful? Is making a consistent place the same as making a beautiful place? What makes a building beautiful? How can design review take heed of the different aesthetic responses that people have? Shall design review view the building as an object, to be judged without reference to its meaning or use or place in the larger site? Shall design review judge only those surficial aspects of the object such as its style or roof line? Shall design review only concern itself with contextual issues like massing and relationship to streets and leave meaning or style alone? How about the message, the "reading" of buildings—if it contributes to our response to the building, can design review judge that as well? If so, how can we give the architect freedom in his or her message? What can possibly serve as criteria for judgment? No wonder it is such a tangle.

Design review principles tend to be abstract and universal, not specific, site-related, or meaningful at the community scale. Along with the use of contextual patterns as design criteria, my survey of cities and towns with design review revealed nearly universal agreement on the elements that cities review: more than 90 percent of towns review fences and buffers, parking lot location and landscaping, signs, screening of loading and trash areas and building height. The most popular principles of good design (with at least 80 percent of towns agreeing) are directed at simple "neatening up": screening service areas and parking lots, reducing the variety of signs, and re-creation and infill of contextual patterns. Ironically, the least popular or irrelevant, according to the planners who responded, were design principles that were more specifically related to building or urban design, for example, encouraging public spaces or fountains. Other than those popular principles directed at the desire to protect a site's natural environment (a finding that slightly conflicts with the same planners' admission that they do not actually review a project's response to microclimate, sunlight and shadows, the generation of pollution, or energy efficiency), most design principles being used extensively are extremely general and transferable from one place to another.

Design review encourages mimicry and the dilution of the authenticity of place. By simplifying

the rules and guidelines, by encouraging banal imitations, by denying originality, creativity, or expression of difference in any way, the design review system eventually creates a dead place, a place without surprises or exigencies of site or landmarks. Fortunately, the city's uncontrollable actors (age, events, change) take care of such superficiality by immediately beginning the process of writing over it. And fortunately, too, design review is usually not that effective and is almost never followed up after a few years. But what of places that are effectively controlled for long periods of time? Some cities that have had stringent design review for long periods of time, like Cincinnati's Mariemont (a village designed in 1921 by John Nolen), *are* completely distinct from their chaotic neighbors, with a serenity that comes only from common architectural expression and homogeneity. It could be argued that the excellent quality of Nolen's original plan for Mariemont, the coherent and consistent design of the original buildings, and the respect that this excellence inspired affected later developments a great deal more than design controls. Nevertheless, Mariemont has resisted any changes through the offices of its design review. It is as if it is frozen in time. The price of its homogeneity is fossilization, an inability to change. In a tiny town like Mariemont, the price is undoubtedly worth it. But in a large, functioning, active city, such rigidity could be functionally, morally, and socially dangerous.

Outside of special historic enclaves like Charleston, South Carolina, Mariemont, or Boston's Beacon Hill, places where extreme control is exerted have a kinship to theme park perfection or urban fantasy and embody an idea that life lived here is not real life fraught with pain and crisis and emotion, but an artificial one, cleaned up, predictable, and safe. Thus the overcontrolled Battery Park City is the Disneyland equivalent of the real New York City—it is New York rendered as a stage set, spooky and unreal because it lacks the scars of urbanity: street people, vendors, handmade signs, noise, and bustle (Russell, 1992). Sadly, this approach also dilutes the meaning of the real space it imitates or preserves under glass. The camouflage of new "old" buildings resulting from misguided design review makes the authentic old buildings disappear and lose their importance and distinction.

Design review is the poor cousin of urban design. Ideally, design review's purpose would be to serve an urban design vision specifically developed for the place, the processes, and the public will. Of particular focus and importance for urban design implementation would be the public investment: streets, sidewalks, plazas, public buildings, maintenance, parks. The use of design review for this purpose is relatively rare. Of the cities with design review, less than 30 percent subject public buildings to design review and only 18 percent review public infrastructure for design.

Design review generally focuses on single projects rather than working from an urban design program. Sometimes, design review is performed in a vacuum, operating as a studio jury, with judgments and critiques rendered on the design merits of a single project, without a concern for its place in the urban ensemble or its impacts on the nature of the surrounding space. (Of those with design review, 26 percent did not use contextualism in any way as a measure of design quality). More often, design review is concerned with surroundings, specifically *context,* which has become confused in meaning. At the current time, planners who use context as a measure agree strongly that contextual fit means that 1) new buildings and rehabs should respect the existing pattern of buildings and open space and 2) designs that diverge widely from surroundings should not be allowed. This, too, though, is not an urban design vision or plan, but simply the recognition of an old, existing pattern that in itself constitutes too simplistic a view of urban design. Planners without physical training may find this a comforting and completely adequate approach to urban design but it negates the importance of design to create urban space, connect places, and create hierarchy and meaning. If urban design were simply a matter of the repetition of old patterns, as it seems the practice of design review encourages, there would be no opportunity to design new responses to changes in the world, like the advent of computer communication and shopping malls.

Design review is a superficial process. Of course, the effectiveness of design review is limited by the type of things commonly reviewed: reviewers focus on the surface materials and stylistic quality of buildings, and the concealment of cars and signs. Yet the condition of the urban and suburban environment has more to do with the use of ubiquitous and automobile-scaled typologies—K-Marts, strip shopping centers, gas stations, fast food chains, endless pavement—than whether K-Mart has blue metal or yellow awnings or even tasteful signs. Landscaping, buffers, fences, and other popular design review requests are just ways of hiding the problem, not fixing it. The catalog of what is wrong with our environment is a catalog of what is wrong with our culture: the dominance of greed and consumption, the lack of public responsibility (on the part of both residents and builders), the deterioration of the inner city from poverty and crime, the energy waste of sprawl and automobile domination, and the abuse of the natural setting. To the extent that government is allowed to think that it is "taking care" of the "ugly" problem through the institution of design review, it is a diversion of political energy from environmental, social, and economic problems and, not insignificantly, it is a diversion from the necessity for genuine urban design. The design review solution is in fact reminiscent of the urban renewal solution: urban renewal postulated that the solution to the unsightly and deteriorating inner city was to tear it down and build new office buildings and high-priced housing.

THE INVITATION TO DEBATE

This is a fascinating topic because there seems to be no end to the ideas it engages: power, freedom, beauty, morality, justice, discretion, authenticity. After five years of being a design reviewer and five years subsequently of studying it, I have come to be concerned with the enormous effect that widespread design review will have on our cities and towns, on the profession of architecture, and on the public life and freedom of our people. These effects are just beginning to be clear. What is not clear is whether design review, a very powerful government tool, can be directed in a way that answers some of the problems addressed above. Its potential for abuse and misdirection is very strong, and even dangerous. Yet the need for thoughtful urban design in American places grows every day, and the rights of the community to expect local government to contribute to good design is unquestionable. Our task in this book is to bring the best minds to bear on the issue of design review, to look at how it is done in various places, and to offer criticism that will bring about better ways of bringing good design to the urban setting.

REFERENCES

Costonis, John. 1982. "Law and Aesthetic Regulation: A Critique and a Reformation of the Dilemma." *Michigan Law Review* 80:355.

Costonis, John. 1989. *Icons and Aliens: Law, Aesthetics and Environmental Change*. Champaign: University of Illinois.

Gordon, Doug. 1992. "Guiding Light or Backseat Driver" *AIA Memo,* December, p. 28.

Poole, Samuel, III. 1987. "Architectural Appearance Review Regulations and the First Amendment: The Good, the Bad and the Consensus Ugly." *Urban Lawyer* 19 (Winter): 287–344.

Russell, Francis. 1992. "Battery Park City: An American Dream of Urbanism." *Proceedings of the International Symposium on Design Review,* p. 315.

Scheer, David. 1992. "Design Performance." *Proceedings of the International Symposium on Design Review,* p. 133.

Williams, Stephen. 1977. "Subjectivity, Expression, and Privacy: Problems of Aesthetic Regulation." *Minnesota Law Review* 62 (November): 1–58.

I
Issues in Design Review

1
Democracy and Design

John Delafons

University of Reading United Kingdom

Is the design of buildings a fit subject for public policy in a democracy? If so, how is that policy to be articulated and how is it to be implemented? This chapter explores these questions from the perspective of both American and British experience, chiefly the former since the methods used in the U.S. are generally more explicit than those used in Britain, although the objectives or motives may be similar. The first part considers the concept of design control. The second part suggests a possible typology, with examples of various approaches to design control. The dilemma is to find a means of control that will serve the public interest while affording the creative designer the freedom of expression that he or she requires. The third part concludes with suggestions for a broader-based approach.

CONCEPT

By "design" in this context we refer to a building's aesthetic concept as expressed through its external appearance and in relation to its context or setting. Hence the term *aesthetic control* is more apt and specific than *design control*, since the latter can extend also to the structural, safety, and internal aspects of building design.

In neither Britain nor America is the concept of aesthetic (or design) control defined very clearly in legal or legislative terms. Indeed it seems to have proved somewhat elusive. In Britain the index to Butterworth's 760-page *Planning Law Handbook* contains no references to "design," aesthetic control, or external appearance. Nor does the index to the 728 pages of Professor Malcolm Grant's standard work *Urban Planning Law*. This is very odd because the British Town and County Planning Acts have contained (at least since the Planning Ace 1932) explicit provisions enabling the local planning authority to control "the size, height, design and external appearance of buildings."

Despite these uncertainties or ambiguities there can be no doubt that the general public *expects* the planning system to exercise effective control over the aesthetic aspect of new development. Indeed it is apparent that the public supports the planning system largely because of the protection that it is believed to afford to neighborhood amenity and private property values. Even the late professor F. A. Hayek, despite his general antipathy to bureaucratic controls, recognised in his hugely influential *The Constitution of Liberty* the need for regulation of development by means of town planning to ameliorate what he called "neighbourhood effects" (Hayek 1960).

Later in this chapter we will consider the various methods of control that are used in America, but essentially it is a *regulatory* system in which the requirements for each type of development are specified in written regulations or ordinances, whereas the British system is essentially *discretionary* in the sense that most applications for planning permission are considered individually on their merits, having regard to the local plan. This distinction was certainly very marked at the time when I wrote my book *Land-Use Controls in the USA* (Delafons, 1969). But in the thirty years since then there has been a growing convergence: in America the traditional regulatory system has been retained but many local ordinances now allow for exceptions through zoning amendments and variations, and for special districts or other devices that depend on the local authority's discretion. On the other hand, in Britain the tendency has been away from untrammeled discretionary control and toward both greater detail in local plans and greater reliance on those plans in deciding individual planning applications: it is now a "plan-led" system. In both countries, despite the pervasive influence of design factors in planning control, the proper extent of aesthetic objectives within the system has not been subject to very searching judicial examination. In Britain there is explicit authority for control of "design" in national legislation, although successive governments since 1932 have discouraged local authorities from exercising it in too detailed and intrusive a manner. The courts have in general confined their attention to whether the reasons for the decision on a particular case were reasonable and adequately expressed.

In America, the relevance of amenity considerations was recognized by the Supreme Court in the first major test of zoning control that came before it in 1926. This was the classic case of *Village of Euclid v. Ambler Reality Co.* It was not until 1954, however, that the Supreme Court had occasion to consider explicitly whether such a zoning ordinance could also deal with matters of design and aesthetic considerations. In the case of *Berman v. Parker* the Supreme Court observed: "The concept of the public welfare is broad and inclusive. . . . The values it represents are spiritual as well as physical, aesthetic as well as monetary. It is within the power of the legislature to determine that the community should be beautiful as well as healthy."

In reaching this conclusion the Supreme Court was echoing (no doubt unconsciously) the words of John Burns nearly fifty years earlier in introducing Britain's first planning legislation—the Housing and Town Planning Act 1909—when he told Parliament that its purpose was "to secure the home healthy, the house beautiful, the town pleasant and the suburb salubrious."

In general, both the Supreme Court and subordinate courts have accepted that traditional zoning powers can be used to impose aesthetic controls in the interests of protecting property values, conserving and enhancing neighborhood character, and promoting a tourist economy by preserving natural beauty and historic areas. There is a strong democratic flavor in this approach, since it rests chiefly on the popular concern for safeguarding property interests and local amenity rather than on any more refined aesthetic sensibility.

Before turning to typology, I must point out that there is nothing new about the attempt to regulate or control the pattern of urban development. There are ample historical precedents in both the U.S. and the U.K., and in many other countries and older civilizations. Those who want to explore that aspect could not do better than read the late Spiro Kostof's splendidly illustrated book *The City Shaped* and its companion volume, *The City Assembled* (Kostof, 1991 and 1992). I take one example from Kostof, concerning the Italian city of Siena. It has often been cited as the classic example of how a city can grow into beauty organically and without the need for controls or regulations. But consider this from the City Council's resolution of 1346, which declared: "It redounds to the beauty of the city of Siena and to the satisfaction of almost all people of the same city that any edifices that are to be made anew anywhere along the public thoroughfares . . . proceed in line with the existing buildings, and one building not stand out beyond another, but that they shall be disposed and arranged equally so as to be of the greatest beauty for the city."

TYPOLOGY

The history and practice of American planning demonstrate a variety of methods of exercising aesthetic control. A possible typology is suggested:

- the regulatory mode
- the stylistic imperative

- the proprietorial injunction
- the authoritative intervention
- the competitive alternative
- the design guidelines

The Regulatory Mode

Zoning—the traditional and universal method of land-use control in the U.S.—imposes its own aesthetic on the American scene. It is still the main determinant of urban form.

The Chicago Zoning Ordinance provides a comprehensive example. It was first adopted in 1923, and the current version was the subject of a major revision about ten years ago. While exhibiting all the features of big-city zoning, it also incorporates a variety of newer techniques, including performance indicators for noise and other environmental factors. It lists twenty-two types of use-district and seventy-one categories of floor-area ratio. The bulk of the ordinance consists of precise dimensional prescription and is based on the conventional health, safety, and welfare criteria that ostensibly provided the legitimacy for traditional zoning control, and which in turn served to restrain unbridled and unneighborly speculative development.

There is no reference in these parts of the Chicago Ordinance to aesthetic objectives or design criteria beyond the dimensional requirements. But it is certainly a "code," and those who advocate the adoption of design codes must ponder whether this form of control is what they want and whether it would achieve the results they desire.

Such dimensional controls may be seen to serve an aesthetic purpose but they give no other indication of design objectives or criteria. The traditional regulatory mode, with its reliance on purely dimensional requirements, imposes its own conformity while having little influence over the quality of the built environment.

The Stylistic Imperative

An alternative to the dimensional type of control or more complex forms of zoning regulation is that which simply dictates adherence to a particular architectural style or vernacular idiom. This device has at least the merit of being easily understood and generally highly popular. A classic example of this mode was that adopted some thirty years ago in Coral Gables, Florida, requiring that "all buildings shall be Spanish, Venetian, Italian or other Mediterranean or similar harmonious type architecture." This "comic opera zoning" might by now have become extinct and of only archaeological interest. But not at all. Quite recently one State Supreme Court upheld a zoning board's insistence that new homes must conform to the character of a particular neighborhood where the existing properties were said to be in "traditional colonial, French provincial and English Tudor style." The mind boggles at this degree of eclecticism.

While enforced stylistic conformity of this kind may seem naive, we will see later that it can still be found within much more sophisticated planning regimes. Those who are now striving to devise subtler but equally effective design guidelines are conscious of the danger of attempting to ensure quality by prescription.

The Proprietorial Injunction

While private landowners and developers commonly resent the imposition of design controls by the public sector, they often adopt even more stringent controls themselves for their own developments. Many of the most famous townscapes in Europe were the product of princely landowners or autocratic landlords. In London, from the end of the seventeenth century to the middle of the nineteenth century much of the new development was initiated by great landlords who instructed their agents to prepare their holdings on the western and northern fringes of the city for development. New streets (often on the grid pattern), squares, and gardens were laid down and plots offered to speculative builders. The unified land ownership, the uniform style adopted by the builders, and the pretensions of their clients all contributed to the "palace fashion" whereby whole terraces of relatively modest houses were given a unified palatial appearance, with the end and center houses often set forward or made slightly taller. This fashion reached its apex with the sequence of Nash terraces around Regent's Park.

This method of development, with the large landowner laying out the land for development and selling off plots to individual builders, is still the normal mode of suburban development in America, whereas in England the roles of developer and builder are more often combined. Paradoxically, the separation of the two functions may produce the better result, as the landowner/developer will want to achieve a high quality of development so as to enhance and maintain land values, whereas the speculative builder may set his sights lower down the market. The landlord thus acts as the "planning authority" for the area and can enforce the style and standards of development that he wants to achieve and in doing so he may well be more demanding and more autocratic than any public authority would dare to be. In many cases, the degree of detail in design and landscaping goes far beyond what any local planning authority would attempt by way of general prescription (except when the authority itself owns the land, in which case it can exercise landlord privilege).

The Authoritative Intervention

Many local authorities find the exercise of aesthetic control a very difficult and very contentious process, and yet it is a responsibility that the local community expects them to undertake. Many take refuge by appointing an independent, or at least separate and supposedly nonpolitical, body to which all or part of that responsibility can be transferred. In some cases that committee or commission may be appointed by mayoral edict and in others it may be provided for in a local ordinance or in state legislation. In some cases legislation may endow the commission with powers of decision but more usually it has only an advisory role.

The city council may choose always, or nearly always, to rest on that advice; or it may treat it with less respect. Sometimes the commission may have only a few cases of major importance referred to it; in others it may act as a panel advising routinely on most new development. Sometimes there may also be other bodies—a historic buildings commission or an arts committee—which have, or assume they have, a similar role. That adds to the confusion or entertainment that this subject generates. In some cases, however, the commission acquires a formidable reputation and is able to intervene authoritatively in the process.

In Britain, one such body—the Royal Fine Art Commission—can act in this manner. The RFAC, founded in 1924, was conceived as an advisory committee to whom the government or "any other authority of standing" could refer for advice on "any artistic question in the open air." For many years the commission pursued a policy of discretion to the point of virtually abstaining from public comment. More recently it has intervened forcefully on many occasions and is now entitled to do so on its own initiative without waiting for its advice to be sought.

The American courts have not been averse in principle to the concept of the architectural review board, but they do not approve of endowing the board with a large measure of discretion. They also look to see whether the board is given reasonably explicit guidance on how they are to act, and whether the developer can have some sense of what they require or regard as good design. The simple criterion of conformity with neighboring property will not suffice. In the New Jersey case *Morristown Road Associates v. Mayor & Common Council 1978,* the plaintiffs complained that the standards set forth in the Ordinance were so vague and broad as to be incapable of being objectively applied. The Superior Court agreed and ruled that a standard based on whether the proposed structure "related harmoniously to the terrain and existing buildings in the vicinity" was unconstitutionally vague. Whatever other form of "authoritative intervention" there may be in the American planning process, the courts certainly possess that capability.

The Competitive Alternative

One method of advancing the cause of good architecture while avoiding regulatory conformity might seem to be the architectural competition. This was a popular procedure for major buildings in Britain in the nineteenth century, and more recently in America. But neither country has gone as far as France, where all public buildings (above a low cost limit) are required to be put out to competition and the process is supervised by the Mission Interministeriel de Qualité des Constructions Publiques (MIQCP). The procedure has the advantage of providing opportunities for the smaller architectural firms, and for younger architects, to compete for work with the big names of the profession. On the other hand, the big firms tend to suffer from competition fatigue and the system seems to encourage a somewhat flashy style of exhibitionist architecture.

The competition process may also help to increase public understanding of the design process and to stimulate public interest in architecture and city planning. Thus what may appear an elitist procedure can serve the interests of democracy, provided that a means can be found to engage the public in the process of adjudication. The results, however, may be paradoxical: it is said that among the entries in the competition for the National Gallery extension in London that were put on public display, Richard Rogers's proposals attracted both the most votes in favor and the most votes against. In the event, all the entries for the competition were abandoned and the job went to the American architect Robert Venturi.

The Design Guidance

Much the most interesting and relevant work that is being done in America on aesthetic control is in those cities that are developing the concept of design guidelines or guidance. ("Guidance" is the preferred term, since "guidelines" may imply more rigidity than is intended.) These cities retain the traditional zoning devices but supplement them by much less rigid and more meaningful design guidance. Developers who need to seek an exception to, or variance from, the normal zoning regime, or who want to benefit from the various "bonuses" that may be on offer (e.g., in the form of increased height or density) must demonstrate that their proposals have taken full account of the guidance.

At present only a few cities adopt this approach. In most cities the guidance focuses on detailed elements of building design, but in the most enlightened cases the emphasis is on the general character and quality of new development, and on "design" in the wider sense of civic enhancement—layout, public facilities, and amenities (open space, works of art, pedestrianized streets, sidewalk improvement, landscaping) and other features that the city would like to see incorporated in new development. This is "design" just as much as the detailed design of individual buildings. Indeed, it may be thought that it is a more valid area for public policy and intervention than the latter. It recalls an older tradition of "civic design" that can be traced back to the early days

of town planning in Britain and to the "City Beautiful" era in America, and which has survived better in the U.S. than in the U.K.

There are many examples that could be cited, but is it impossible within the confines of this chapter to give any detailed excerpts from the guidance, which often needs to be read together with the city master plan and zoning ordinance. It is also true that those drafting such guidance come up against the limitations of language in describing aesthetic qualities and objectives—illustrations, diagrams, and actual examples are also needed.

San Diego provides an interesting example but also a cautionary one. Its guidance for various neighborhoods has evolved in close consultation with committees of local residents—and it shows. It tends to recall the Coral Gables approach referred to earlier. The guidance for the historic area of Golden Hill, for example, requires that each building shall incorporate specified features from one of four styles—Victorian, Craftsman, Spanish, and contemporary. The specification for the Victorian style includes such delights as "turrets or cupolas, scalloped shingles, crafted open stickwork" and a quarter of all windows facing a street should be "bays, half-round, elliptical Gothic, oval or Palladian shapes, quatrefoils, bull's eyes, and stained glass (geometric, lattice or opalescent)." There is a great deal more in the same vein. It shows the direction in which such an approach may lead, especially when drafted by groups of "concerned citizens."

San Francisco has pursued somewhat similar objectives in preparing guidance for redevelopment in its older neighborhoods and for the city center, but in a much subtler manner. The city's basic zoning controls contain a lot of immensely detailed dimensional requirements but more recently it has adopted a much less restrictive approach. It seeks to identify the distinctive qualities and characteristics of an area, and to describe these in terms that leave plenty of scope for designers to relate buildings to their contexts without aiming at detailed replication. It is fine-grain local planning without undue restriction. The relevant section of the downtown plan states: "These guidelines establish minimum criteria for neighborhood compatibility, not the maximum expectations for good design."

In its guidance, Portland, Oregon, largely eschews detailed architectural prescription and concentrates instead on attempting to define and explain the qualities that need to be preserved and enhanced. And the city does this by examining not just the buildings but the types of activity that each area generates and other features that contribute to its character and that new development should respect and enhance. The introduction to the guidelines concisely expresses their purpose: "The Guidelines herein focus on relationships of buildings, space and people. They are used to coordinate and enhance the diversity of activities taking place in the downtown area. Many ways of meeting a particular guideline exist, and since it is not our intent to prescribe any specific solution, the Commission encourages a diversity of imaginative solutions to issues raised by the guidelines." This is indeed a highly sophisticated policy, and one that is difficult to elucidate and explain in terms that developers can comprehend. But it is a far more enlightened approach than the regulatory mode or the stylistic imperative.

Portland, however, does not rely solely on the initiative of individual developers and their architects to achieve its objectives. The city has a long tradition of civic enhancement and accepts responsibility for the quality of public space and the street scene. In the city center the street furniture, bus shelters, direction signs, street names, traffic lights, tree planting and other landscape features, fountains, paving, curbs, and every such item is superbly designed, used consistently throughout the city center, and of the highest quality. It adds great distinction to the city and is paid for largely by developers and established businesses that appreciate the commercial benefits of a well-designed and well-managed city center. It is surely the best approach to aesthetic control.

CONCLUSION

It could be forcefully argued that only those controls should be enforced that can be strictly justified in terms of the traditional police power—public health, safety, and welfare (taking a narrow view of "welfare"). The whole idea of "aesthetic" control offends one's libertarian instincts. Good design (like good writing or good music) is the exception rather than the rule. It results from cre-

ativity and cannot be achieved by prescriptive regulations. An autocratic "design code" would certainly do more harm than good. But these evasions will not do. Architecture is a public art and invites inspection and criticism. It is too important to be left to the architects, still less to developers.

The trouble with traditional methods of control, whether the regulatory American one or the discretionary British one, is not that they are too restrictive but that they are too mundane—too pedestrian, too bureaucratic, *devoid of vision*. The fact that the British planning system relies so heavily on ad hoc detailed control of individual building proposals means that it is very difficult (usually impossible) to discern any underlying principles or general objectives, or to evaluate its success in achieving them. The process focuses attention on the development that is the subject of the planning application. Each proposal is examined separately and often in great detail but without reference to any specific policies or criteria, and usually with a view only to assessing potential objections from neighboring owners or local opinion. Nor are developers and their architects given any prior indication as to what the local planning authority is looking for or will find acceptable. No wonder the results are so meager.

The advantage of the American system (or systems) is that its objectives and methods are more explicit. Moreover, in a system where everything is left to local decision, with no control or intervention by central government, there is ample scope for local variations and experiment. So far as planning and design are concerned, America is not so much a melting pot as a laboratory.

Much the most interesting aspect of aesthetic control in the American context is where the city planning authority no longer relies exclusively on the traditional regulatory methods but evolves policies and practices that evoke a positive and creative response from developers and architects. The most successful examples of *design policy* in American cities are those that rely on *design guidance* rather than on regulatory controls.

This type of approach has three main components. The first component involves the careful and detailed analysis of the existing scene, the distinctive qualities of each district and neighborhood, its local characteristics and incidental landmarks. This analysis is not limited to the architectural dimension; it includes also the mix of uses and types of business that generate its character and its place in the life of the city. This very deliberate endeavor to understand and delineate the nature of each area provides the basis for the second component: the development of a design policy for the area and its incorporation in design guidance, in the preparation of which the local community must be closely involved. The third component is to enforce the guidance through negotiations with developers and in consultation with their architects. It is a difficult task, and not worth doing unless it is well done. But it is the only valid way forward.

I term this method *mandatory design guidance*. The guidance is mandatory not in the usual prescriptive and regulatory sense but because developers and architects *must* take account of that guidance in preparing their proposals, and the local planning authority *must* have regard to it in reaching their decision whether or not to approve those proposals.

This type of design guidance is based on a close and sensitive assessment of the character and qualities of the area to which it relates, and it should concentrate on matters of context, scale, density, the relationship between buildings and the spaces between them, the enhancement of public areas, ease of access, pedestrian safety, and where relevant, the appropriate use of locally derived materials, building techniques, and architectural features, not in the form of replication or pastiche but to assist in achieving congruity and a lively sense of continuity.

The adoption of design guidance for the purpose of aesthetic control is not in itself a sufficient means of achieving quality in the built environment. Those policies must apply to the public sector too. And policies to promote good design must comprehend the whole range of municipal activities that affect the visual environment. That means rigorous attention to good housekeeping—parade-ground discipline in street cleaning and the prevention of litter. It means highly professional standards of public landscaping and maintenance of parks and gardens. It can include redesigning street crossings, sidewalks, and parking spaces, decorative paving, high-quality street furniture, bus shelters, kiosks, traffic signs, and so on, all to a consistent "house style," good design, and

materials. It requires a deliberate and sustained policy of civic enhancement, new public spaces, tree planting, fountains, water features—all immaculately maintained.

If all of this is done well, it may be concluded that the design of individual buildings is of less consequence—or, at least, that aesthetic control can be applied with a lighter touch. When the public domain is seen to be cared for and progressively improved, private developers and property owners will begin to respond with more than grudging compliance. When that situation prevails, not only will they be prepared to raise their own standards but they may well be prepared to undertake an increasing share of the cost of maintenance and enhancement. Only if the public sector is seen to be committed will the private sector contribute. It requires public sector initiative to evoke a private sector response.

The aim of aesthetic control must be to ensure that new development benefits, and does not damage, the community to whom the local environment belongs. That assessment must be based on the building's *context,* not only on its design *concept.* It is a great mistake to focus solely on the design of the individual building instead of on its setting and the impact that it will have on the local environment. Above all, the methods used must be democratic and involve the local community, not dictate to it. The result must be practical, which means it will not be perfect. Aesthetic control of this kind is a proper concern of public policy in a democracy.

REFERENCES

Aesthetic Control (Monograph 41). Berkeley: Institute of Urban and Regional Development, University of California.

Delafons, John. 1969. *Land-Use Controls in the USA.* Cambridge, Mass: M.I.T. Press. See also Delafons, John. 1990

Hayek, F.A. 1960. *The Constitution of Liberty.* London: Routledge and Kegan Paul.

Kostof, Spiro. 1991. *The City Shaped.* London: Thames and Hudson.

Kostof, Spiro. 1992. *The City Assembled.* London: Thames and Hudson.

2
Reviewing New Design in Historic Districts

Ellen Beasley

Historic Preservation Consultant, Houston, Texas

One resident described the historic review board meetings in Santa Fe, New Mexico, as "the most democratic forum in town" because "it equalizes everybody. Some big-shot architect from Albuquerque comes strutting in and just gets spit out. It is citizens governing the community at its best."

Needless to say, the architect from Albuquerque might refute that conclusion, but democratic or not, one of the most active arenas of design review in the United States has been the locally designated historic district, the first of these being Charleston, South Carolina, in 1931. There are now approximately 1800 such districts, a number that was just 500 in 1976 (USPCIP, 1992). The majority of these districts are residential, commercial, or mixed-use in character. In age and architectural content, they range from eighteenth-century rural villages in New England to twentieth-century inner-city neighborhoods in California. What distinguishes design review in the historic district from many other situations is the setting: there is an existing, established context with determined boundaries to which the community attributes identified cultural values and meanings.

The local zoning ordinance is the legal means by which these municipalities designate a historic district. A preservation commission or review board (various names are used) is appointed to review proposed alterations, changes, and demolitions to existing buildings and new construction projects within district boundaries. Usually, the commissions consist of five to nine members with representatives from the design, preservation, legal, and real estate professions, and district property owners. Nondesigner members are in the majority.

The author first became interested in design review in the early 1970s after moving to Galveston, Texas, and observing the local review board as it agonized over applications for new construction projects in the forty-block residential historic district. The board was often forced to juggle the unspoken agendas of politics and economics as well as that aspect of a project for which it was actually responsible—the design.

Was the plight of the Galveston board similar to that of commissions around the country? (fig. 2-1) To answer that question, the local design review process and its specific relation to the issue of new construction in historic districts was documented in nine communities around the country in 1977–78. Eight years later, the same communities were revisited to analyze the evolution of the review process, including its impact on new design in the districts over a period of time and how the process and the results were perceived by the communities (Beasley, 1980 and 1987).

The nine cities and towns that serve as case studies were chosen because they typified the resources available to the majority of communities that practiced design review in a historic district. Design review had been in place for varying

Figure 2-1. Savannah, Ga., vacant lot on Oglethorpe Square. (Photo: Ellen Beasley, 1986.)

Figure 2-2. Beaufort, S.C., bank building, riverside facade, Thomas & Denzinger, 1977–78. (Photo: Ellen Beasley, 1986.)

lengths of time in the districts that could be described as primarily residential and small-scale in character.

1. The smallest community was Arrow Rock, Missouri, now a village of 80 people but once a major commercial river town of 1,000. Its historic district, established in 1974, included most of the town limits and abutted a state park.
2. The largest was Indianapolis, Indiana, population close to one million. In 1968, the city designated its first historic district, Lockerbie Square, a six-block neighborhood with a mix of nineteenth-century residential building types and within walking distance of downtown Indianapolis.
3. Alexandria, Virginia, had the oldest historic zoning ordinance, passed in 1946, and had experienced a large volume of new construction, both residential and commercial, in the district, much of it part of an urban renewal program.
4. Beaufort, South Carolina, a town of 10,000, established its historic district in 1967. There was the potential for a considerable amount of new construction, although little had been built as of 1977. The review board had ap-

proved a bank building that was the most contemporary and controversial example of infill in any of the case studies (fig. 2-2).
5. Galveston, Texas, adopted its historic zoning in 1971, and as of 1977, had one district.
6. In 1962, Mobile, Alabama, passed its historic ordinance, which stipulated that three of the five members of the reviewing body had to be registered architects, a higher percentage than usual. In 1977, there were three historic districts in the city.
7. The Santa Fe, New Mexico, ordinance passed in 1957 defined a strict design approach—two historic styles—for new construction. As in Alexandria, the review board in Santa Fe had reviewed a high volume of new construction.
8. Savannah, Georgia, was recognized as having one of the most successful preservation programs in the country in 1977, due to the activities of the Historic Savannah Foundation, a private organization. The city administered design review in the historic district, which was created in 1973.
9. Telluride, Colorado, a small mining town, was in the early stages of shifting to a ski and tourist economy. The town adopted its historic zoning in 1972, as it was facing tremendous development pressures.

Figure 2-3. Alexandria, Va., rowhouses, 1977. (Photo: Ellen Beasley, 1977.)

THE PICTURE IN 1977–78

When beginning the study, it was assumed that new construction projects would prove to be easier to review for those commissions that had been in existence the longest periods of time. Such was not the case. First of all, most of the commissions were struggling with basic administrative and procedural matters. There was an appalling lack of support materials such as surveys, plans, design guidelines, and standard operational procedures. Aside from Indianapolis, where the Historic Preservation Commission had an office and staff, staff support was either nonexistent as in Arrow Rock or minimal even in such preservation gurus as Savannah and Santa Fe, where the commissions were staffed by reluctant building inspectors. Interviews with citizens ranging from elected officials to building contractors suggested that the nine review boards were considered, without exception, the toughest local board on which to serve.

With respect to new construction in the districts, board members confessed to being lenient with initial requests not only because of timidity and ignorance but also because they felt that most of the districts desperately needed *any* sign of construction—whatever the design. Most new construction since the creation of the districts had been residential in use and made some allusion to historic styles, although there was a wide swath to this approach. The strictest adherence was in Alexandria and Santa Fe, where the historic zoning ordinances reinforced long-standing community attitudes (fig. 2-3; see also Harry Moul's chapter about Santa Fe). Whereas the Santa Fe ordinance specified the "old Santa Fe style" and the "new Santa Fe style," the "colonial" preference in Alexandria was more implied than clearly stated.

Projects in other districts also keyed off local historic buildings, as in Mobile, where it was the two-story brick residence with wrought-iron trim (fig. 2-4), and in Savannah, where it was the two-story Greek Revival row house. Variations of these building types had been built repeatedly in their respective districts. Local precedence, however, was not always a requirement as in Arrow Rock, where it could be selecting something "Colonial" from a house-plan catalog. In most communities, there was at least one example of a contemporary design, the strongest of these being the bank building in Beaufort.

Interviews with people in the communities revealed that everyone—the design and building professions, preservationists, commission members, the general public—was groping for a con-

Figure 2-4. Mobile, Ala., office building in DeTonti Square Historic District, 1969. (Photo: Ellen Beasley, 1977.)

sensus of what was "appropriate" or "compatible" new design for historic districts. Clearly, the general public preferred designs that made some gesture to historic styles. Design professionals and preservationists advocated new buildings that respected the scale of a district but were "products of their time." Although there were many people who supported the latter, at least in conversation, many had concluded that it was better to have "a good copy than a bad original." Certainly, what had been built in the districts with commission approval represented an architectural mix and experimentation.

JUST EIGHT YEARS LATER, A DIFFERENT PICTURE

The picture had changed by the time the communities were revisited. All the commissions presented a more confident, secure attitude that could be attributed not only to experience but also to greater public support, an increase in staff and budget for most of them, and a strengthening of such procedural and planning tools as surveys, plans, design guidelines, and application requirements. Many decisions pertaining to renovation projects had become routine and although new construction remained the most difficult projects for all the commissions to review, they felt more secure about those decisions as well.

During those interim years, all nine commissions reviewed applications for new construction but in varying quantities. Alexandria, Santa Fe, and Telluride experienced a tremendous amount

of new construction as did Lockerbie Square in Indianapolis, where the population in the district more than doubled because of new construction and renovation projects. In Galveston there were very few vacant lots left in the historic district and new construction consisted primarily of garages and garage/apartments. In one Mobile district, there was limited new development even though there were large parcels of vacant land: the economics and the marketability of the district simply did not support it.

Although some single-family dwellings were built in the districts, the applications for new construction were now dominated by larger-scale multi-unit residential projects that ranged anywhere from two to over fifty units (fig. 2-5) and nonresidential and/or mixed-use projects. And although there was considerably more new construction in the districts collectively, there was less architectural variety than seen in the infill buildings that predated 1977–78. The newer buildings, those that postdated 1977–78, made a more direct reference (or deference) to a historic style or an agglomeration of styles. No new structure had been built in any of the districts that was comparable to the bank building in Beaufort. The greatest contrasts between old and new were reserved for additions to existing buildings (fig. 2-6).

The interviews—which included people who were interviewed for the original study—were no longer dominated by a discussion of what constituted acceptable new design for the historic districts. Quite clearly, a consensus had evolved and was shared by all the communities. By the mid-1980s, professionals and nonprofessionals alike were at least comfortable with, if not ecstatic about, much of what was being built in the historic districts. There was a perceptible relief that a solution had been found to the design dilemma that had existed in the late 1970s, but to attribute this consensus to the local design review process is much too simple a conclusion.

EXPLAINING THE SHIFT: THE NATIONAL SCENE

New construction projects in historic districts, even those projects that are relatively simple and noncontroversial (the ones one never hears about),

Figure 2-5. Alexandria, Va., residential development, Kyes, Condon, & Florance in association with Metcalf & Associates, 1984–85. (Photo: Ellen Beasley, 1987.)

Figure 2-6. Indianapolis, Ind., 1835 house moved to Lockerbie Square in 1977, addition and garage, Perry Associates, 1985. (Photo: Ellen Beasley, 1986.)

reflect a complicated interweaving of tangible and intangible influences and a melding of the design and the design review processes. For starters, any explanation of what was built in the districts of the nine communities during those interim years

has to be placed within the context of national events and trends.

The period between visits saw the convergence of the postmodern style in architecture, the glowing aftermath of the Bicentennial, and a new economic rationale for preservation advanced by the Bicentennial celebration and passage of the 1976 and subsequent tax acts. The Bicentennial and the accompanying swelling of preservation activities paralleled a period when the public was already developing a greater design consciousness. A historic layer was inserted into the growing concern for the environment, both natural and man-made. The public had become not only more articulate but also more militant, "more macho" as one person said, about design issues and in response, architects and other designers became, willingly or unwillingly, more responsive to public opinion. Elected officials and other governmental entities responded by increasing budgets and staffs for preservation-related programs, including local landmark commissions and review boards.

Figure 2-7. Beaufort, S.C., retail building, Thomas & Denzinger, 1985. (Photo: Ellen Beasley, 1986.)

The general public has always viewed pseudo-historic styles as the preferred design solution for new structures in historic districts, and events from the mid-1970s to the mid-1980s advanced the popular view. The Bicentennial and the tax acts also reinforced the attitude of the marketplace which, like the general public, has always identified imitative-style structures as being the most marketable for historic areas (or for that matter, for many nonhistoric areas). By the late 1970s, "historic" had become big business and had acquired an unprecedented economic justification and business-world respectability. Many architects and designers were seduced into the fold by the aesthetics of postmodernism which gave professional credence to architectural expressions of historicism, and by the economics of preservation-related projects which were often the major, if not the only, development projects in town. Professionals and nonprofessionals had given considerably more thought to the specific issue of new construction in historic areas.

The jargon also shifted. The 1970s requirement that new buildings be "compatible" with their historic settings was replaced with the demand that they be "contextual" in the 1980s, a shift symbolized by the bank building in Beaufort and a later retail building designed by the same architectural firm (fig. 2-2 and fig. 2-7). Although the meanings of the two words were similar and they both placed an importance on the fit of a structure with its surroundings, they did not (and do not) mean the same thing. "Compatible," as used in the 1970s, placed a greater emphasis on scale, mass, and materials than on details. By the mid-1980s, the word had acquired something of a negative meaning, as summarized by one Mobilian who described a building as "compatible but that's all you can say for it." In contrast, "contextual" gave far greater importance to a borrowing, exact or not, of shapes, detailing, and surface treatment from historic structures and styles, local or not. People had become, as stated by one architect, "passionately interested in context." As such, the word was (and is) used not only as a descriptive term for the design of new structures in historic areas but equally important, it also contributed to moving new design for that setting toward a more imitative and literal expression of historic styles.

ADD THE LOCAL SCENE

The period during which the nine communities were documented was unique on the national level: the country was celebrating the major historical and cultural event of the century. In many respects, the Bicentennial and all the attendant

Figure 2-8. Mobile, Ala., clinic in Old Dauphin Way Historic District, Derry Hargett, 1981–82. (Photo: Ellen Beasley, 1985.)

hoopla simply sanctified and legitimated what the communities had been doing for years.

At the same time, there are local forces and attitudes *continuously* at play in the local design review process that impact the design of buildings on that local level—and the period under study is no exception. Among these forces are local architectural expressions that may be of varying duration. In Mobile, the popularity of the two-story brick residences with iron trim had waned but several elongated and strikingly similar "Gulf Coast cottages" had been constructed for office use in the districts (fig. 2-8). Savannah, however, continued to build the two-story Greek Revival row houses even in its more recently designated Victorian district. Local trends were more mercurial in Telluride, where "this year, it's log—last year, it was bay windows."

Previous decisions of a design review board will influence property owners, beginning with their selection of an architect, which may in part be based on a firm's reputation for guiding proposals through the review process. Buildings that have the stamp of approval first by a board and then by the public's acceptance once they are built shape subsequent projects which is one explanation for the popularity of the row houses in Savan-

nah. A negative reaction to a building also molds subsequent designs, as was the case in Beaufort, where one observer stated that "the bank has always regretted that it didn't build a pseudo-Colonial number," as did one of its competitors down the street.

Acceptable new design in a historic district can reflect local perceptions of and aspirations for an area, as in Arrow Rock and Telluride, where the townspeople had become increasingly conscious of appealing to what they believe are tourists' expectations and to which they tie their economic livelihood. In this respect, the two towns are not unlike Alexandria and Santa Fe, only several decades behind and less town-specific in what they consider to be acceptable new design.

Maintaining and/or improving property values is a major concern of residents in historic districts. It is generally believed that new buildings offering minimal contrast to surrounding historic structures are most likely to enhance property values. This was among the concerns of residents in a Savannah neighborhood when they objected to what they believed was too contemporary a design for a multi-unit townhouse complex that had been approved by the review board. Under pressure, the developers/architects redesigned the project so it was "more aesthetically pleasing to the neighbors as well as [the] Historic Savannah [Foundation]."

Many design-related decisions pertaining to such elements as square footage, setbacks, density, and parking are determined by nonhistoric zoning regulations that must be accommodated in new construction projects. These requirements, some of which are also driven by the market, may result in design elements that are alien to historic forms and streetscapes, such as meeting parking requirements and attendant—and growing—security concerns that pose a continuing design problem for row-house development in Alexandria, Savannah, and Indianapolis.

Nonhistoric zoning also determines building size, which is also closely tied to the economics of a historic district. Projects of a *much* larger scale were built in the districts during the interim years. In most instances, the zoning in the districts would have allowed construction of such projects at a *much* earlier date but the economics and appeal of the districts did not support maximum development until the later period. As one Telluride property owner offered rather smugly, "When your property value goes from $35,000 to $1.5 million, *that* changes your attitude."

AND FINALLY, ADD THE REVIEW PROCESS

By the time a new construction project actually enters the public review arena, the design has been shaped by a good many forces including national and local architectural trends and attitudes, economics, a combination of zoning regulations, the property owner's motivations and tastes, and the designer's ability. Added to these are the factors—both tangible and intangible—that are imposed by the public design review process itself.

The tangible factors include support materials such as design guidelines which six commissions had written or revised during those interim years. Although the newer guidelines placed a greater emphasis on urban design issues than did previous guidelines, they also demonstrate how difficult it is to write and illustrate sections pertaining to new construction in a historic district without sug-

gesting by inference, if not example, that the only design option for new buildings is to mimic existing buildings.

A commission's response to a project at a meeting—in other words, the design review process—is a reactionary one but that, too, can be handled differently and in ways that affect the design of a project. The Mobile and Arrow Rock boards made specific design suggestions and changes because they feel that one of their functions is to provide design assistance. Several of the boards rejected or approved applications by making only minimal, if any, design recommendations and tying their decisions to specific guidelines. In fact, most of the boards were making a deliberate effort to move in this direction but rejecting a project without offering any design alternative was difficult for all of them.

When projects are submitted for actual review, they are affected by the psychology—the intangibles—of the meeting: who makes the presentation, their previous experience with the commission, at what point during the meeting a project is considered, the complexity and controversy of other projects on the docket, the chair's style in conducting meetings, the quality of presentation materials, the mood of the audience. All these elements and more can have a subtle or not so subtle impact on what transpires.

Frequently, it is at the public design review stage that projects are presented for the first time in such a way that the general public can visualize and assess their impact. As a result, most of the nine commissions, like those in many other communities, found themselves at one time or another being held accountable for such highly charged and emotional issues as growth management and control. In such situations, the project in question and the review process assume a broader importance than simply design.

The Santa Fean's sentiment that the review board meetings were "the most democratic forum in town," was expressed by others as well. The *Indianapolis Star* likened the meetings of that city's Historic Preservation Commission to New England town board meetings and cited a special hearing that lasted three and a half hours, during which time the commission "proved that it is one of the most accessible commissions anywhere . . . asking for public comment each step of the way."

Figure 2-9. Telluride, Colo., new development outside historic area but subject to design review. (Photo: Ellen Beasley, 1986.)

HAS DESIGN REVIEW MADE A DIFFERENCE?

Unquestionably, the review of new construction for historic districts is a complicated process but has it made a difference in these communities?

The nine communities themselves may provide at least a part of the answer. The strongest testament in favor of the review process is that eight of the communities (Beaufort being the exception) had enlarged their original districts and/or had designated additional districts in those interim years. However, this was not because people were so enamored with historic districts but rather, because they saw the accompanying design review as a means of having some control over change and development, and the quality of change and development, in their neighborhood or community. The underlying motivations for historic districts today are issues of growth and design, not historic association, as suggested by the fact that several boards have been given responsibility for design review in outlying, undeveloped areas (fig. 2-9).

The increase in the number of projects for which professional designers were engaged could be viewed as another indicator of the positive impact that the design review process has had on the districts in the nine communities. In the 1980s, an architect was far more likely to be involved in the design of a new project than in the 1970s. The shadow of public scrutiny—a shadow that loomed larger as the commissions gained status—pushed property owners and developers toward a stronger commitment to design. As one commission member (also an architect) stated: "We have become more effective over the years because people know that they have to get approval so they bring better designs before the commission to begin with. This alone has improved design."

The age-old complaint that design review "stifles creativity" was voiced as often in the 1980s as in the 1970s and will be heard as long as design review is practiced. The process does have a leveling impact to some degree but it is one that touches both ends of the spectrum. If one believes that the initial design for most buildings falls in the mediocre and lower end of the spectrum and that replicative design is the most satisfactory solution that most architects and designers can offer, then design review will be seen as having a positive impact.

On the one hand, the review process denied the obvious intrusions of an A-frame in Arrow Rock and a two-story barrackslike apartment complex in Galveston in the 1970s. Neither project would even be proposed for those districts today, and for many, this is reason enough for design review. On the other hand, a building comparable to the bank building in Beaufort probably would not be approved by many local commissions either, even if an architect's client wanted a strong contemporary statement—which in itself is unlikely. The review process may result in the occasional loss of an exceptionally designed building, but is that more a question of their not being proposed than their being denied by the boards?

An evaluation of the effectiveness of design review in the historic districts must be made within the total context of the communities and not just the district boundaries. If historic zoning, design review, design guidelines, and commissions hinder good design, then it should be possible to simply step outside the district boundaries and find a wealth of well-designed new projects. It is not. One may not always be enthusiastic about the specifics or the style of new projects that were subjected to design review but they will usually exhibit greater attention to their setting, placement, detailing, materials, landscaping, and parking than do projects outside the districts.

MAKING JUDGMENTS

This raises yet another question. How should one judge these projects that reflect this "most democratic" of forums? This was brought into focus when the author was asked several years ago to comment on a recently completed project in a neighborhood (not in one of the nine communities) that not too long before was loosing its late nineteenth-century housing stock to demolitions and the building of multistory box-apartment complexes.

Enroute to the district, the guide described the project, which consisted of a series of detached two- and three-story, small-scale, multi-unit residential buildings with which "everyone was thrilled." The city's review process had worked the smoothest it ever had. Everyone felt that the buildings were compatible with the neighborhood and that they fit the design guidelines for the district. The neighborhood association felt that it had won a victory because the developer, as a courtesy, had asked the group to review the plans. The developer was happy because the units had sold. The architect was pleased because the completed project was built essentially as he had designed it.

When seeing the project, it was not what was expected, but knowing all those factors that went into the building of the project, it crystallized those questions of judgment:

1. Should judgment be based on the contextual or compatible fit of a project with the existing structures and streetscape?
2. Should it be judged solely on design?
3. What would have been built had there *not* been historic district designation, design review, and (as in some instances) neighborhood involvement?
4. Should it be based on what the architectural community is or is not capable of designing?
5. Should it be based on success in the marketplace?
6. Should it be based on acceptance by the people who will look at it and walk by it on a daily basis?
7. Or should it be judged on the passive realization that time will soothe and foliage will hide at least some of the mistakes?

Once again, there is no simple or single answer, but then, how could one expect that? After all, there is no simple explanation to the psychology of the design review process, just as there is no single solution for the design of a new structure in the historic setting.

REFERENCES

The numbers were reported in the United States Preservation Commission Identification Project conducted from March 1991 to March 1992. It was coordinated by Pratt Cassidy, Executive Director of the National Alliance of Preservation Commissions and Preservation

Services Coordinator for the University of Georgia School of Environmental Design.

Beasley, Ellen. 1980. "New Construction in Residential Historic Districts." In *Old and New Architecture: Design Relationship,* Washington, D.C.: Preservation Press, National Trust for Historic Preservation, pp. 229–56.
———. 1987. *The Impact of the Public Review Process on New Design in Historic Districts in the United States.* Vol. 1, Symposium Papers of the 8th General Assembly and International Symposium, *Old Cultures in New Worlds,* October 10–15, 1987. Washington, D.C.: U.S. Committee of the International Council on Monuments and Sites. Funding for the update study was provided by the Design Arts Program of the National Endowment for the Arts, the Graham Foundation for Advanced Studies in the Fine Arts, and several of the communities. The ongoing study is in its third stage.

3
Can the Process of Architectural Design Review Withstand Constitutional Scrutiny?

Richard Tseng-yu Lai

Arizona State University

In his dissent from the majority in *City of Los Angeles v. Taxpayers for Vincent* (466 U.S. 789, 1984), Supreme Court Justice William J. Brennan, Jr., cited the opening statement of a law review article by New York University law professor John J. Costonis:

> Aesthetic policy, as currently formulated and implemented at the federal, state and local levels, often partakes more of high farce than of the rule of law. Its purposes are seldom accurately or candidly portrayed, let alone understood, by its most vehement champions. Its diversion to dubious or flatly deplorable social ends undermines the credit that it may merit when soundly conceived and executed. Its indiscriminate, often quixotic demands have overwhelmed legal institutions, which all too frequently have compromised the integrity of legislative, administrative, and judicial processes in the name of "beauty" (Costonis, 1982, 356).

In the case before him, Justice Brennan was protesting what he viewed as a diminution of the First Amendment guarantee of free speech in the Court's decision to uphold a city ordinance that prohibited the posting of political signs on public property to avoid "visual clutter." It is likely that Brennan would find Costonis's condemnation of aesthetic policy even more applicable to design review of architecture. Certainly the prevailing practice of design review under the police power has not only befuddled the courts and confused

well-meaning members of review boards and elected community officials, it has furthermore deprived property owners and architects of their fundamental right of free design expression and, in the owners' case, their legitimate use of property as well. At the heart of the problem is the need for a method or process of design review that can define the boundaries of discretionary authority in review, while both fulfilling the legitimate community purpose of design regulation and preserving the applicant's rights under the Constitution.

In *The Road to Serfdom*, his prize-winning thesis written while a refugee from the totalitarianism of Nazi Germany, Nobel Laureate Friedrich A. Hayek observed:

> Nothing distinguishes more clearly conditions in a free country from those in a country under arbitrary government than the observance in the former of the great principles known as the Rule of Law. Stripped of all technicalities, this means that government in all its actions is bound by rules fixed and announced beforehand—rules which make it possible to foresee with fair certainty how the authority will use its coercive powers in given circumstances and to plan one's individual affairs on the basis of this knowledge (Hayek, 1944, 72).

The Supreme Court has affirmed the principle of "fair certainty" by requiring administrative discretion to be constrained by standards or guidelines. In 1966 in *Giacco v. Pennsylvania,* it said:

> It is established that a law fails to meet the requirements of the Due Process Clause if it is so vague and standardless that it leaves the public uncertain as to the conduct it prohibits or leaves judges and jurors free to decide, without any legally fixed standards, what is prohibited and what is not in each particular case (382 U.S. 399, 1966, 402–3).

The requirement for standards to guide discretion has indeed become so axiomatic in law that the reference, *American Law Reports,* states as dictum a rule that draws from words enunciated by Justice Benjamin N. Cardozo in not one but two Supreme Court cases (*Schechter Poultry Corp. v. United States,* 295 U.S. 495, 1935, 551; *Panama Refining Co. v. Ryan,* 293 U.S. 388, 1934, 440):

> The rule is generally accepted that the legislature must ordinarily lay down some standards sufficient to canalize the administrative discretion so as to avoid committing decisions affecting the right of property owners to the purely arbitrary choice of the administrator (*ALR* 2d 58, 1087).

But how have architectural boards and reviewing courts observed these admonitions? Consider these following instances.

THE FOLLY OF UNFETTERED DISCRETION UPHELD

In *Reid v. Architectural Board of Review of the City of Cleveland Heights,* a case decided by an Ohio appellate court in 1963, Mrs. Reid had hired an architect to design a house for her in an affluent, wooded neighborhood of Cleveland Heights. Houses in the area were, in the words of the court, "in the main, dignified, stately and conventional structures, two and one-half stories high." The proposal, which the board conceded to be "in a class, cost-wise, with other houses in the neighborhood," was for a modern single-story residence, which from the street appeared only as a ten-foot high wall with no indication of what lay behind it.

Although the board agreed that the structure would be a very interesting house in a different setting, it disapproved the project for a building permit, stating that the design "does not maintain the high character of community development in that it does not conform to the character of the houses in the area." The court upheld the decision of the review board, citing the board's purpose to protect property, to maintain high character of community development, and to protect real estate from impairment and destruction of value. It said that criteria and standards used by the board in regulating design were matters of "proper architectural principles" to be adjudged by a board of "highly trained experts in the field of architecture." Protested Judge J. J. Corrigan in his dissent opinion:

> Should the appellant be required to sacrifice her choice of architectural plan for her property under the official municipal juggernaut of conformity in this case? Should her aesthetic sensibilities in connection with her selection of design for her proposed home be stifled because of the apparent belief in this community of the group as a source of creativity? Is she to sublimate herself in this group and suffer the frustration of individual creative aspirations? Is her artistic spirit to be imprisoned by the apparent beneficence of community life in Cleveland Heights? This member of the court thinks not (192 N.E. 74, Ohio App., 1963, 81).

Seven years later, in 1970, the issue of design review came before the Missouri Supreme Court in *State ex rel. Stoyanoff v. Berkeley* and met with much the same conclusion as in *Reid.* The case arose from the refusal of the architectural board of review of the city of Ladue, one of the more exclusive suburbs of metropolitan St. Louis, to issue a permit to Dimiter Stoyanoff, a registered architect, to build a house of his own design for his personal use. In response, the applicant's lawyers noted that, although the proposed residence was unusual in design, it nevertheless complied with all existing city building or zoning regulations and ordinances. The ordinances establishing the architectural board of review they challenged as being "unconstitutional in that they are vague and provide no standard nor uniform rule by which to guide the architectural board" (458 S.W. 2d 305, Mo., 1970, 306–7). The court, however, ruled in favor of the board and its enabling ordinances, thereby upholding the ban on Stoyanoff's proposed design.

In reviewing the decision for the *Missouri Law Review*, Ronald R. McMillin worried that the case opens a "Pandora's box of problems" in its recognition of a municipality's power to regulate exterior building design and, in particular, that to give the term "general welfare," on which the police power is based, "too broad a meaning would seemingly make the three preceding terms of 'health, safety, and public morals' superfluous" (McMillin, 1971, 426–27). As for the argument that the unusual design did not conform with the traditional style of existing houses in the vicinity, Harvard law professor Frank Michelman poses an interesting hypothesis and query:

> What A does is to build a deck house in B's neighborhood, which so far is populated only by Tudor-style, Georgian-style, and New England Colonial-style homes. Can it really be said that by buying into such a neighborhood, B somehow staked out a claim not to be exposed to contemporary architecture? (Michelman, 1969, 41).

If the court decisions in the *Reid* and *Stoyanoff* cases are correct, then such a preemptive claim would indeed have validity. And then might not a Colonial house be logically excluded from a neighborhood of modern homes, and a postmodern house also? Or an English Tudor home from an area of Mediterranean-style homes?

A third instance differed from the preceding two in that the review was not conducted by a board acting under the police power. Nor was the case recorded in a law reporter, but rather it became the subject of a three full-page essay in a 1969 issue of *Life* magazine. In a Virginia community outside of Washington, D.C., Brockhurst C. Eustice, an architect, purchased a lot in a subdivision of conventional, ranch-style houses and began construction of a residence of a modern, cubistic design for his own use. When the house was almost fully constructed, John Q. Binford, a next-door neighbor, filed for an injunction to prevent its completion, charging that the house was ugly and resembled "orange crates." Another neighbor agreed that the house "just ruins the neighborhood" and said that "the only remedy I can see is to tear it down" (Neary, 1969).

Although no public board of architectural review was involved, the deed to the lot provided for design review by a committee in the subdivision.

However, all original members had resigned, the committee had never functioned, and no house in the subdivision had ever been subject to review. With no review board at hand, Judge Charles Russell devolved the function of design critic and censor upon himself. After visiting the site and viewing the nearly finished residence he found the house to be "not harmonious" with other houses in the subdivision and in violation of a "mutual compact, binding on all lots, for good or ill, to a scheme of relative uniformity." He issued a permanent injunction to prevent its full completion. An appeal found the Virginia Supreme Court evenly divided, and Russell's decision stood (181 S.E. 2d 634, 1971).

H. Rutherford Turnbull III, writing in the *Wake Forest Law Review*, characterized *Eustice v. Binford* as "one of the most outrageous cases of judicial meddling and misconstruction of residential covenants" involving "grievous . . . rewriting of the covenant to include the standard of 'relative uniformity' . . . a term that contains gross contradictions . . . not appear[ing] to have been contemplated by the covenant at all" (Turnbull, 1971, 239–40). While quick to judge on architectural merits, Judge Russell seemed less inclined to deliberate on such legal issues as the lack of uniformity in enforcement of the covenant, the investment already made by Eustice in the construction of his house, his rights of private property, and his prerogative as an individual not to conform. As in the *Stoyanoff* case, Eustice was an architect building a house for himself after his own design, an act of self-expression deserving full consideration of First Amendment guarantees. Especially pertinent was the just compensation requirements of the Fifth Amendment, particularly in view of the judge's decision virtually requiring removal of a practically complete structure.

In consideration of Friedrich Hayek's admonition that a cardinal principle of the Rule of Law is that rules should be known beforehand, Eustice had his house design conform to all known building restrictions then under enforcement, and Russell's proscription had resulted only from "litigation after the event." In 1956, a New Jersey court had asserted that one's right to use his property in good faith "should not depend upon the outcome of litigation after the event in which a provision, which he apparently fully meets, assumes a new and different significance by a process of refined interpretation" *Jantausch v. Borough of Verona* (124 A. 2d 14, N.J. Sup'r., 1956, 22).

A fourth instance of architectural review did not result in litigation but is instructive nonetheless, especially in view of the high profile of the project and the players involved. For years the American Institute of Architects had housed its national headquarters in Washington, D.C., at the Octagon, a historic brick house that dated to the eighteenth century. In 1967 the institute held a competition for the design of a new office building on the grounds behind the landmark. The winning design selected by a jury of nationally known architects was the entry of the architectural firm of Mitchell-Guirgola. At the time, Romaldo Guirgola was chairman of the division of architecture at Columbia University; Ehrman B. Mitchell, Jr., would later become president of the AIA itself. The work of the firm, and of Guirgola in particular, was identified with the school of architectural postmodernism, a movement now dominant in design theory but considered at the time to be reactionary to the tradition of modernism and the International Style, which had prevailed in design from about the 1930s to the 1970s.

Following the jury selection, a modified version of the winning design was submitted for approval by the Washington Fine Arts Commission, the board of architectural review for historic areas of the capital city. The commission rejected the proposal. Said Gordon Bunshaft, a member of the commission and senior design partner of the architectural firm of Skidmore Owings and Merrill, "The design concept is totally out of scale with the existing building on the site. This new building makes the buildings and garden look like a toy" (*Progressive Architecture,* 1967, 136). Mitchell-Guirgola subsequently submitted several modifications of the design for approval, but each scheme was turned down. Finally, in frustration, they resigned, and the firm of TAC (The Architects Collaborative) was commissioned to design the now-existing headquarters building. Whether coincidentally or not, commission-member Bunshaft, his firm of Skidmore Owings and Merrill, and TAC are all eminently associated with the design theories of modernism and the International Style, the design tradition philosophically at odds with the newer, reactionary theories of architectural postmodernism represented in the aborted Mitchell-Guirgola scheme.

Ada Louise Huxtable, architectural critic for the *New York Times,* compares the built TAC design unfavorably with the rejected Mitchell-Guirgola proposal. She was especially critical of the owner, the American Institute of Architects, which she faulted for not standing up for the project selected by its own blue-ribbon jury, and for failing to contribute affirmatively to the design review process:

> The AIA's reaction was either chicken or preposterous. Whatever the design's shortcomings may have been, and whatever the Commission's reservations may have been, the scheme was conscientious, concerned, and able, not a speculator's destructive, free-wheeling horror. In retrospect, the Fine Arts Commission seems to have been guilty of an overbearing misinterpretation of its role for an extraordinary and dubious imposition of its own taste. On these grounds, the AIA should, and could, have stood firm, without compromising its belief in the review board function. It could, in fact, have helped to clarify that function constructively and appropriately, and aided in the proper definition of review board responsibilities. It is understandable that at this point Mitchell-Giurgola resigned (Huxtable, 1976, 173–74).

Said lawyer H. P. Kucera in 1960, "Aesthetics should not concern itself with the distinction between the smell of a rose and smell of a lily, but certainly should concern itself with the smell of a rose and the smell of a barnyard" (Kucera, 1960, 48–49). Surely to judge between the Mitchell-Guirgola proposal and the design finally constructed is to distinguish between a rose and a lily.

It would appear that, through such decisions as *Reid* and *Stoyanoff* and episodes like *Eustice* and the AIA imbroglio, the process of design review has won de facto court vindication. However, in view of the criticism of authorities in law as well as design, much less the admonishments of Supreme Court justices and Nobel laureates alike calling for "fair certainty" and guidelines to channel administrative discretion, it would also seem that explicit standards to guide the design effort of applicants as well as the review process of boards would be an appropriate remedy. However, when communities attempt in good faith to conceive and enforce just such standards, their efforts are often thwarted by the same judicial system that confers approval to the unfettered board discretion evident in *Reid* and *Stoyanoff*.

DESIGN STANDARDS HELD INADEQUATE AND "VOID FOR VAGUENESS"

Consider the result of two cases, *Pacesetter Homes, Inc. v. Village of Olympia Fields* in 1968 and *Morristown Road Associates v. Mayor and Common Council and the Planning Board of the Borough of Bernardsville* in 1978. In *Pacesetter,* the issue concerned an ordinance enacted by the Village of Olympia Fields that prohibited architectural design from exhibiting "excessive similarity, dissimilarity or inappropriateness in exterior design and appearance of property" (244 N.E. 2d 369, Ill. App., 1968, 37). Design characteristics subject to review included such elements as the building facade, opening and breaks in the facade, cubical content, floor area, roof line, height, construction, material, and site relationship. Also to be considered were the "quality" of the design and any "inappropriateness" in relation to the context of the neighborhood. Although widely held to be considerable in its detail—certainly in comparison with the standards upheld in *Reid* and *Stoyanoff*—the Olympia Fields ordinance was nevertheless voided by an Illinois appellate court for its failure to prescribe adequate standards to guide the actions of the village architectural advisory committee and for allowing it too broad a discretion.

Ten years after *Pacesetter,* a New Jersey court used similar reasoning in *Morristown Road* to reject a zoning ordinance establishing a design review committee and providing design standards for review of site plans. Although the ordinance included an extensive description of site and building design considerations, to assure that a proposal project relates "harmoniously to the terrain and to existing buildings in the vicinity," the standards were deemed by the court to be "so broad and vague as to be incapable of being objectively applied, thereby permitting arbitrary action . . . in the review of site plan applications" (394 A. 2d 157, N.J. Sup'r., 1978, 162–63). Despite pleas by the borough that the standards were "as precise as the subject matter of the regulations permits," the court agreed with the developer's assertion that the standards invited "arbitrary determination and unbridled discretion on the part of the reviewing agency."

Dolores Dalton writes of the Olympia Fields ordinance struck down in *Pacesetter*: "It is difficult to imagine a more specific set of standards, yet the court held the ordinance conferred uncontrolled discretion on the Committee. The court invalidated the ordinance on unlawful delegation grounds" (Dalton, 1979, 964). Dalton compares this outcome with *Stoyanoff,* in which an ordinance was upheld that allowed for determination by a board of professional architects, based only on "proper architectural standards in appearance and design . . . and general conformity with the style and design of surrounding structures." In *Pacesetter* as well as in *Morristown Road,* the suggested criteria contained in the ordinances were rejected by the courts as being conceptual, vague, and investing too broad a discretion on review. It is certainly arguable that the terms—including "excessive similarity," "harmony," and "displeasing monotony"—are indeed qualitative and subject to interpretation rather than precise determination, and that despite their enumeration in the ordinances, they were no more or less definitive or exacting than the terms used in consideration of *Stoyanoff* and *Reid*.

THE CONUNDRUM OF RECONCILING DESIGN AESTHETICS WITH LEGAL STANDARDS

It is an anomaly that on the one hand predetermined, evaluative design standards are aspired to and even made requisite by law. Yet even apparently scrupulous attempts to delineate design standards and criteria have failed to pass court scrutiny for reason of being "void for vagueness" (*Giacco v. Pennsylvania*, 382 U.S. 399, 1966, 401). On the other hand, though free discretion in design review can reasonably be construed as violating reasonable certainty, in several of the cases examined here, such discretionary review has enjoyed court approval.

Where rejection of a certain design by a public review board has been upheld by a court, the assumption has been that architecture as art is guided by established aesthetic principles subscribed to by the architectural profession at large. The court in *Reid,* for instance, defended the review process on the assumption that a board of "highly trained experts in the field of architecture" could make definitive aesthetic judgments based on "proper architectural principles." The apparent feeling was that, even if courts and the lay public could not judge on design aesthetics, "highly trained" architects could interpret and agree on "proper architectural principles" well enough to use them as a definitive standard for aesthetic judgment. This Pythagorean assumption of absolute principles and standards in architectural judgment is based on an illusion of definitive expertise in matters of aesthetics. Philip Selznick points to such deference as "the retreat to technology" (Selznick, 1957, 74) and Alan Altschuler similarly refers to the apparent invulnerability of expertness in the layman's eyes (Altshuler, 1969, 334 ff.). However, given the human nature of all professionals, expertness can just as easily be a cloak for dogma and subjectivity as a basis for disinterested objectivity.

It should also be pointed out that community design review boards are usually less interested in promoting "proper architectural principles" and its implication of esoteric design theory than in "associational harmony" with the existing cultural and architectural context of a community, whether or not of critical value—an end not without merit even in terms of "proper architectural principles." As Costonis observes, people tend to want "cultural stability-identity" in their environment, whether to maintain historic architecture or to recreate familiar, if somewhat counterfeit, traditional-style surroundings. He notes that "associational harmony, not visual beauty, is what community groups primarily seek from aesthetic regulation." It is ironic that the term "proper architectural principles" cited in the Cleveland Heights ordinance constituted the rationale justifying the actions of the community's review board in the *Reid* case. However, the values of the board seemed to be less "proper architectural principles" as taught in most schools of architecture or evidenced by the types of projects cited by professional organizations and journals than traditional design values held by neighboring homeowners seeking to perpetuate familiar "associational harmony" in the interests of "cultural stability-identity" (Costonis, 1982, 424). Even then, as noted by the Rhode

Island court in *Hayes v. Smith,* the police power can only require a project architect to take reasonable account of the aesthetic context of the surroundings and to make his design proposal compatible, "even if not so compatible as the commission [deems] advisable (167 A. 2d 546, R.I., 1961, 550).

Notwithstanding attempts to apply sociopsychological, economic, and other criteria to justify and guide official design review, the difficult search for standards is exacerbated by the nature of architecture as artistic expression. Just as design legislation and set formulae cannot substitute for architectural creativity, so design judgment defies the measurable specificity demanded by the law. As art critic Lionello Venturi observed, "There is not a science of beauty but only a criticism of it" (Venturi, 1964, 190–91). Huxtable puts the issue in the following terms:

> The problem with law and the design of amenities and any attempt to deal with the quality of the design involved is that such judgments cannot be quantified—they are unavoidably subjective, although responsible judgment rests on a very specific set of standards and their interpretations. . . . A textbook could be written . . . but there seems to be no way to translate such language into the measurable specifics required by law (Huxtable, 1978).

John W. Wade, in his 1977 analysis *Architecture, Problems, and Purposes* (Wade, 1977, 15), points out that modern architectural criticism as practiced by such professional critics as design professors is made in response to a "gestalt." Deriving from the maxim of modern architecture generally attributed to Louis Sullivan that "form follows function," the gestalt perception of contemporary design judgment conceives architecture as an integrated totality. The aesthetic quality of a building is regarded as a part of a holistic composition, not as an element that can be abstracted and considered separately. This gestalt conception makes narrow consideration of the aesthetic quality of a building's exterior virtually meaningless from a critical standpoint. Compounded by the ethereal nature of aesthetics itself, this view makes even more difficult the judicial demand for definitiveness and precision in prescribing standards in architectural aesthetics.

The propensity of architects to judge design

as a gestalt and of lawyers and judges to favor judgment based on precisely defined standards leads not only to special difficulty for official design review but is symptomatic of a basic disparity between the approaches of the design and legal professions. Like all disciplines, architecture and law each have distinctive values, methodologies, and semantic practices peculiar to themselves. In contrast to the law, which places high esteem on accepted doctrine and historic precedent, architecture assigns its highest premiums to originality and innovation. Whereas in law the judicial ethic is impartiality, often in architecture, as in other media of artistic expression, the more creative and established the individual, the stronger his convictions in a certain design philosophy. Moreover, members of review boards are generally quite ignorant of the limitations imposed over their actions by the First Amendment. By appointing distinguished design professionals to review boards, the public may find itself, whether deliberately or unwittingly, lending a particular design ideology its police power, as apparent in the AIA case.

Whereas legal thinking has precision and definiteness as its standards, architecture as artistic expression is judged on more ethereal, intangible criteria that defy explicit definition. The difference between the two is particularly evident in considering the judicial response to the precision (or lack of it) in the design standards at bar in the *Pacesetter* and *Morristown Road* cases. In all likelihood, it would also be revealed were the law to scrutinize the discretionary reasoning process used by the architectural review boards in evaluating the design proposals in *Reid* and *Stoyanoff*.

With their own training and professional life steeped in the legal approach, judges are accustomed to demanding definitiveness and precision in representations by lawyers, whether in factual evidence, legal arguments, public legislation, or in the judicial opinions of their colleagues. Not surprisingly, legal thinking is probably at its weakest in dealing with other disciplinary processes totally alien to its own, hence the propensity of some courts to defer judgments on such consideration as architectural aesthetics to professional architects sitting on boards of review. When courts do exert their influence on design controls, the precise standards they demand are in the explicit idiom of law, and often seem in-

compatible with the nature of the creative design process.

Lawyer James L. Bross cites Wade in tracing the absence of a common ground for communication between law and design to the classroom.

> Architectural teaching differs from law teaching in other respects which are critical in their implications for design review. In comparison to law professors who purportedly apply Occam's Razor to cut down unsupported generalities to precise terms, teachers of architecture "respond to the 'Gestalt,' the perceived totality of the project being presented." Because architecture teachers respond to the "Gestalt," there is considerable flexibility in the weighting of critical values applied. . . . ["I]n the judgment process there is no explicit weighting of the judgmental values. There is no explicit proportioning of importance among the many issues that architectural criticism addresses."

Thus, the existing system of architectural education fails to properly articulate substantive standards to balance the competing values in design review. This system also falls short of the legal procedural requirements that decisions be made with "articulate consistency," and with discretion properly structured to insure fair, regular and consistent decisions. "Design criticism has tended to be random and disordered" (Bross, 1979, 226–27).

ADMINISTRATIVE AND PROCEDURAL REFORM OF DESIGN REVIEW

The difficulty of articulating standards for architectural review that would afford free design expression yet satisfy the requirement of law for precise, predefined criteria has led legal commentators to point to the apparent incongruity and futility of the task. With recognition that creative, high-quality design cannot be attained through mechanical application of legislative standards, many observers have concluded that design regulation must ultimately depend on knowledge and considered judgment. Law professor Jesse J. Dukeminier writes:

> What we need . . . to solve a value problem is not an illusion of an absolute standard but decision-makers whose technical training and knowledge of human beings are sufficiently extensive to qualify them to pass judgment on the particular problem

and to develop rational techniques for implementing our generalized, flexible, relativistic community values (Dukeminier, 1955, 229).

Kenneth Culp Davis shares Dukeminier's view but is more specific in recommendations. In his authoritative *Administrative Law Treatise,* he writes:

> The problem is not whether we want to prevent arbitrariness but how to do it. Putting some words into a statute that a court can call a legislative standard is not a very good protection against arbitrariness. The protections that are effective are hearings with procedural safeguards, legislative supervision, and judicial review (Davis, 1958, 108).

In *Discretionary Justice* he concludes, "The hope lies, I think, not in better statutory standards, but in earlier and more elaborate administrative rule-making and in better structuring and checking of discretionary power" (Davis, 1969, 219).

Davis's ideas are picked up by lawyer George Lefcoe, who points to the particular difficulty of attempting predetermined standards in architectural review and suggests the solution lies not in the application of standards but in improved administrative procedure in the conduct of board business. He writes: "As for design review, if what courts fear is favoritism or a lack of predictability for architects and developers, the best way to meet these concerns is not by elaborate formulas in statutes or ordinances but in administrative systems so structured as to minimize precisely these risks" (Lefcoe, 1974, 50). Lefcoe continues by making three specific suggestions.

First is that any party with substantial interest in a design proposal be allowed the opportunity to challenge review-board members whom they believe to be biased and incapable of impartial judgment. Obviously, the fairness of the review process can be compromised if evaluation is made by board officials who are, for example, associates or adversaries of the applicant, whether in design philosophy or in business competition.

Second is the proposed adoption of the judicial practice of opinion writing to the design review process. The idea is favored by architect Robert Venturi and his associates, who argue that review boards should be held accountable for their decisions. Like judges, who are also given great discretionary power, review boards should state the reasons for their decisions in written opinions. This, according to Venturi and his associates, is "a great protection" (Venturi, 1972, 188). Their view is also shared by Davis, who reasons:

> Statement of findings and reasons will not assure fairness of the decision, but it will pull in that direction. A member who merely votes yes or no, with no findings or reasons, may in human fashion give in to notions or whims. Subjecting his findings and reasons to the view of outside critics—and inside critics—may cause him to try to make his action appear rational, and the easiest way to appear rational is usually to be rational (Davis, 1969, 131).

In dissenting from the majority in the *Reid* case, Judge Corrigan showed implicit dissatisfaction with the reason given by a review-board member for rejecting Mrs. Reid's proposed design, to wit: "We don't like the appearance of the house in this neighborhood" (192 N.E. 2d 74, Ohio App., 1963, 79). As in the law, the practice of opinion writing by review-board members would open their actions to the same kind of scrutiny to which the design itself is subject, thus providing an appropriate degree of protection against arbitrary decision making by the public body. Certainly a requirement of review boards to furnish written evaluations and opinions to support their findings publicly would increase the likelihood of substantive professionalism in design judgment.

Finally, with a well-maintained and open record of past board decisions and written opinions, Lefcoe suggests, a procedural model for future board actions can borrow from "common law tradition itself" by deriving principles empirically from precedent decisions (Lefcoe, 1974, 14). This idea was proposed by Davis, who writes: "Building law through adjudication is a sound and necessary process; the great bulk of American law is the product of that process" (Davis, 1969, 57).

There is no diminishing the complexity of aesthetic questions and the difficulty of abstracting meaningful standards from common-law-style procedure. However, a suggestion by Davis may aid in mitigating the problem:

> Seeing all around a complex subject is not a prerequisite to making a sound rule, because a rule need not be in the form of an abstract generalization; a

rule can be limited to resolving one or more hypothetical cases, without generalizing. . . .

An agency which uses three tools for making law—adjudication, rules in the form of generalizations, and rules in the form of hypotheticals—is much better equipped to serve the public interest than an agency which limits itself to the first two of the three tools (Ibid., 60–61).

Lefcoe applies Davis's concept of using "hypotheticals" to the process of architectural design review:

An administrative board can take the essential ingredients of cases it has decided, and convert them into hypotheticals for its annual report. After stating the facts in the examples it has chosen, the board can next explain the problem raised by the facts, and indicate its answer to the problem. Finally, the board should supply reasons for its positions. In this way, guidelines will be evolved which do not tie the board's hands as much as general pronouncements might (Lefcoe, 1974, 14).

It might furthermore be kept in mind that the American system of precedent case law indeed makes no attempt at generalization or even periodic abstraction; and in fact, in consideration of a case at bar, any precedent can be regarded somewhat as a de facto "hypothetical" from which a governing rule can be derived.

Accordingly, notwithstanding the complex nature of aesthetic questions, a definitive and open process of design evaluation, including written opinions, a recording of precedent decisions, and a periodic, public review of past actions, can yield principles to structure the exercise of discretion in board review and clarify board actions before interested parties, the public, and the courts. From this empirical process can emerge principles that might afford the "fair certainty" associated by Hayek with the Rule of Law as well as freedom for creative architectural expression so difficult to reconcile with more definitive design standards.

In proposing a model ordinance for local design review, Lefcoe further suggests a rule to delimit board interference with a development proposal:

[The suggested ordinance] seeks to embody something analogous to a distinction familiar to lawyers between a de novo and a "reasonableness" review.

When a court hears a dispute de novo, it makes all factual determinations afresh. On a "reasonableness" standard the reviewing court only ascertains whether those primarily responsible for the decision have taken all necessary considerations into account. This distinction has a counterpart in grading systems that differentiate between pass-fail work and honors. It is not the function of the review board under this model to compel all projects to receive an "honors" rating. Their authority is solely to make sure that certain items have been treated passably well. When boards attempt to do more than that, they inevitably find themselves substituting their personal views for those of the architect (Ibid., 38).

Davis further amplifies the distinction between a check and de novo review:

Paradoxically, the principle of check is often at its best when it is limited to correction of arbitrariness or illegality, and it may be relatively ineffective when it includes de novo review. This is because of the important fact, sometimes overlooked, that a de novo determination may itself introduce arbitrariness or illegality for the first time and not be checked, whereas a check may be limited to the one objective of eliminating arbitrariness or illegality, so that almost all final action is subject to a check for arbitrariness or illegality. The recognized superiority of a check to a de novo determination is one of the main reasons that the mainstay of judicial review of administrative action is a review of limited scope, not de novo review, although in some circumstances de novo review may be desirable (Davis, 1969, 142–43).

BRENNAN'S RULE

In addition to these suggested reforms in review procedures is a requirement advocated by Supreme Court Justice Brennan, that if adopted would lend both legitimacy and substance to any form of aesthetic regulation. Brennan made these recommendations not once but twice, first in 1981 in his concurrence with the court in *Metromedia, Inc. v. City of San Diego* and again in 1984 in his dissent from the majority in *Taxpayers for Vincent*. In *Metromedia*, the justice wrote:

Of course, it is not for a court to impose its own notion of beauty on San Diego. But before deferring to a city's judgment, a court must be convinced that the city is seriously and comprehensively addressing aesthetic concerns with respect to its environment. Here, San Diego has failed to demonstrate a comprehensive coordinated effort in its commercial and industrial areas to address other obvious contributors to an unattractive environment. In this sense the ordinance is underinclusive. Of course, this is not to say that the city must address all aesthetic problems at the same time, or none at all. Indeed, from a planning point of view, attacking the problem incrementally and sequentially may represent the most sensible solution. On the other hand, if billboards alone are banned and no further steps are contemplated or likely, the commitment of the city to improving its physical environment is placed in doubt. By showing a comprehensive commitment to making its physical environment in commercial and industrial areas more attractive, and by allowing only narrowly tailored exceptions, if any, San Diego could demonstrate that its interest in creating an aesthetically pleasing environment is genuine and substantial. This is a requirement where, as here, there is an infringement of important constitutional consequence (453 U.S. 490, 1981, 531–33).

In other words, Brennan suggests that a court would—and should—approve a municipality's regulation of aesthetic considerations only on the condition that the community demonstrate a "comprehensive coordinated effort" at addressing the overall problem of environmental aesthetics. The inference is that aesthetic regulation, including design review of private development, should be predicated on a demonstrated comprehensive commitment by local government to community attractiveness. Logically, any public effort to beautify the community must entail a plan of urban design, regardless of the ultimate course of action chosen. In the *Vincent* case three years following *Metromedia,* Brennan was even more explicit:

> In cases like this, where a total ban is imposed on a particularly valuable method of communication, a court should require the government to provide tangible proof of the legitimacy and substantiality of its aesthetic objective. Justifications for such restrictions articulated by the government should be critically examined to determine whether the government has committed itself to addressing the identified aesthetic problem.
>
> In my view, such statements of aesthetic objectives should be accepted as substantial and unrelated to the suppression of speech only if the government

demonstrates that it is pursuing an identified objective seriously and comprehensively and in ways that are unrelated to the restriction of speech. Without such a demonstration, I would invalidate the restriction as violative of the First Amendment. By requiring this type of showing, courts can ensure that governmental regulation of the aesthetic environments remains within the constraints established by the First Amendment. First, we would have a reasonably reliable indication that it is not the content or communicative aspect of speech that the government finds unaesthetic. Second, when a restriction of speech is part of a comprehensive and seriously pursued program to promote an aesthetic objective, we have a more reliable indication of the government's own assessment of the substantiality of its objective. And finally, when an aesthetic objective is pursued on more than one front, we have a better basis upon which to ascertain its precise nature and thereby determine whether the means selected are the least restrictive ones for achieving the objective (466 U.S. 789, 1984, 827–29).

Brennan's rule, by requiring the community to demonstrate a comprehensive plan and program, of which design review could be a part, could produce a standard by which private design could be measured. The requirement for such a plan might be met, for example, by such design guidelines as adopted by any of the communities whose regulatory devices are discussed later in this book (see Part Two, Design Review in Practice). The design of any private development could be evaluated in terms of its compatibility with the plan and whether it advances or detracts from the stated community objective in design. A requirement for a community to have such a plan should scarcely be regarded as an impediment to the design review process, for indeed its existence would invariably strengthen the legitimacy and substance of review. Clear articulation of a community's policy goals in urban design would increase the likelihood that a requirement for private development to conform to a community's urban design objectives would be sustained on substantive grounds and not on the confused premises of some past decisions.

In conclusion, it seems appropriate that architectural design review should be considered less in terms of individual buildings and more in context of the urban design of a community as a whole. Considering the counsel of scholars and jurists from Hayek to Brennan, it is only reasonable that a prerequisite for design regulation and review be adoption of a public policy and plan that specify in advance the precise urban design objectives and standards that the community is committed to enforce and against which the design of private development can be gauged without prejudice or arbitrariness.

REFERENCES

This chapter is adapted from the book by Richard Tseng-yu Lai. 1988. *Law in Urban Design and Planning: The Invisible Web*. New York: Van Nostrand Reinhold.

"A.I.A. Headquarters: Headquarters for Architecture?" 1967. *Progressive Architecture* 48 (December): 136.

Altshuler, Alan A. 1965. *The City Planning Process: A Political Analysis*. Reprint 1969. Ithaca, N.Y.: Cornell University Press.

American Law Reports 2d 58. 1958. Rochester, N.Y.: The Lawyers Co-operative Publishing Co.

Bross, James L. 1979. "Taking Design Review Beyond the Beauty Part." *Environmental Law* 9:211.

Costonis, John J. 1982. "Law and Aesthetics: A Critique and a Reformulation of the Dilemma." *Michigan Law Review* 80:355.

Dalton, Dolores Ann. 1979. "San Francisco's Residential Zoning: Architectural Controls in Central City Neighborhoods." *University of San Francisco Law Review* 13:945.

Davis, Kenneth C. 1958. *Administrative Law Treatise*. St. Paul: West Publishing Co.

———. 1969. *Discretionary Justice*. Louisiana State University Press. Reprint 1980. Westport, Ct.: Greenwood Press.

Dukeminier, J. J., Jr. 1955. "Zoning for Aesthetic Objectives: A Reappraisal." *Law and Contemporary Problems* 20:218.

Hayek, Friedrich A. 1944. *The Road to Serfdom*. Reprint 1960. Chicago: University of Chicago Press.

Huxtable, Ada Louise. 1976. *Kicked a Building Lately?* New York: Quadrangle Books.

———, personal letter, March 28, 1978. Quoted by Clifford L. Weaver and Richard F. Babcock. 1979. *City Zoning: The Once and Future Frontier*. Chicago and Washington: Planners Press 301.

Kucera, H. P. 1960. "The Legal Aspects of Aesthetics in Zoning." *Institute of Planning and Zoning* 1:21. Quoted in respondent's brief, *Oregon City v. Hartke*, 400 p. 2d 255, Ore., 1965. See *Harvard Law Review* 71 (1966): 1321.

Lefcoe, George. 1974. *Design Review Boards: A Handbook for Communities*. Washington, D.C.: American Institute of Architects.

McMillin, Ronald R. 1971. "Community Wide Architectural Controls in Missouri." *Missouri Law Review* 36:423.

Michelman, Frank. 1969. "Toward a Practical Standard for Aesthetic Regulation." *Practical Lawyer* 15:36.

Neary, John. 1969. "A Cube House vs. The Squares." *Life* (November 14): 83–86.

Selznick, Philip. 1957. *Leadership in Administration*. New York: Harper and Row.

Turnbull, H. Rutherford III. 1971. "Aesthetic Zoning." *Wake Forest Law Review*. 7:230.

Venturi, Lionello. 1936. *History of Art Criticism*. Translated by Charles Marriott. Reprint 1964. New York: Dutton.

Venturi, Robert; Denise Scott Brown; and Steven Izenour. 1972. *Learning from Las Vegas*. Cambridge: M.I.T. Press.

Wade, John W. 1977. *Architecture, Problems, and Purposes*. New York: John Wiley.

4

The Abuse of Discretionary Power

Brian W. Blaesser, Esq.

Rudnick & Wolfe, Attorneys, Chicago, IL

> *The Appearance Commission attempted to negotiate us down from what was acceptable per the code [10' × 10'], to a five foot wide sign. After much discussion, we finally agreed on an eight foot wide sign, which they approved. I asked them if we had any other choice in the matter, and they commented that our proposal could be tabled again until next month.*

> —Letter of a shopping center developer to
> a village mayor in suburban Illinois

Perhaps one the most ubiquitous of the various types of advisory bodies found in local communities is the appearance committee. The appearance committee, or commission, with its charge to serve as the aesthetic watchdog for the community, has become a fixture in many communities. Developers find it easier to accommodate this body's requests than to challenge it.[1] The exasperated and resigned shopping center developer whose letter of frustration to the village mayor is quoted above is not alone in feeling that this type of action by an advisory body is an abuse of discretionary authority at the local level.

With the aid of two U.S. Supreme Court decisions,[2] courts generally have taken a more permissive attitude toward land use regulations that address "aesthetic" concerns of a community. Although these two decisions upheld the regulation of signs for aesthetic and traffic safety reasons, the language from these cases helped move many state courts toward the view that aesthetics alone is a legitimate governmental purpose in land use regulation.[3] These state and federal court decisions also encouraged local governments to adopt regulations focusing on the aesthetic impacts of "ugly" signs, loss of open space, and erosion of community "character." In these regulations, communities are increasingly adopting discretionary review approaches to design review issues ranging from fences in neighborhoods to office buildings in downtown areas.

THE MEANING OF DISCRETION

Discretion refers to the exercise by a legislative or administrative body of judgment, within the limits of power delegated to it, to make substantive and procedural choices for the purpose for

---

1. For the handful of cases involving challenges to such bodies, see *Wakelin v. Town of Yarmouth*, 523 A.2d 575 (Me., 1987); *Morristown Road Associates v. Mayor and Common Council*, 394 A.2d 157 (N.J., 1978). See also Poole and Kobert, "Architectural Appearance Review Regulations and the First Amendment: The Constitutionally Infirm 'Excessive Difference' Test," *Zoning and Planning Law Report* 12 (January 1989).

2. *Metromedia, Inc. v. City of San Diego*, 453 U.S. 490 (1981); *Members of City Council v. Taxpayers for Vincent*, 466 U.S. 789 (1984).

3. See, e.g., *Donrey Communications Co. v. City of Fayetteville*, 660 S.W.2d 900 (Ark., 1983, cert. denied, 466 U.S. 959 (1984); *Metromedia, Inc. v. City of San Diego*, 610 P.2d 407 (Cal., 1980), rev'd on other grounds, 453 U.S. 490 (1981); *City of Lake Wales v. Lamar Adv. Ass'n*, 414 So.2d 1030 (Fla., 1982); *John Donnelly & Sons v. Outdoor Adv. Bd.*, 339 N.E.2d 709 (Mass., 1975); *Cromwell v. Ferrier, 225 N.E.2d 748 (N.Y., 1967)*; *State v. Jones*, 290 S.E.2d 675 (N.C., 1982); *Oregon City v. Hartke*, 400 P.2d 255 (Or., 1965); *State v. Smith*, 618 S.W.2d 474 (Tenn., 1981); *LaSalle National Bank v. County of Lake*, 325 N.E.2d 105, 110 (Ill., 1975).

which the power was delegated.[4] In the context of land use and urban design, discretion is exercised to make design respond to the appearance, architectural design, or historic character of the surrounding area.

ABUSE OF DISCRETIONARY POWER

An abuse of discretion means action taken that is inconsistent with the intent and policy of a statute or implementing ordinance, as applied to the facts and circumstances of a case. More often than not, the discretionary review approach to design review fosters abuses of discretion at both the administrative and the legislative levels. At the administrative level this occurs because frequently an advisory committee's "recommendation" that a permit be denied, or conditioned upon compliance with specific design modifications, is given the force of a final decision by virtue of the local legislative body's routine affirmance of, or extreme reluctance to overturn, such recommendation. Because the village board or city council usually acts by ordinance to approve the recommendations of such reviewing commissions and committees, depending upon the state jurisdiction, it is viewed as acting in its "legislative" capacity and does not have to follow precise standards.[5] If there are insufficient standards and procedures to guide the exercise of discretion by the "advisory" commission or committee, the legislative body's subsequent affirmance of a recommendation by ordinance only compounds the applicant's burden of proving the decision was arbitrary. Moreover, the procedural steps under the ordinance that establishes such an advisory commission or committee may have the effect of making that advisory body a final decision maker. When combined with imprecise standards, this latter circumstance is disastrous to an applicant with a controversial development proposal.

Legislative bodies can also engage in abuses of "legislative" discretion by imposing additional conditions of approval, and subjecting as-of-right uses to discretionary review procedures through which aesthetic considerations may be imposed.

CONSTITUTIONAL LIMITATIONS ON THE EXERCISE OF DISCRETION

At issue in these two governmental approaches to discretionary review is fundamental fairness—the heart of due process. This central principle of the Fifth and Fourteenth Amendments to the Constitution requires that citizens be protected from the fluctuations of legislative policy.[6] Because the right to develop property is a valuable property right,[7] the failure to articulate clear, workable standards reduces the property owner to a state of uncertainty and effectively deprives the owner of that right. Failure to establish standards to guide the exercise of discretion at the administrative level also risks uneven treatment, a denial of equal protection. At worst, as expressed by the Supreme Court of Maine in *Waterville Hotel Corp. v. Board of Zoning Appeals,*[8] standardless administration of a zoning ordinance can encourage roving discrimination:

> Without definite standards an ordinance becomes an open door to favoritism and discrimination, a ready tool for the suppression of competition through the granting of authority to one and the withholding from another. . . . A zoning ordinance cannot permit administrative officers or boards to pick and choose the recipients of their favors.[9]

The two key constitutional doctrines that limit the exercise of discretion, and hence its abuse, in the imposition of land-use controls, are the doctrines of nondelegation of legislative power and void for vagueness.[10]

---

4. See generally Kenneth C. Davis, *Discretionary Justice* (Louisiana State University Press; Baton Rouge reprint, Urbana, Ill.: University of Illinois Press, 1979).

5. *LaSalle National Bank v. County of Lake,* 325 N.E.2d 105, 110 (Ill., 1975).

6. *West Main Assocs. v. Bellevue,* 720 P.2d 782 (Wash., 1986), citing the Federalist No. 44, at 301 (J. Madison) (J. Cooke, ed., 1961).

7. *Louthan v. King Cy.,* 617 P.2d 977 (Wash., 1980).

8. 241 A.2d 50, 53 (Me., 1968).

9. *Id.* at 53, quoting the Michigan Supreme Court in *Osius v. City of St. Clair Shores,* 75 N.W.2d 25 (Mich., 1956).

10. For general discussion of these principles, see Blaesser & Weinstein, eds., *Land Use and the Constitution* (Planners Press, 1989).

Nondelegation of Power

Local legislative bodies may not delegate their legislative or policy-making power to administrative boards, commissions, or committees. Legislative bodies may, however, delegate to such administrative bodies the authority to exercise discretion provided that the delegation is accompanied by standards and specific procedural guidelines.[11] The delegation issue also implicates the ability of a local legislative body itself to act as an administrative body. The courts in many states hold that a village board or city council acts in a legislative capacity when it is authorized to approve special uses or planned unit developments. Therefore no precise standards are necessary.[12] Nor is the village board or city council bound by the recommendations of its staff or experts on such matters.[13]

Void for Vagueness

The void-for-vagueness doctrine is derived from the due process clause of the Fourteenth Amendment, specifically, the procedural due process requirement of notice. The doctrine concerns the lack of clarity or certainty in the language of regulation. Its purpose is to place a limit upon arbitrary and discretionary enforcement of the law.[14] Local courts, when presented with a void-for-vagueness challenge to a regulation most frequently echo the U.S. Supreme Court's language in *Broadrick v. Oklahoma*,[15] namely, that "[a]n ordinance is unconstitutionally vague when men of common intelligence must necessarily guess at its meaning."[16] In other words, due process of law in legislation requires definiteness or certainty.

Limitation on "Legislative" Discretion

Although the delegation and vagueness doctrines are most frequently discussed with emphasis on the exercise of discretion by local administrative bodies, it is the local legislative body, in the first instance, that creates the constitutional issue by either improperly delegating its policy-making powers or adopting an ordinance containing vague regulations. In its enthusiasm for discretionary review procedures that lend themselves to analyses of development "impact," a local government often overlooks the well-established legal principle that the *adopting* by a local legislative body of zoning classifications with related terms, standards, and requirements applicable to all persons is, in fact, its fundamental exercise of discretion: "The acts of administering a zoning ordinance do not go back to the questions of policy and discretion which were settled at the time of the adoption of the ordinance."[17]

DESIGN REVIEW AND THE EXERCISE OF DISCRETION

Before addressing current design review models, it is important to describe certain regulatory settings that most frequently lead to abuses of discretion in aesthetic regulation.

Regulatory Settings That Invite Abuses of Discretion

The regulatory circumstances that most easily invite abuses of discretion in aesthetic regulation may be defined in four categories: (1) regulations that allow as-of-right uses to be converted to special or conditional uses and subjected to design review; (2) vague regulatory statements of purpose and accompanying standards; (3) "advisory" citizen-based commissions or committees whose recommendations are guided by few standards but given great weight by the legislative body; (4) approval procedures that give those "advisory" commissions or committees virtual veto power over development requests. The following discus-

---

11. *Montgomery County v. Woodward & Lothrop. Inc.*, 376 A.2d 483, 500 (1977), citing 8 McQuillin, *Municipal Corporations* Section 25.35 *et seq.* (3rd ed. rev., 1976).

12. See e.g., *LaSalle National Bank v. County of Lake*, 325 N.E.2d 105, 110 (Ill., 1975).

13. *Minnetonka Congregation of Jehovah's Witnesses, Inc. v. Svee*, 226 N.W.2d 306 (Minn., 1975).

14. *Burien Bark Supply v. King County*, 725 P.2d 994, 996 (Wash., 1986) citing *State v. White*, 640 P.2d 1061 (Wash., 1982).

15. 413 U.S. 601 (1973).

16. *Union National Bank & Trust v. Village of New Lenox*, 505 N.E.2d 1, 3 (Ill. App., 1987).

---

17. *Valley View Industrial Park v. City of Redmond*, 733 P.2d 182, 192 (Wash., 1987), quoting *State ex rel. Ogden v. Bellevue*, 275 P.2d 899 (Wash., 1954).

sion details the regulatory scenarios that give rise to such opportunities for discretionary abuse.

"Automatic" Conversions to Conditional Use

An example of local government administrative actions that attempt to "convert" a permitted use to a "conditional use" and then impose conditions through design review after an applicant has demonstrated compliance with all zoning code requirements for a permitted-use is found in *Chase v. City of Minneapolis*.[18] The applicant in that case sought approval for a convenience-food restaurant, which was listed as a permitted use in the zoning district, subject to specific performance standards. His application complied with all site plan requirements for curb cuts, safety, signage, lighting, landscaping, parking, screening of view, and architectural appearance. However, at the public hearing, neighborhood residents expressed the desire that the property be used for residential use rather than a commercial use and argued that the restaurant was inconsistent with the area's proresidential comprehensive plan. Following a discussion of how the proposal was "inappropriately" commercial and inconsistent with the comprehensive plan, the planning commission voted to deny the building permit on the basis of noncompliance with the following provision f the Minneapolis Zoning Code:

> The architectural appearance and functional plan of the building shall not be so dissimilar to existing buildings as to cause impairment in property values within reasonable distance of applicant's zoning lot.

However, no facts regarding dissimilar architectural design or impairment of property values were presented at the hearing to rebut the applicant's evidence on these issues. In the subsequent mandamus proceeding brought by the developer, the city argued that the conditions placed on the approval of the permit under the ordinance "recharacterized" the requested use as conditional, which gave the city discretion to consider it in light of the general welfare and city's planning goals. The court, however, ruled that the city could not arbitrarily convert the permitted use to a conditional

use in such a manner. Because the application complied with the zoning code in all respects, approval was required as a matter of right.[19]

Vague Statements and Standards

Vague statements of purpose and vague performance standards as applied to development requests are also open invitations to abuse of discretion. The following statement of sign criteria was held in *Diller and Fisher Company, Inc. v. Architectural Review Board of Borough of Stone Harbor*,[20] to be impermissibly vague, inviting mischievous results:

> Signs that demand public attention rather than invite attention should be discouraged. Color should be selected to harmonize with the overall building or scheme to create a mood and reinforce symbolically the sign's primary communication message. . . . Care must be taken not to introduce too many colors into a sign. A restricted use of color will maintain the communication function of the sign and create a visually pleasing element as an integral part of the texture of the street.

Undue Legislative Weight Given to Advisory Body Recommendations

Although it is easy to argue that the subject matter of appearance and architectural review committees is inherently subjective, it is hard to believe that better standards than those invalidated in *Morristown Road Associates v. Mayor and Common Council*[21] could not have been written. There, the ordinance establishing a design review committee relied upon the basic criterion of "harmony" with existing structures and terrain for applying design review. More specifically, it provided that "proposed structures shall be related harmoniously to the terrain and to existing buildings in the vicinity that have a visual relationship to the proposed buildings."

In addition, the ordinance provided that "[e]xcessive similarity of appearance and the repetitiveness of features resulting in displeasing monotony of design shall not be permitted."[22] But

---

18. 401 N.W.2d 408 (Minn. App., 1987).

19. *Id.* at 413.
20. 587 A.2d 674 (N.J., 1970).
21. 394 A.2d 157 (N.J., 1978).
22. *Id.* at 159.

because the ordinance lacked definitions of such critical terms as "harmonious" and "displeasing" the court, not surprisingly, concluded that this basic "harmony" standard "[did] not adequately circumscribe the process of administrative decision" and vested the design review committee "with too broad discretion," permitting "determinations based upon whim, caprice or subjective considerations."[23]

Is the Administrative Body Truly "Advisory"?

Because a local government often characterizes its appearance committee as "advisory" only, it is more difficult to address the extent to which specific standards must be established to guide the decisions of such a committee. There are recognized principles of administrative law that distinguish between decisions that are "declaratory" in nature and those that are "advisory" only. Advisory decisions generally are not reviewable and do not have a binding effect, except where estoppel can be demonstrated. By contrast, declaratory decisions are binding upon applicants and are also appealable.[24]

Ordinance language, however, does not always clearly establish the "advisory" or "declaratory" role that the particular committee plays in the decision-making process. For example, in *Pacesetter Homes, Inc. v. Village of Olympia Fields*,[25] the developer's application to construct a single-family residence was referred to the Architectural Advisory Committee, which determined that because the residence was "architecturally similar" to other buildings in the area, the application should be disallowed. The committee's action was authorized under an ordinance that provided that (1) if the committee determined that the permit should be *approved*, then the village board had no authority in the matter; (2) if the committee determined that the permit should be *disapproved*, then the building permit could not be issued unless expressly authorized by the village board on appeal. The court held that the Architectural Advisory Committee's function un-

der those procedures was declaratory rather than advisory and that therefore the principles governing the delegation of legislative powers to administrative bodies were applicable.[26]

MODELS OF CURRENT DESIGN REVIEW PROCESSES

Presented below are five models of design review processes. Some of these models are in fact in existence or about to be implemented in certain jurisdictions. Others, as will be discussed, represent ways in which the process could be structured depending on the constraints and opportunities within a particular jurisdiction.

From the perspective of local government, *Model No. 1* represents an ideal design review process. The structure reflects the existence of state legislation authorizing the establishment of a separate design review entity to implement design review plans and policies. Presumably, the state legislation also requires that the local government take certain steps, including a careful planning study that identifies the critical design elements of a geographic area, followed by the adoption of standards and procedures to implement the plan.

Model No. 2 ties the objectives of design review to economic development policy by empowering a local development authority, enabled under state legislation, to carry out economic development policies as well as design review policies in order to further the overall economic viability of specific areas of a city, such as a downtown. This model can be found in Kentucky's legislation (KRS 82.660–82.670), authorizing the establishment of "overlay districts" to provide additional regulations for design standards and development in areas that have historical, architectural, natural, or cultural significance that is suitable for preservation or conservation.

Under the legislation, the local legislative body is authorized to delegate the implementation of overlay district regulations to a department or agency of the city or to a nonprofit corporation established by the city. For example, the City of Louisville, which is considering utilizing overlay districts as one means to implement its adopted downtown development plan, has established a

23. *Id.* at 163.

24. See Davis, Administrative Law Treatise, vol. 1, section 4.09

25. 244 N.E.2d 369 (Ill., 1968).

26. *Id.* at 372.

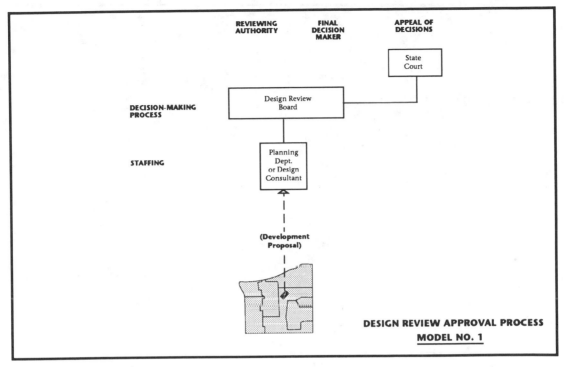

Figure 4-1. Design review approval process, Model No. 1.

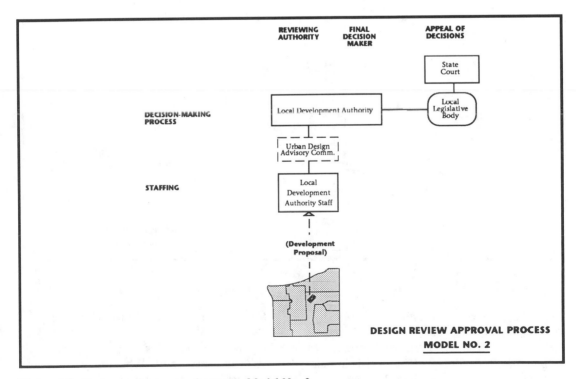

Figure 4-2. Design review approval process, Model No. 2.

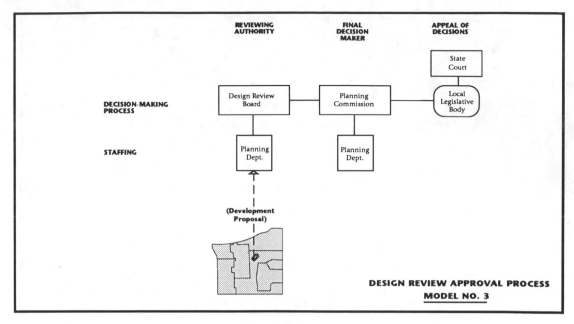

Figure 4-3. Design review approval process, Model No. 3.

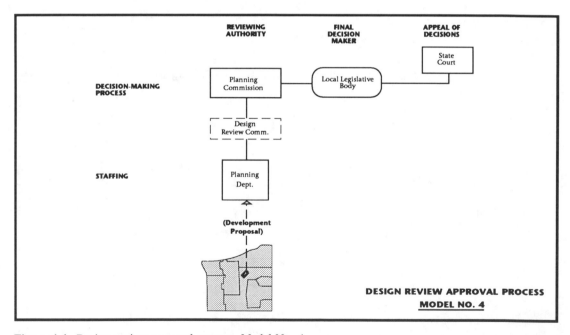

Figure 4-4. Design review approval process, Model No. 4.

Louisville Development Authority (LDA). It is expected that the responsibility for implementing overlay districts will be delegated to the LDA by the board of aldermen. The legislation also requires that an "advisory body" be established to assist the administrative body that administers the provisions of the overlay district ordinance.

Finally, the legislation provides that appeals of decisions by the administrative body may be taken first to the local legislative body, and from there to the state court. While having the local legislative body hear appeals is not always desirable, depending upon the political climate of the particular jurisdiction, it can prove to be a safety

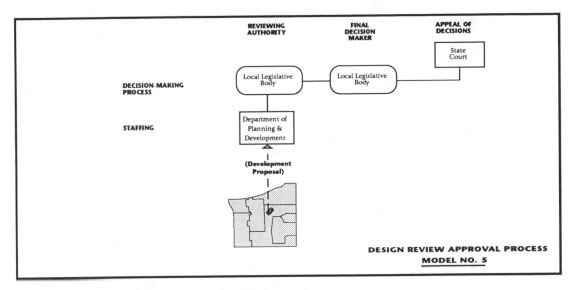

Figure 4-5. Design review approval process, Model No. 5.

valve for resolving issues before they reach the litigation stage.

Model No. 3 is structured to reflect the situation that typically constrains jurisdictions desiring to implement design review processes. Provided the state legislation recognizes aesthetics as a legitimate object of the police power, it is usually possible to establish a design review board to advise the body that in most jurisdictions is authorized by statute to make certain discretionary decisions—the planning commission. This structure has the advantage of limiting the design review board to an advisory role. Provided there are adequate standards, the planning commission can utilize either a conditional use mechanism or some other statutorily or judicially recognized mechanism through which to apply conditions that reflect certain aesthetic considerations. In addition, the appeal to the local legislative body is often desirable in this instance because, as in Model No. 2, it provides a safety valve through which disputes can be resolved administratively.

Model No. 4 reflects the reality that is prevalent in some jurisdictions, namely, that the planning commission does not have the authority to make final decisions on matters involving aesthetic considerations or even conditional uses. Under such circumstances, it is the local legislative body that acts as the final decision maker on most land-use approvals. This model is typical of many villages and small cities.

Model No. 5 has potential application in those circumstances, usually a downtown, where a city has retained control of certain parcels of land through urban renewal or other means. This model sets up the local legislative body as the final decision maker on development projects that may involve a public subsidy in one form or another. Usually because projects involving design review within a downtown involve significant sites, large structures with very visible benefits or detriments to the downtown, the local legislative body desires to be involved from the beginning. This model allows for that involvement, but its success depends upon how well staff can present the relevant issues on design review to the local legislators.

LIMITING THE POTENTIAL FOR ABUSE OF DISCRETION IN DESIGN REVIEW

In the face of the many invitations to abuse of discretion that take place in the context of design review and aesthetic regulation, safeguards are needed. The following is a brief prescription.

Principles for Drafting Design Review Standards and Guidelines

At the outset, a local government should decide what level of control it wishes to exercise through design review and whether state law (statutory or judicial decisions) authorizes that level of control. Mandatory controls that have design implications are usually limited to such judicially accepted areas as build-to lines, height, bulk, and setbacks. Whether the scope of mandatory aesthetic regulation may be broadened will depend upon the existence of specific studies or plans to support such additional requirements and the extent to which state law can be read to authorize such prescriptions. By contrast, design "guidelines" express the design outcomes that are desired ("should"), but which are not mandatory. Whether mandatory or desirable, certain principles should be kept in mind. Specifically, the standards or guidelines should be *detailed,* not visionary, and employ *precise language.* For example, a guideline stating that "signage should enhance the pedestrian experience" is not specific enough to be meaningfully applied and creates a vagueness problem. At the same time, the drafter must avoid being too design-prescriptive. For example, simple pen-and-ink seating drawings for a plaza, coupled with a statement of how many linear feet of seating should be provided for each thirty square feet, convey the basic intent of seating without being too design-prescriptive—stiffling creative design responses.

In the case of design guidelines, it is also helpful to first state the *design principle* and then the guidelines that implement that principle. This simple hierarchy provides a foundation and rationale that is easily followed and aids the interpretation of how guidelines are to be applied. To that end, it is also important that if guidelines are articulated in an ordinance, that the ordinance explain the *weight* or *effect* that should be attached to them. The courts have emphasized that this is necessary to provide sufficient guidance to the decision maker.[27]

LIMITING THE POTENTIAL FOR ABUSE OF DISCRETION

Since it is the states from whom local governments receive the delegation of police power to exercise land-use controls, the states have the responsibility to ensure that local governments act fairly in imposing design regulations on development. State legislatures should mandate certain minimum requirements for discretionary decision-making processes. These requirements should apply regardless of whether the process for arriving at a design review determination starts with an administrative body vested with final authority or an "advisory" body. For example, state statutes could provide that standards utilized in discretionary decision making must provide for the *minimum discretion necessary* to accomplish the stated public purposes. Such statutes could also require that in addition to established administrative bodies, any citizen advisory body, such as the appearance committee described above, must go beyond general perceptions or conclusory findings in arriving at recommendations and make written findings of fact that tie those facts to clear standards and justify its recommendations. By mandating these changes in the conduct of discretionary review processes and ensuring careful drafting of standards and procedures at the local level, the objectives of design review can be realized without the abuse of discretionary power.

---

27. See, e.g., *Chandler v. Town of Pittsfield,* 496 A.2d 1058 (Me., 1985); *Pace Resources, Inc. v. Shrewsbury Township Planning Commission,* 492 A.2d 818 (Pa., 1985); *Sherman v. Colorado Springs Planning Commission,* 763 P.2d 292 (Colo., 1988).

5

Design Review and Conservation in England: Historical Development and Contemporary Relationships

John V. Punter

University of Strathclyde, Glasgow, Scotland

Design review, design control, or aesthetic control, as it is conventionally known, has always been an integral part of the development control system in the United Kingdom. It has an eighty-year history, although it only became applied to all parts of the country in 1947. Since the late 1960s in particular it has been a major bone of contention between the public and the development industry, between planners and architects, and between central and local government. Certainly there are many similarities with current controversies in the U.S., and it may be that an examination of the history of control in the U.K. will serve to clarify key issues for debate and resolution in design control at large.

Thus this chapter begins by outlining key differences between the British and American planning systems and the role of design control in each, as a prelude to explaining the evolution of control in several distinct phases: 1909–46, 1947–66, 1967–74, and 1975 to the present (Punter, 1986–87). The preoccupations of control are isolated and the key arguments explained with particular attention paid to the relationship between design control and urban conservation. Design control offers an important route to raising design standards but needs more effective policies and prescriptions, more skilled controllers, a broadening of concern beyond architectural character, and stronger support from central government to improve its effectiveness.

THE BRITISH AND AMERICAN PLANNING SYSTEMS: KEY FACTORS

It is important to appreciate the key differences between the British and American planning systems in order to understand the context of design control. In Britain, central government exercises considerable control over local planning practice maintaining control of both legislation and policy, the latter through circulars and guidance notes. Government advice can be enforced through an appeal process that allows aggrieved developers (but not third parties) to appeal to the Secretary of State for the Environment against a refusal of planning permission, and to have their case decided by an Inspectorate, who will usually place great emphasis upon the advice in prevailing circulars (30,000 such appeals were lodged in England in 1989).

A second key aspect of the British planning system is its discretionary nature. In contrast with Western Europe and America, where conformity to a development/zoning plan guarantees a planning permission, the British approach is to treat each application for planning permission on its merits. The legislation (1990 Act, section 70) requires local authorities to "have regard to the provisions of the development plan, so far as material to the application, and to any other material considerations." Such considerations may include

51

external appearance, layout, surroundings, physical impact, circulation, access, traffic, and so on, but also more strategic considerations of location, coordination and phasing, and desirable precedent. Even where a development plan exists it will usually only set very broad guidelines for a site. So not only are the basic planning parameters of development often very vague, but design control almost invariably becomes embroiled with more fundamental considerations of planning policy.

A third key issue is that it is the elected members in the form of the local council (or a subcommittee) who take the decisions upon planning applications, although they are in all cases advised by professional planners employed by the local authority. It is the planners' task to consult a wide variety of bodies, including district and county planning authorities, utilities, and the public, whether it be immediate neighbors, residents, or specialist amenity groups.

So design control or design review is in no sense separable from other aspects of the development control process, and it has political, professional, and participative components. Nor is it a matter for local authorities alone, and central government has been directly concerned to limit the extent of design control in the interests of the speed of decision making and the supposed efficiency of the economy at large, especially since 1979. Finally, design considerations have very rarely been fully codified in a plan, although a variety of policies and guidance have been produced on selected aspects of development.

Early History, 1909–47

The early history of control was marked by a series of local initiatives to inject design control into the regulation of suburban development but central government showed great suspicion about such initiatives. In 1932 legislation gave local authorities unequivocal powers to regulate design and external appearance, but an accompanying central government circular followed the architectural profession's advice in arguing that this should only be used to "prevent outrages." The circular also emphasised that it was important to judge proposed designs against the character of the surrounding area.

During the 1930s design control came into the

public eye through a series of celebrated appeal cases where largely Conservative lay planning committees sought to prevent the construction of modernist houses. However, the greatest influence on design was the peculiar combination of garden city site planning with neo-Georgian and Queen Anne revival house styles developed by Raymond Unwin and others, and promulgated by central government housing manuals for public housing estates (Punter, 1986).

The neo-Georgian found particular favor as a style for public buildings, an expression of utterly English "good manners" in design (Edwards, 1924). Like the struggle over housing styles, this, too, was an expression of a general reaction against the "stylistic excesses" of Victorian architecture. While design control has been seen as an expression of a collectivistic ethic (and was often accused of being totalitarian), it was, in this period, much more an expression of establishment views about the timeless values of classicism against Victorian eclecticism or the emergent modernism, and conservative-escapist values about good taste and the value of unspoiled countryside and historic townscapes (Brett, 1949).

The Impetus for Conservation, 1947–73

In 1947, in the aftermath of the Second World War, a Labour government provided local authorities with the power to refuse development (without compensation) unless it had received planning permission and introduced comprehensive town planning. While the legislation scarcely mentioned design control, it was clear that control of the design and external appearance of development was one of the "material considerations" that could influence the grant of planning permission. Government advice on central area redevelopment promoted the principles of modernism with an emphasis upon segregation of land uses, the principles of open planning and sunlighting, and efficient traffic circulation and parking, leaving only isolated "historic buildings" as landmarks (Ministry of Town and Country Planning, 1947). In residential development prewar design principles were extended with hybrid modernist versions of the neo-Georgian and new car-oriented patterns of layout (MHLG, 1953), but these were gradually replaced with advice on how to achieve ever-higher densities.

Disillusionment with the results of control was being widely expressed in the design professions by the mid 1950s (Nairn, 1957). Widespread public concern with the quality of redevelopment and the loss of familiar townscapes began to be expressed through the local amenity movement. The Civic Trust, formed as the umbrella organization for these groups, took up the mantle of the "Townscapists," like Cullen and Nairn, in a series of largely cosmetic facelift schemes in historic towns. But it was soon inspired by the 1962 Malraux Act in France (which created the French equivalent of Conservation Areas) to campaign for conservation legislation as a means of protecting historic townscapes (Dobby, 1978).

Historic Preservation and Conservation Areas

In rural areas the designation of National Parks and "Areas of Outstanding Natural Beauty" gave a greater impetus to rural than to urban conservation in the early postwar years. These designations now cover 23 percent of the land surface of England and Wales, while county councils have added further protective designations in their Metropolitan Green Belts and more remote "Areas of Great Landscape Value" to spread the presumption of conservation much wider (Blunden and Curry, 1988). In terms of the built environment, ancient monument protection dates back to 1888, but protection for individual historic buildings was introduced in 1944, when central government undertook to draw up lists of buildings of architectural or historic interest. This meant that anyone wishing to alter the character of, or demolish, a listed building needed a specific consent, although the government did not produce the first complete list until 1968 (Dobby, 1978). No compensation was payable for the loss of development rights implied by listing or later conservation controls.

The criteria for listing are of interest because they emphasize the value of antiquity per se, and the "principal works of principal architects" or buildings displaying technological innovation. Relevance to social history and association with well-known characters of events are two other criteria influencing selection, as is "group value," though the latter is supposed to be, but rarely is, directed toward town planning history (DoE, 1987). Criticisms of the criteria, particularly the

failure to acknowledge matters of local significance, must be tempered by the fact that in recent years listings have been generous, with a fourfold increase since 1968; the total now stands at 530,000 in England alone (Page, 1990). The 1968 act not only provided the means of preventing demolition of such buildings but also their alteration. The accompanying policy note in 1969 also presented the setting of each listed building (MHLG, 1969).

The 1967 Civic Amenities Act extended protection to whole areas of historic townscapes by allowing local authorities "to designate areas of special architectural or historic interest, the character or appearance of which it is desirable to preserve or enhance." The act also established the principle of much tighter *detailed* design control (and from 1971 demolition control) in such areas. A new pump-priming grant regime was established and tree protection was given additional emphasis in development control. Perhaps even more important, the Civic Amenities Act introduced the concept of public participation in the control process. By encouraging local people to participate in control in conservation areas the government unwittingly stimulated public interest in control decisions everywhere. In 1973 it conceded the basic principle "that opinion should be able to declare itself" before permissions were granted (Punter, 1987). Central government gave local authorities the power to designate whatever conservation areas they saw fit and the result is that some 7000 such areas have now been designated in England, and designations continue to increase at the rate of five percent per annum.

Meanwhile, outside of conservation areas and designated rural areas central government continued to restrain design control. Campaigns by the Royal Institute of British Architects in the 1950s and 1960s reinforced the view that architectural advice should carry greater weight than the "subjective views of planners, committees or the general public" (Punter, 1987). The Ministry revealed that in the design debate it was "usually on the side of the new and different conscious always that development must go on and that new techniques of building however hideous they may seem must be accepted—and perhaps one day will be admired" (Sharp, 1969).

The Conservation Movement and the drive for improved design control was given great impetus by the consequences of the 1968–73 development boom and the early 1960s high-rise public housing movement (Amery and Cruickshank, 1976). The desire to return to "traditional" garden city or terraced forms of housing in the public sector and the demand for more sensitive redevelopment in inner and central cities were manifested in public, professional, and political comment in the control process (Punter, 1987).

A key expression of the desire for improved control was the 1973 Essex *Design Guide for Residential Areas,* an attempt to codify a new approach to suburban design that was more responsive to the character of the locality, and that rejected the controlling influence of highway, parking, and layout standards, and the "anyplace" architecture of the mass house builders (Essex CC, 1973). A few local authorities produced guidance of similar quality, but regrettably the Essex guide was also widely and unthinkingly plagiarized by many authorities. After a House of Commons investigation into the whole issue of development control (HOC, 1977), the government wrote a new circular further clarifying its position on design. It was given a new twist by the election of a Conservative government bent on deregulation and by an environment minister, Michael Heseltine, who passionately believed in individual initiative against all forms of collective control.

Government's Restraint on Design Control

Circular 22/80, entitled *Development Control: Policy and Practice,* contained only four paragraphs on design (aesthetic) control. It opened with a quotation from the minister deriding democracy "as an arbiter of taste or as a judge of aesthetic . . . standards" and then reverted to the now-familiar refrain that "aesthetics is an extremely subjective matter." It argued that "developers should not be compelled to conform to the fashion of the moment at the expense of individuality, originality or traditional styles," nor be asked to adopt "unpopular" designs. Despite the "subjectivity" of aesthetics it was suggested that the views of architects or professionally qualified advisers should be given special weight, while planning authorities should confine their attentions to "rejecting obviously poor designs, out of

scale or character with their surroundings. Only exceptionally should they control details." Design guides were grudgingly accepted if they were not used as detailed rule books. Control of external appearance, however, was considered to be important in environmentally sensitive areas, including designated rural and urban landscapes, thus establishing a two-tier system where detailed control could be retained in high-quality "heritage" areas, but a largely laissez-faire system had to operate elsewhere.

Analyzing central government advice on control, in 1980 and in all the preceding circulars, one can detect three possible interpretations of the government position. It is possible to see the refusal to tackle issues of design quality seriously as a defeatist orthodoxy ("aesthetics is subjective!") in the gifted amateur tradition of the British civil service. Or the position could be interpreted as a bureaucratic convenience to facilitate the operation of the planning system ("avoid detail!"), and to allow central government to enforce a hands-off attitude through the appeal system. Or it could be seen as a convenient smokescreen to allow commercial interests the freedom to fashion the built environment to their own ends ("leave it to developers!") (Punter, 1987). In fact all three interpretations seem to have some validity, while the very existence of design control, however weak, actually helps to legitimate much poor-quality development and to bring the planning system into disrepute with the public ("the planners approved it!").

Through the 1980s local authorities had to struggle with the essential negativism of Circular 22/80 as they sought to improve the practice of design control. Some (such as Bristol) designated and extended conservation areas and campaigned for the addition of historic buildings to the official list to defend detailed control (Punter, 1990). Others (such as Reading) succumbed to the threats of appeals and costs and retreated to a more laissez-faire system (Punter, 1986). The number of developers' appeals against refusals of planning permission in England rose sharply in 1980 with the Conservatives taking power, and increased a further 40 percent between 1983 and 1988. More significantly the success rate of major appeals rose from 38 percent in 1980 to an all-time high of 54 percent in 1986, with major office development reaching 62 percent (DoE, 1980–89).

THE CONSERVATIVE COMMITMENT TO CONSERVATION

Despite widespread and persistent attacks on planning controls the Conservatives upheld their commitment to conservation, emphasizing one of the essential contradictions of Conservatism. They commissioned a new listing in 1982 that doubled the numbers of protected buildings, accepted a register of historic parks and gardens, and greatly strengthened archaeological considerations in planning (Suddards, 1988; Page, 1990). The loss of listed buildings slowed to a trickle (less than 20 per annum over the decade) but there remained the problem of securing their future. A 1992 survey revealed that 7 percent of these were in imminent danger and a further 13 percent vulnerable (English Heritage, 1992). Similarly, the sheer number of conservation areas has contributed to one of the key failures of the conservation legislation—the lack of formulation of positive proposals for enhancement and resources for the same (Morton, 1991). Estimates of the 1980s showed central funds of only £16 per listed building and £80 per conservation area annually (Sales, 1983). This is not to deny the overall success of conservation designations, for more sensitive forms of reuse, conversion, and redevelopment and better standards of design of infill have been achieved through improved design control. Nonetheless, criticisms of the quality of development in conservation areas, and of failures to enforce conservation controls, are common (Robinson, 1991). A legal challenge to the failure to ensure that development genuinely "preserved or enhanced" the character of conservation areas raised hopes of a strengthening of conservation powers, but these were recently dashed by a 1992 House of Lords decision that stated that "preventing harm" constituted preservation (Stubbs and Lavers, 1991). Pragmatism prevails.

The extent of designations has now become a bone of contention and a rallying point for all opponents of the planning system and proponents of laissez-faire enterprise. Criticisms have been made by developers and architects, who clearly have a vested interest in a less constrained development system, but also by critics on the political left who see conservation and the "Heritage Industry" as elitist, as protecting the positional goods of the affluent, and preventing necessary physical change (Wright, 1985; Hewison, 1987). Both groups see Britain as wallowing in nostalgia and bidding to retain existing townscapes and landscapes as a refuge from economic decline, modernization, and social change. But even a government bent on deregulation has been forced to concede that "public opinion is now overwhelmingly in favour of conserving and enhancing the familiar and cherished local scene" (DoE, 1987). Local communities recognize the sheer difference in quality of pre-1914 building as opposed to that evident in postwar developments. They want to retain the fabric of their areas, recognizing the threat to character and quality posed by contemporary development and the need to force developers and house holders to take more care with their surroundings.

Conservation as the Learning Vehicle for Design Control

It can be argued convincingly that participative and practical approaches to design control since the 1970s have been informed and refined largely by the practice of development control in conservation areas. Conservation practice also brought in skilled advice, initially at the county level, that could offer an informed architectural historian's perspective on control. The ideas of townscape study and morphological analysis developed from the Townscape School of Cullen through the conservation work of Worskett and others to define principles for locality analysis, design policies, and the design of infill.

The history of design control shows that the question of how a development relates to its surroundings is the key issue and central government has always endorsed this perspective as the only sound basis of judging design quality. Conservation areas have provided valuable experience in developing more sophisticated approaches to control examining "bulk, height, materials, colour, vertical or horizontal emphasis and grain of design" (MHLG, 1968). But of course the government has sought to confine such preoccupation with detail to designated areas. One obvious response from local authorities has been to extend their existing conservation areas and designate many new ones (Punter, 1990).

It can be argued that for a long time these

conservation-based approaches precluded an embrace of the more social-usage-oriented concepts of urban design that focused upon streets and spaces, and the comfort and safety of the public realm (Jarvis, 1980). But some local authorities have been able to develop a much more thoroughgoing contextualism, incorporating morphological/typological analysis with analyses of movement systems, public space, land use, and local ecology. They have also been able to harness amenity and resident group opinion and activism into enhancement programs and policy formulation to begin the development of community-based design sensibility (Punter, 1990).

THE INTERVENTIONS OF THE PRINCE OF WALES, RTPI, AND RFAC

As the Conservative government implemented their two-tier system of control in the 1980s, academic and practitioner criticism made little impact upon government policy makers and it was interventions of the Prince of Wales that gave new impetus to the debate. In 1984 he accused "some planners and architects of consistently ignoring the feelings and wishes of the mass of ordinary people in this country" and argued that the public welcomed a return to traditional scales, facades, ornaments, and soft materials. By 1987 he was comparing the British system unfavorably with French design and conservation controls, and he argued that all that was needed was adherence to a simple set of rules, characteristically phrased as a sort of "Ten Commandments" (Jencks, 1988; HRH Prince of Wales, 1988). It was his particular advocacy of classical architecture that refocused the debate over design control onto a question of an appropriate style, reviving debates that had taken place in every decade in England since the 1850s. Throughout its history design control has been associated, often unfairly, with the advocacy of a particular style—neo-Georgian and stripped classical in the 1920s and 1930s, modernist in the 1950s, neovernacular in the 1970s, and even postmodern styles now (Punter, 1986–87). Such associations have always undermined professional designer support for design control and the debate over appropriate style remains largely irrelevant to questions of environmental quality.

The Prince's critique of design control significantly raised the profile of the debate and created an opportunity for others to increase the pressure on central government, most notably the Royal Town Planning Institute president, Francis Tibbalds, and the Royal Fine Art Commission (Tibbalds, 1989; Hillman, 1990). Their idea of a new, positive circular received a much more sympathetic hearing from Chris Patten, M.P., who was Secretary of State for the Environment during most of 1990. But his replacement, Michael Heseltine, the man who had put his own personal gloss on Circular 22/80, was much less enthusiastic. As in 1980, he sought an agreed statement between the architectural and planning professions on the issue before reconsidering the government's position, knowing how much this would deflect the issue.

The architectural and planning professions produced a seven-point statement that at least acknowledged design as a material consideration in development control, something that had previously only been implicit, and called attention to the importance of spaces and landscape in development. Otherwise it largely repeated long-standing government advice, though critics have argued that the planning-profession leaders seem prepared to concede detailed design almost entirely to architects (Tugnutt, 1991). The replacement of the word *control* by the pejorative term *interference* in the accord itself is particularly significant in this regard. The continuing muddle as to what actually constitutes detail compounds the problem since there is a dispute as to whether aspects of design like fenestration, materials, and modeling are by implication minor issues that should be left entirely to the architect. A key Department of the Environment amendment to the accord noted that "the aim should be for any development to result in a 'gain' in environmental and landscape terms" (DoE, 1992). This promises to be a key phrase likely to generate endless discussion. As with the similar concepts of "preserve" and "enhance" in conservation legislation, it is unlikely to be given genuine positive reinforcement at appeal. The exact terminology and interpretation of such generalized statements may seem irrelevant to American observers, but in fact they are critical to the whole practice of design control since they are minutely dissected and analyzed hundreds of times a year by the best legal advice in the country acting for major developers on large-scale schemes at appeal.

But there are two other key issues raised by the accord. The first is the tendency of government and professionals to treat the whole issue as if it were merely a professional competence or demarcation dispute about elevations rather than environmental quality at large; the second, the corollary, is that public preferences, and their expression through public participation, are ignored in the new advice. These blind spots have always been characteristic of design control in Britain and show no signs of being resolved (Penny, 1980). We will return to discuss these key issues in the conclusion.

Finally, in the recent evolution of design review policy, a key legislative change in the Planning and Compensation Act 1991 (section 26) has given an enhanced status to the development plan. Now "the determination (of planning applications) shall be made in accordance with the plan unless material considerations indicate otherwise." Thus new design policies have to be developed for inclusion in such plans if local authorities are to pursue design control seriously, and it is now a requirement that every local authority have a district-wide development plan.

The design content of development plans has frequently been both vague and ill-considered with highly generalized statements ("there shall be a high standard of design . . .") the norm. Set alongside the absence of zoning to control basic land use, density, building volumes, and footprints, these have been largely useless in enforcing higher design standards (hence the resort to design guides and so forth). In the late 1970s a number of London boroughs initiated and developed some much more fundamental thinking, including attempts to develop performance criteria, and some have built on this experience over the last decade to produce very sophisticated conservation and urban design policies in their new plan (Westminster, City, Kensington). Others have had their design expertise decimated by budget cuts so that a third of London boroughs only have small teams of urban designers, while a further third only have a single specialist conservation officer (Gould, 1991). This underlines the general paucity of skills in design control in Britain, since elsewhere even less design expertise is generally available.

Key Themes in the Debate over Design and Conservation

The key contemporary issues in the evolution of design control can be conceptualized as a set of interlinked arguments, or sometimes a set of polarities, in the debate. Central government has exercised significant restraint on the exercise of design control at the local level in the interests of the development industry, the architectural/engineering professions, and efficient decision making (DoE, 1992). The minimal controls conceded outside designated areas—defined as an ability to reject "obviously poor" designs and to take into consideration scale, bulk, height, and effect on the character of the neighborhood—have frequently limited design intervention, discouraged painstaking control, and been a recipe for mediocrity. It can be argued that such restraint is necessary given the NIMBY (Not In My Back Yard) and conservationist stance of most localities, but the official discouragement of design control has led to minimal design research and education, and a failure to develop effective control policies and good prescriptive skills in practice. This is only now beginning to be corrected.

Whether or not there has been an excessive designation of urban and rural conservation areas and listed buildings is a contentious point, with development interests arguing that there has and community interests arguing that there has not. It certainly can be argued that central government restraint on design intervention, and the failure to provide general controls on demolition (until 1991) outside conservation areas have contributed to extensive designations. Against the extent of designations it can be argued that the actual impact of conservation controls is not that dramatic because of the essential pragmatism shown with the widespread acceptance of facadism, facsimiles, and intensification of development. The general lack of enhancement proposals emphasizes the reliance on negative development controls to "preserve and enhance," while the favored legal interpretation of such a clause seems to be the rather negative prevention of harm.

Meanwhile a potent mix of anti-urbanism, anti-industrialism, rural fundamentalism, snobbery against suburbia, and antimodernism have created a set of two-dimensional (green belts, village envelopes, and so on) and sometimes three-dimensional (listed buildings, design guides, and the like) planning polices that are preoccupied with the preservation of the visual landscape and thereby often the positional goods of the affluent. This is often at the expense of the need to create modern townscapes and landscapes that improve living and working conditions for a wider section of the community, provide more access to nature and create usable public spaces, and ensure sustainable developments.

As a corollary to their preoccupation with conservation, the English continue to demonstrate a strong antipathy toward modern architecture, certainly stronger than elsewhere in Anglo-America or Western Europe. The planning system's tendency to express this preference clearly by rejecting functional or innovative designs is one of the main sources of its tension with the architectural profession—which seems greater than that prevailing in the United States (Schuster, 1990)—which feels it has few enough genuine commissions as it is. A key problem for planning and design control is that much of the public blames practicing planners as much as the developers for the poor-quality buildings of the late 1960s and 1970s and continues to have little confidence in development control (and modern architecture) as a result.

If modernism remains largely out of favor, stylistic debates have continued unabated since the mid-nineteenth century in Britain and show few signs of diminishing. But when design control becomes embroiled in stylistic issues, it is generally missing the key issues in environmental quality. An appropriate style is the preoccupation of patrician taste makers, totalitarian leaders, or evangelizing architects or critics, and the choice usually reveals one of the key architectural fallacies—mechanical, ethical, aesthetic, purposive, or biological (Scott, 1914). It fails to acknowledge that architecture can and should express structure, function, symbol, memory, and context without having to resort to a particular style or architectural language, and that a healthy stylistic pluralism should prevail commensurate with a diverse society (Crook, 1989). Such a view also puts context in its place as only one, albeit key, element in developing architectural expression.

Contextualism has become the watchword of design control in England, just as it has become a key theme of postmodern architecture every-

where. Design control has always been primarily concerned with a development's relationship to its surroundings, and the phrase "keeping in keeping" summarises the kind of good manners the English have always expected of their developments. Contextualism has developed as the *modus vivendi* of design control largely from conservation practice. At its best it begins with the analysis of context at the micro and macro scales (including morphology, vernacular character, visual relationships) and moves on to the principles of townscape. At its worst, as in many American communities, it relies upon repetition of and similarity to neighborhood styles (Habe, 1989). Contextualism is capable of development into three-dimensional prescription and can embrace many of the themes of a desirable "critical regionalism"—resisting placelessness, reasserting the importance of the public domain, responding to the locality and the full range of human senses (Frampton, 1986). However, without strong contextual clues design control often struggles to define the qualities that it is seeking to achieve, perhaps particularly in suburbia.

The very preoccupation with architecture or elevations as the focus for design control has been criticised and arguments have been made for a broader conception of urban design to take its place. Certainly there is a feeling, in England and America, that once controllers get away from building elevations, the subjectivity of design control decreases, it is easier to define principles for control, and its relevance to the public increases (Habe, 1989). British traditions of civic design and townscape have been quite slow to absorb the more North American perspectives of Jacobs, Whyte, Lynch, Alexander, and others (Jarvis, 1980), and concern with the continuity, safety, comfort, and quality of the public realm is only now beginning to get the emphasis it deserves in design control. Regrettably, it is doing so when public resources have never been more impoverished. The change in focus from buildings to spaces is taking place as the design agenda shifts to embrace issues of landscape and sustainable development.

These initiatives will have to be synthesized and given expression in the new generation of unitary and district-wide development plans. British planning has been particularly bad in developing proactive design advice, partly because it is not a zoning-based system where the plan enshrines development rights. The most progressive local authorities have developed sophisticated design guidance, briefs, and conservation policies and are now attempting to write general design policies that will provide useful guidance and be robust at appeal. The United States has a much longer and better understood tradition, but not one without its problems and oversights. Even here locality analysis, community participation, and the integration of ecological with urban design concern are the exception rather than the rule (Southworth, 1989).

As the policy-writing skills of designers come under scrutiny, so their competence as controllers is being questioned. The number of architect-planners in the planning profession has declined from 40 to 10 percent between 1965 and 1986, and less than 10 percent of local planning authorities have architects in their staff. Less than 3 percent of planners entering the profession have architectural training (Bloch, 1986). Planning education has tended to downplay design to favor a stronger social science and managerial orientation contributing to a significant distrust in the architectural profession of local authorities' competence. The planning profession and planning education need to give much more attention to the requisite skills and training required. Planners also need to consider whether they do not need to develop much more effective mechanisms for public participation in plan making and control. Design education must be a two-way process, especially given the gap between lay and professional preferences.

Finally it has been argued in this chapter that, despite extensive architectural lobbying to the contrary, there is evidence that design control has raised the standard of design across the country, particularly in Conservation Areas and National Parks but also in many locations where local communities have insisted upon higher-quality design (Davison, 1991). Design control would achieve more with appropriate backing from central government, but one must conclude by arguing that there is a limit to what negative controls can achieve. Real improvements are dependent upon changes in the development process. Key structural factors in the British development industry have undermined imaginative and responsive design—the highly speculative nature of the development process, the lack of custom building, short-term profit motives, the general lack of patronage and recognition that good design pays for itself, the limited horizons of house holders and businesses, the conservativism of the funders, the monopoly of the mass house builders, and the particular governmental failure to commission fine architecture in public buildings being foremost among them. Most developers, large and small, institutional or house holder, simply do not give architectural quality or environmental impact the priority they deserve. Instead, design tends to be dominated by expediency, cheapness, and speed, and clients remain ignorant both of better ways of achieving the same end product and of improving their developments' contribution to the environment. As in the United States, design control can only disguise the realities of the contemporary development process and cannot solve the problems it creates.

It is in this sense that, to quote the familiar cliché, the English "get the architecture they deserve," and it is in this sense that environmental and architectural education have the furthest to go. On numerous occasions over the last eighty years, government, architects, and planners have voiced the opinion that a rise in design standards is dependent upon the development of higher levels of visual and environmental literacy throughout the nation. It is worth remembering that the design control process does actually provide the best, most direct education process available for prospective developers and affected citizens alike. Stronger positive controls, better practitioners, a more participative design process, and a more informed debate all offer some hope for an improved urban environment.

CONCLUSION

Design control in England remains an integral part of an essentially discretionary development control system. It has developed in close association with urban conservation practice, which has helped define not only the principles of contextual design but also the practice of involving the local community in the decision process. It is a reasoned, accountable, and transparent process that has raised the standard of design by forcing developers to take more care with their developments.

These great strengths are offset by significant weaknesses, which include continued confusion between the principle and scale of development and its detailed design, the general failure to develop soundly based prescriptive advice (especially in suburbia), a shortage of design skills (other than "experience") amongst controllers, a preoccupation with elevations rather than environmental quality, and a general prejudice against modern design. The effectiveness of design control depends very much upon central government support. The 1990s have seen some positive moves to broaden the scope and increase the effectiveness of design control. It remains to be seen to what extent the Conservatives place citizen control, local character, and environmental quality ahead of the imperatives of a largely speculative development industry. Little change is expected.

REFERENCES

Amery, Colin, and Dan Cruickshank. 1975. *The Rape of Britain*. London: Paul Elek.

Bloch, Colin. 1986. "Planners' Gain is Architects' Loss." *Architects' Journal* 184(2):22–23.

Blunden, John, and Nigel Curry. 1988. *A Future for our Countryside*. Oxford: Blackwell.

Brett, Lionel. 1949. "Second Thoughts on Planning." *Royal Institute of British Architects Journal* 57:44.

Civic Trust. 1976. *The Local Amenity Movement*. London: Civic Trust.

Crook, J. Mordaunt. 1989. *The Dilemma of Style: Architectural Ideas from the Picturesque to the Post-Modern*. London: John Murray.

Cullen, Gordon. 1961. *Townscape*. London: Architectural Press.

Davison, Ian. 1991. *Good Design in Housing: A Discussion Paper*. London: HBF/RIBA.

Department of the Environment (DoE). 1980—present. *Chief Planning Inspector's Report*. London: HMSO.

———. 1980. Circular 22/80, *Development Control: Policy and Practice*. London: HMSO.

———. 1987. Circular 8/87, *Conservation Areas and Listed Buildings*. London: HMSO.

———. 1990. *Planning Policy Guidance Note 16: Archaeology and Planning*. London: HMSO.

———. 1991. *Time for Design*. London. HMSO.

———. 1992. *Planning Policy Guidance Note 1: General Policy and Principles*. London: HMSO.

Dobby, Alan. 1978. *Conservation in Planning*. London: Hutchinson.

Edwards, A. Trystan. 1924. *Good and Bad Manners in Architecture*. London: Phillip Allan.

Edwards, Arthur M. 1981. *The Design of Suburbia*. London: Pembridge Press.

English Heritage. 1992. *Buildings at Risk: A Sample Survey*. London: E.H.

Essex County Council. 1973. *A Design Guide for Residential Areas*. Chelmsford: Essex County Council.

Frampton, Kenneth. 1985. *Modern Architecture: A Critical History*. London: Thames & Hudson.

Gould, Stephen. 1991. "Design Policy in London's Unitary Development Plans." Master's thesis, University of Reading, School of Planning Studies.

Habe, Reiko. 1989. "Public Design Control in American Communities: Design Guidelines/Design Review." *Town Planning Review* 62(2):195–219.

Hewison, Roger. 1988. *The Heritage Industry*. London: Methuen.

Hillman, Judy. 1990. *Planning for Beauty*. London: HMSO.

House of Commons. 1977. *Eighth Report from the Expenditure Committee: Session 1976–77: Planning Procedures*. London: HMSO.

HRH Prince of Wales. 1988. *A Vision of Britain*. London. Doubleday.

Jarvis, Bob. 1980. "Urban Environments as Visual Art or Social Settings? A Review." *Town Planning Review*. 51(1):51–66.

Jencks, Charles. 1988. *The Prince, the Architects, and New Wave Monarchy*. London: Academy Editions.

London Borough of Camden. 1979. *A Plan for Camden: The Environmental Code*. London: LB Camden.

Ministry of Housing and Local Government (MHLG). 1953. *Design in Town and Village*. London: HMSO.

———. 1969. *Development Control Policy Note No. 10: Design*. London: HMSO.

———. 1968. Circular 61, *Town and Country Planning Act 1968; Part V: Historic Buildings and Conservation*. London: HMSO.

Ministry of Town and Country Planning. 1947. *Advisory Handbook on the Redevelopment of Central Areas*. London: HMSO.

Morton, David. 1991. "Conservation Areas: Has Saturation Point Been Reached?" *Planner* 77(17):5–8.

Nairn, Ian. 1957. *Counter Attack Against Subtopia*. London: Architectural Press.

Page, Jennifer. 1990. "The Historic Heritage." In *Material Considerations in Town and Country Planning Decisions, Journal of Planning and Environmental Law*. Occasional Paper no. 17:52–65.

Penny, Leith. 1980. "The Aesthetics of Development: A Professional Issue?" *Planner* 66(9):114.

Planning and Land Compensation Act. 1991. Section 54A. Department of the Environment. 1991. *op. cit.* paragraph 21.

Punter, John. 1986–87. "A History of Aesthetic Control, 1909–1985." *Town Planning Review*, 57(4):351–81; 58(1):26–62.

———. 1986. "Aesthetic Control within the Development Control Process: A Case Study. *Land Development Studies* 3:197–212.

———. 1990. *Design Control in Bristol, 1940–1990.* Bristol: Redcliffe Press.

Robinson, John M. 1991. Civic Offence. *Architects' Journal* 192(2):24–27.

Royal Town Planning Institute (RTPI). 1990. *Planning Policy Guidance: Design and Planning Control.* London: RTPI (mimeo).

Sales, Richard. 1983. "The Historic Buildings' Council for England. An Assessment." Master's thesis, University of Reading, School of Planning Studies:

Schuster, J. Mark, D. 1990. *Design Review. The View from the Architecture Profession.* Boston, MIT/AIA/BSA.

Scott, Geoffrey. 1914. *The Architecture of Humanism.* London: Constable.

Sharp, Dame Evelyn. 1969. *Ministry of Housing and Local Government*. (New Whitehall Series no. 14). London: Allen & Unwin.

Southworth, Michael. 1989. "Theory and Practice of Contemporary Urban Design: A Review of Urban Design Plans in the United States." *Town Planning Review*. 60(4):389–402.

Stubbs, Michael. and Lavers, Anthony. 1991. "Steinberg and After: Decision Making and Development Control in Conservation Areas." *Journal of Planning and Environment Law,* 9–19.

Suddards, Roger W. 1988. "Listed Buildings: Have We Listed Too Far?" *Journal of Planning and Environment Law,* 523–28.

Tibbalds, Francis. 1989. "Mind the Gap! A Personal View of the Value of Urban Design in the Late Twentieth Century." *Planner* 74(3):11–15.

Tugnutt, Anthony. 1991. "Design Control or Interference?" *Planner* 77(38):6–7.

Worskett, Roy. 1979. *The Character of Towns: An Approach to Conservation.* London: Architectural Press.

Wright, Patrick. 1985. *On Living in an Old Country.* London: Verso.

———. 1981. "The Debate over Aesthetic Control." *Estates Gazette* 256:1271–72. 257:179–180.

———. 1992. "Lakeland Case Outcome Puts Steinberg to Rest." *Planning* 955:3.

6
Design Review from the Inside

Bernard J. Frieden

Massachusetts Institute of Technology, Cambridge, MA

City governments have redefined their relationship to real estate development. Instead of regulating real estate ventures from a distance, many now act as coinvestors or cosponsors with private companies. City redevelopment agencies, for example, assemble land, contribute financing, and build infrastructure for private projects they want to promote. Port authorities, transportation agencies, and public land development corporations also act as codevelopers of private projects that are intended to serve a public purpose.

This style of public sector development has opened a new way for local governments to shape the built environment. Public agencies that assist private projects want to be consulted on major planning and design decisions. In effect, they use city assistance to buy a place at the bargaining table together with the developer, key tenants, private investors, and the architect. Design plans for these projects evolve over time; the first plan is almost never the one that is actually built. During a period of several years, developers revise their plans to suit changing conditions in real estate markets and in the economy. Unexpected crises invariably buffet these projects, sending the participants back to the drawing board to find another solution. In public-private projects, the city usually has a strong voice throughout the process of reaching decisions.

These projects represent only a small proportion of all city development ventures, but they are usually highly visible and important ones, such as Battery Park City in New York, Copley Place in Boston, the renovated Union Station in Washington, D.C., Nicollet Mall in Minneapolis, Bunker Hill in Los Angeles, and Mission Bay in San Diego. When public officials influence the design of places such as these, they can have a major impact on the character of a city.

City representatives who negotiate the design of public-private projects are taking part in a special kind of design review. Their function is to bring a public interest point of view to bear on design decisions that would otherwise reflect only the private-market perspective of developers, lenders, and key tenants. In this respect their role is similar to that of more conventional design review bodies, such as citizen advisory committees or city design review boards. Yet they differ from conventional review boards in several respects. First, the city negotiators are professional staff members or in some cases elected officials, not ordinary citizens with an interest in design. Although they are usually attentive to public opinion and especially to organized interest groups, the public interests they advocate may have more to do with city-hall priorities. Further, these city negotiators have direct channels into decision making on projects and therefore greater potential leverage than most design review boards. As a result, they represent an extension of the design review function into a new arena that merits attention.

PUBLIC SECTOR DEVELOPMENT: POLITICS, ECONOMICS, AND DESIGN

How do city governments use their leverage as insiders to shape project designs? What are their interests in design decisions, and how do they act on these interests? To answer these questions requires a look behind the scenes at how the public-private projects take shape. As background research for a recent book, *Downtown, Inc.: How America Rebuilds Cities,* Lynne Sagalyn and I prepared five in-depth case histories of public-private projects and collected less detailed information on numerous others. This research shows city negotiators using their insider position to limit the size of projects, incorporate features that will attract the public at large, make clear connections to nearby streets, preserve landmark and historic structures, and encourage unconventional design as a strategy to help city projects cope with suburban competition.

The cases we investigated covered retail and mixed-use centers that were key elements of city efforts to rebuild downtown (Frieden and Sagalyn, 1989). But the rebuilding of downtown had been long and hard, with many aborted plans along the way. As a result, a basic priority in almost every case was simply to get a project built. For that purpose, the design would have to be functional and economically viable above all. Whatever demands the project made for governmental contributions would have to be within the limits of a city's fund-raising capacity. A design that was going to require expensive construction or lavish use of space would come under careful scrutiny.

City negotiators had a political bottom line as well as an economic one: projects would have to be acceptable to elected officials and to the public at large. One design feature that flowed directly from this consideration was the restricted size of most downtown projects. Cities in the 1950s and 1960s had tried to rebuild downtown by bulldozing entire neighborhoods. Projects of thirty, forty, or fifty acres in the heart of the city were not uncommon then. The results were often disastrous. Families were uprooted by the thousands, cut off from familiar people and institutions, given little help in finding other places to live and little compensation for the rent increases most had to pay. Numerous small businesses were also destroyed in the process; on average more than a third of those evicted went out of business. Then the land usually lay idle for years while renewal agencies searched desperately for developers willing to take on large projects. The political protests that followed taught city government to minimize disruptions by working with small projects.

When cities chose sites for their retail centers in the 1970s and 1980s, most set a framework for compact design. Boston's Faneuil Hall Marketplace fits within six and a half acres, Baltimore's Harborplace is just over three acres, Cincinnati's Fountain Square Plaza is less than two acres, and the exceptionally large site of Horton Plaza in San Diego is eleven and a half acres. Of seventy-one downtown retail centers for which information is available, nearly half took up fewer than five acres; the median size was 5.7 acres.

These sites tend to be located near existing attractions or centers of activity: next to large stores, close to established shopping areas, or near waterfronts or historic districts in many cities. Favorable locations improve the prospect of finding a suitable developer; at the same time, they set the stage for design schemes that emphasize connections to nearby places.

Political and economic considerations also affect the types of aid that cities offer to developers, with direct consequences for design decisions. For certain kinds of projects, such as retail centers, development and operating costs are so much higher in the city than in the suburbs that city governments usually close part of the gap by providing subsidies to the project they want to promote. The aid can take many forms, but politically it is useful for the city to supply something that citizens will recognize as a public amenity in itself, such as a parking garage.

When St. Paul started planning for the Town Square/St. Paul Center mixed-use project, downtown was in such poor shape that no developer would risk building a project of this kind without generous help. The city undertook typical forms of aid, including land assembly and write-down, garage construction, and street improvements. But more was necessary. City officials decided to act as developer for a public part of the shopping-office-hotel complex. Originally they planned to build a glass-roofed galleria that would pass through the building and form a main shopping axis. When space changes forced a redesign, they substituted a series of other public spaces: pathways between the stores on the three shopping levels, and a 30,000-square-foot park enclosed on the rooftop. For all these components of the project, the city took responsibility for financing, design, construction, ownership, and operation.

This arrangement suited both the developer and the city. It relieved the developer of some $13 million in development costs for circulation areas to bring customers to the stores, and it added a novel indoor park that would help attract visitors to the project. At the same time it put the city in charge of a large public space that suited Mayor George Latimer's purpose of creating a civic showpiece. The public spaces and park in that showpiece would be much easier to justify politically than turning over a check for $13 million to the developer. And by taking over the pathways and the interior park, city officials were also positioning themselves to determine the design of key elements of a public-private project.

ADJUSTING DESIGNS TO FIT THE CITY

In addition to balancing political and economic considerations, cities also have more focused objectives. As a rule, city governments do not want to promote self-contained projects, but rather to build projects that will strengthen an entire area. For this purpose, they tend to resist the inward-focused plans of typical shopping malls, which have blank walls facing the street. City negotiators usually want interesting street frontages, clear connections to streets and nearby points of activity, good pedestrian circulation between a project and its surroundings, and activities on more than a nine-to-five schedule.

The planning of Plaza Pasadena, a shopping mall in the center of an old downtown near Los Angeles, illustrates the way city negotiators use their leverage to change a conventional design into one that fits better within its urban context. City officials decided in the early 1970s to fight the decline in downtown retailing by bringing in a modern shopping mall. They chose a leading California developer, the Hahn Company, to build an adaptation of the typical suburban mall. To make the mall concept work in a downtown setting

where land was too scarce and costly for open parking lots, they planned two underground parking levels directly beneath the mall and a multi-level garage just across the street.

Within this parking plan, Hahn's designers proposed a typical mall layout: a rectangle with a department store at each end and two rows of small shops connecting them. An interior pathway running the length of the rectangle between the small shops would funnel shoppers from one end to the other, concentrating the flow of pedestrian traffic in the center of a two-level, enclosed, air-conditioned structure with blank exterior walls facing the street.

The redevelopment authority had problems with this mall design. It had carved out a site consisting of three square blocks along the south side of Colorado Boulevard, Pasadena's main street. The renowned Tournament of Roses parade, a nationally televised event and a civic institution dating back many years, follows this route down Colorado Boulevard every New Year's day preceding the Rose Bowl football game. The visible deterioration of businesses on Colorado Boulevard was becoming an embarrassment, especially when it was apparent on national television. One of the motives for the revitalization effort was to make the main street more presentable, and a blank wall was unacceptable as a solution. City negotiators pressed instead for street-front stores on the Colorado Boulevard side of the complex.

Hahn Company staff who had never built a mall with stores facing outward raised serious objections. If they made the interior shops deep enough to reach the exterior walls of the building, that would destroy space needed for the customary delivery and service corridor concealed behind the stores. Further, having windows and entrances along the street posed security problems: anyone who broke into a store-front at night would have access to the entire interior of the mall. As an alternative, if they built a row of shallow stores along the street that did not connect to the inside of the mall, these shops would be too far from the mainstream of pedestrian traffic to generate much rental income (Fig. 6-1). Pressed hard by redevelopment authority executives and the city's project architects, the developer eventually agreed to line the Colorado Boulevard frontage with a row of shallow stores.

Figure 6-1. Adjusting to the urban context: Street-front stores lining the Colorado Boulevard frontage of Plaza Pasadena.

Another design conflict took much longer to resolve. To create a rectangular construction site out of three city blocks, the city would have to close two small streets perpendicular to Colorado Boulevard between those blocks. One of these streets was a visual and traffic link between the civic center north of Colorado Boulevard and the civic auditorium one block to the south. The buildings in question were unified architecturally as well as functionally; the entire grouping had high symbolic meaning to Pasadena. Many local groups protested any plan that would cut the connection; these included the planning commission, the design review body responsible for the civic center zone, the local American Institute of Architects chapter, and numerous public organizations. The redevelopment authority, mindful of opposition to the project, took these objections very seriously and held firm to its position that there would have to be a design that allowed people to see through the mall structure and to walk through it, across the main pedestrian flow, from Colorado Boulevard to the civic auditorium.

The project architect, Paul Curran of Charles Kober Associates, tried a design for an open passageway through the mall, but this would have interrupted the enclosure needed for air conditioning and cut off one of the anchor department stores from the rest of the mall. After several years of give-and-take, he came up with a design for an arcade covered by a series of monumental archways passing through the mall to provide a visual connection, sealed by glass panels at either end to maintain the enclosure (Figs. 6-2, 6-3). The city

retained a measure of control over the passageway beneath these arches, including the right to keep it open at hours when the rest of the mall was closed. This solution posed tricky functional issues for the department store at that end of the mall, whose executives had rejected any plan that cut them off from the other stores. It also posed legal issues raised by the project's mortgage lenders, who worried that the corridor might amount to a public right-of-way that would compromise the developer's control of the property and create security problems. City officials negotiated detailed legal agreements spelling out responsibilities for security in the passageway and clarifying the arrangement as not implying a public dedication of the area.

The episode is significant for design review policies in several respects. First, the city as a negotiating partner in this project had the ability to press its demands for both the street-front stores and the civic-center connection over a long period of time, and to explore possible solutions in great detail. Other decision makers who were opposed also had great influence, particularly the mortgage lenders and department store executives. By dealing face to face and coming to grips with the legal issues as well as the architectural ones, city officials were able to find solutions acceptable to all the major interests. Further, these departures from the suburban prototype became the distinguishing features of the project, earning it special recognition in professional circles and a *Progressive Architecture* award. Frictions resulting from the public-private negotiations led to design innovations that helped the project fit into its downtown context.

The project has been both a civic and a commercial success. The city intended it to serve as a catalyst for further downtown development, and a surge of new construction and historic renovation followed in the same area within a few years after it opened. As a commercial venture it produced a high sales volume for the mall tenants and satisfactory returns for the owners. There is no way to know how much the design innovations contributed to this success, but the steady flow of customers suggests that the public is comfortable with the results.

The enclosed passageway, however, has continued to generate controversy. In 1988, eight years after the opening of Plaza Pasadena, design

Figure 6-2. Resolving a design conflict: The arched passageway through Plaza Pasadena, connecting the civic center on one side of the mall to the civic auditorium on the other.

consultants who prepared a new master plan for the civic center raised objections to the glass panels that seal both ends of the passageway. They argued that a combination of glare and distracting door frames block the visual connection through the mall. The master plan, as a result, proposes removing these glass enclosures and converting the passageway into the open gallery that had been proposed earlier, with glass walls on either side of it to allow for air-conditioning within the retail parts of the mall (Lyndon/Buchanan Associates 1988).

DESIGNS TO DRAW CROWDS

City officials also want pleasant, usable public spaces downtown. The projects they assist are usually intended as public attractions: part of the justification for city funding is that they will be open and inviting to the public, visually satisfying, and comfortable to be in. This sense of purpose is a contrast to earlier approaches toward the rebuilding of city centers. During the urban renewal era, many projects were designed for isolation from the rest of the city: surrounded by dead spaces that kept neighboring activity at a distance, segregated into single-purpose office or residential complexes, lacking features that would

Figure 6-3. The visual link: A view from inside Plaza Pasadena through the glass-enclosed arch toward the civic center.

draw visitors, and providing no sitting areas or casual gathering places. Recently, however, a driving force behind much downtown development has been the search for "people-places" that will bring back the crowds to city streets. As a result the city team that works on public-private projects often gives much thought to design elements that promise to attract visitors.

When St. Paul officials worked on the enclosed park they built as part of the Town Square/St. Paul Center project, they tried to simplify construction by hiring the developer's architects, who were designing the retail levels below the park and the office towers above. These architects came up with a plan for the park that featured the flexibility of an open area easily rearranged for different functions but lacking any quality that might attract people. Its hard surfaces and barren look suggested a cold lobby more than the green oasis the city staff had in mind. St. Paul's development chief promptly tracked down the architect of a similar project in Calgary whose rooftop park exploited water and landscaping to create an appealing garden, and got him to prepare a new sketch plan for Town Square. With the sketch in hand, he prevailed on the original architects to draw a new plan including water, plants, and distinct spaces for recreation, exhibits, and public events. Still worried about their fondness for austere modern designs, he arbitrarily doubled the number of plants they specified and placed several more orders before opening day. The result was a park with no fewer than 250 types of plants, with trees and shrubs alongside moving water to create the sense of a greenhouse even on cold winter days, and with water splashing between the escalators down through two retail levels and into a collecting pool in the below-ground food court—all this thanks to the design leverage city negotiators had as codevelopers of the project.

The park has proven to be more successful than the rest of the project. Six years after the project opened in 1980 the development company that built it sold it to new owners who grappled with lackluster retail sales and vacancies in the office towers and then went into default. The park, meanwhile, continued to be a popular attraction, and both the owner and the city made further investments to bring in a historic carousel. The park continues to draw large numbers of visitors, but neither the retail mall nor the office towers have lived up to financial expectations (Brooks, 1992).

PROTECTING LANDMARKS

Some cities act as protectors of traditional and historic places against design schemes that threaten to damage them. The concern of city officials to have workable, economically viable projects has made them willing to consider adaptations of landmark buildings but with an underlying sense of the limits of acceptable change. The renovation of the Faneuil Hall markets in Boston led the city to accept some changes in the historic buildings but to draw the line against others. In this case, the main objective of city government was to preserve the landmark structures; there was little expectation in the planning stages that the project might ever generate a high volume of retail sales.

To preserve the market meant finding some economic use of the buildings that would produce enough income to compensate a developer for the high cost of repairing and maintaining them. The most credible proposal came from developer James Rouse and architect Ben Thompson. It called for many interior changes to convert the stalls and storage areas of several dozen wholesale food merchants into two levels of modern retail space and leasable offices above. To design a food arcade on the first floor of the central Quincy Market building, Rouse and Thompson proposed to remove all partitions between the market stalls and to cut a large circular hole in the ceiling for a two-story rotunda under the great dome. To get still more rental space, they would also rearrange basement layouts and add more entrances. Further, they would change the exterior appearance by building steel and glass canopies extending out from either side of Quincy Market to add room for several rows of small stands and restaurant seating areas (Fig. 6-4).

These alterations were part of a plan to fit a workable retail complex into the tight spaces of the historic structures. Inevitably, they would change the character of the traditional produce market. Historic preservationists objected, but city officials went along with Rouse and Thompson. Still, there were limits to how many design changes the city was willing to accept. Before

Figure 6-4. Blending historic preservation with contemporary retailing: The renovated Quincy Market Building with glass-covered extensions adding rental space to the original structure in Faneuil Hall Marketplace.

Mayor Kevin White made a final decision on who would develop the project, he told Rouse he wanted to be involved in the design enough "to be sure they didn't muck it up with neon signs on the roof or something like that." Rouse offered to work closely with him: "I'll meet with you once a week to report on everything we're doing. You can watch it all the way." Rouse never proposed neon signs on the roof, but at an early stage he wanted to build partial roof extensions connecting the three market buildings in order to shelter visitors from the rain and snow. Thompson was vehemently opposed but could not block the idea on his own. Instead, Kevin White intervened to settle the matter quickly by ruling out an enclosure.

This novel project, with its blend of historic architecture and late twentieth-century retailing, has been one of the great successes of recent city building in the United States. In 1978, the first year the center was fully open, it drew ten million visitors. By the mid-1980s it was drawing sixteen million visitors a year, as many as visited Great Britain and three times as many as Mexico or Hawaii. The usual measure of retail performance—sales per square foot of floor space—was off the scale in comparison with typical shopping centers. For the city, its attendance figures far exceeded all expectations and it became an internationally renowned showpiece as well as a clear stimulus to further downtown investment.

PROMOTING UNCONVENTIONAL DESIGN

Roof and interior decisions are characteristic of the fine grain of recent city involvement in project design. In the case of Faneuil Hall Marketplace, the city had a special claim to participate in design decisions by virtue of its ownership of the land and buildings, which are leased to the Rouse Company for ninety-nine years. When city government takes responsibility for building and managing parts of a project, its control can extend to decisions on the number and types of shrubs to order, as in St. Paul. When the city takes a position as coinvestor, as in Plaza Pasadena, it can also negotiate decisions from a position of strength. And in one project after another, city officials have used their leverage to press for designs that are innovative and sometimes unique. Innovation results in part from city pressure on developers to cope with demands that conventional design solutions overlook. But innovation also serves another purpose: the city government urge to bring back crowds can itself argue for unusual design as a basic strategy. City and developer interests tend to converge in the drive to create "people places." In-town projects almost always have to compete against already established suburban alternatives, and design innovation is an important competitive tool.

Horton Plaza in San Diego illustrates the way many of these considerations come together in a complex project. When San Diego decided in the 1970s to revitalize the heart of downtown, it was dealing with the remnants of a decayed city center that had long been abandoned to run-down stores, cheap hotels, and a large porno district. Developer Ernest Hahn's proposal for a major retail center ran up against formidable suburban competition and against the extreme reluctance of business investors to gamble on a downtown revival. For downtown retailing to assemble enough customers, it would have to draw suburban residents past the ring of modern shopping malls surrounding the city center. They would need special reasons to go downtown, some of which might have to do with unconventional design.

The notion of unconventional design as a competitive strategy emerged only gradually, however. Hahn's first proposal was geared to the difficulty of attracting anchor department stores to the crumbling surroundings of central San Diego. His company operated on the principle that department store executives would be put off by the double negatives of an unconventional site and an unconventional design. Since the location was unconventional in the extreme, they encouraged their architect Frank Hope to reproduce the familiar characteristics of suburban malls in his project design. City officials, however, were dismayed. The design review committee criticized the proposed megastructure for looking inward, for presenting a stark building facade at street level, and for not integrating three historic buildings marked for preservation. The city council voiced its misgivings by making its approval of the preliminary plan conditional on a series of changes: more street-level activity, an attractive frontage for adjoining development, and the addition of nighttime activities. Then the draft environmental impact report gave the plan another slap by noting that the "fortresslike" retail center would fit poorly with other downtown redevelopment and with the restored historic buildings.

Hahn responded by getting a new architect. He replaced Hope with Jon Jerde, an experienced designer of retail projects and renovator of old buildings. Jerde was determined to replace Hope's monolithic structure with something livelier than the suburban prototype. He, too, started with the idea of an enclosed mall, but proposed to add an ice-skating rink, a hotel, restaurants, pubs, housing, offices, and recreation areas. By that time, two years after the Hope plan, there was enough interest from department stores to persuade Hahn that a conventional design was no longer necessary.

Economic pressures soon led to further changes. In June 1978, California voters enacted a statewide tax-cutting measure known as Proposition 13. San Diego faced the immediate prospect of reduced property-tax collections from the project area, and without this income the city could no longer afford to pay for its share of the project. The original plan called for enough parking spaces for Horton Plaza to meet conventional suburban retail standards, with the city paying for most of it. After Proposition 13 Hahn agreed to take over some of the city's responsibility for parking, and both Hahn and the city decided to cut the total

amount of parking. Hahn promised the department stores that he would arrange for shuttle service to other downtown parking during peak periods, and store executives who earlier would have insisted on more parking for their customers were now committed enough to go along with fewer spaces. As construction costs escalated in the next few years, Hahn took over full responsibility for the parking but made a further cut in the total. City officials did not object: they considered suburban parking standards excessive and hoped to attract more riders to public transportation. Further, large garages walled off some of the project from adjoining streets; reducing their size would help integrate Horton Plaza with the rest of downtown.

The city's development chief for Horton Plaza, Gerald Trimble, took steps to increase tax revenues from the project. He negotiated with other developers to bring an office tower and a hotel into the project: both would improve the balance sheet by paying for their sites and by generating property-tax revenues. And they would meet some of the criticisms directed at the earlier plan by diversifying activities and adding nighttime functions. Later, in response to public pressure, the redevelopment agency urged Hahn to add a performing arts theater to the project. Jerde also recommended it as a way to add variety to the center and to reinforce other nighttime activities. Hahn eventually agreed to build the shell of a theater to be leased to a nonprofit company.

The Hahn company followed Trimble's strategy of adding value to the project by building more floor space within the existing site. To make room, they cut the dimensions of the department store building pads, forcing the anchor stores to build three levels of shopping instead of their usual two. As merchant interest grew, these changes proved acceptable; two more department stores joined the project even after these changes in layout and the loss of parking spaces. The total retail area grew from 536,000 square feet in the original agreement to 885,000 as actually built. As the site became more crowded, Jerde first moved the location of the ice rink and then had to eliminate it altogether. Then, to save on both construction and operating costs, Hahn once more affronted industry standards by scrapping his long-standing plan to enclose and air-condition the mall.

From the city's perspective an open mall was well suited to the mild climate of San Diego; and taking away the enclosure would help integrate the project more closely with surrounding streets and buildings. The design changes Hahn and Jerde wanted—a larger but more compact development, on more levels, without an air-conditioned enclosure—met his company's financial needs without upsetting city officials.

There was a general recognition that innovative design could be a strong selling point for Horton Plaza in competition with the conventional malls of suburban San Diego. The decision to do without an enclosure and air-conditioning was not only a money-saver but also an opportunity to make this project different by giving Jerde exceptional design freedom in an open-air setting. Jerde and the city negotiators both understood that the project was to be designed as an integral part of the city. To be sure that retail tenants got the same message, the Hahn company made use of a developer's customary control over store designs to demand individuality. The design criteria given to tenants said: "Horton Plaza is an outdoor urban mall with a . . . design theme built around a vision of the mall as an extension of the city street system. Standard store designs that have been developed for suburban shopping center locations will not be appropriate." Instead, the design guide urged them to create a "one-of-a-kind retail environment" (Fig. 6-5). By the time tenant rules were drawn up, the spirit of unconventional design suited the developer's objectives as well as the city's.

That spirit seemed to suit the public, too. Horton Plaza drew fourteen million visitors in its first year of operations and rang up some of the highest sales in the Hahn company's extensive portfolio of retail centers. It soon became one of San Diego's leading tourist attractions and an important contributor to its ambitious plans for a new downtown.

LIMITS OF INSIDER REVIEW

Managing development by public-private negotiation has opened many opportunities for city government to shape the design of projects. Yet this result is almost an accident. Cities did not become coinvestors in real estate ventures for the sake of

Figure 6-5. A one-of-a-kind retail setting with maze-like pathways in the open-air mall at Horton Plaza.

design objectives. They did it as an implementation strategy: after an era of urban renewal marked by aborted projects and empty rubble fields they were determined to get deeply enough involved to be sure that projects would be finished. But once they became involved, they often discovered important design issues to negotiate. As important, they found that they had the legitimacy and the leverage to get the changes they wanted.

Are there drawbacks to this internal form of design review? It offers opportunities for significant public input into design decisions, but no guarantees about how cities will use their insider influence. Some may not use it effectively to achieve the design results they want. Cincinnati, for example, invested some $21 million in the Fountain Square South office-hotel-retail complex but, according to newspaper reports soon after the opening, failed in its intention to have an interior atrium designed and managed as a public gathering place.

Cities may also rank design decisions below other priorities. When New York invited proposals for an office complex on the Coliseum site in Columbus Circle in 1986, the city encouraged an outsized project damaging to its surroundings—with more floor space than the Empire State Building—in order to get maximum financial benefits from the developer. City negotiators stretched the zoning regulations to the limit, then added a 20 percent bonus in exchange for requiring the developer to renovate a subway station. The bidding invitation was vague on design guidelines but clear about size, sending a message that what the city wanted most was top dollar for the site. Later the state supreme court ruled that the city had acted improperly in negotiating a sale price for the land based on a zoning change to be made by city government; what might have been an opportunity to press for design sensitivity instead became an effort to put up a zoning decision for sale.

A further weakness of internal design review is that city negotiators may become too entangled with a private developer to act forcefully on design issues. City design staff in St. Paul recognized that the developer's plan for Town Square/St. Paul Center gave the appearance of a gray-walled fortress at street level. Mayor Latimer asked the developer to reconsider the design to make it more inviting, but could get no more than minor concessions. The president of the development company had, however, been so cooperative in solving many critical problems up to that point that the mayor was unwilling to start a battle over the street-level design.

These few instances demonstrate that insider influence over design decisions has its limits. Public-sector development can create a new channel for city influence over what would otherwise be private design decisions, but cities will not always make the most of their opportunities. In many cases where city negotiators were effective, it was because local groups created demonstrable political pressure over design considerations. A climate of public concern is probably the best assurance that city negotiators will be attentive to design when they swing their new-found weight at the bargaining table.

REFERENCES

Brooks, Ronnie. Former Executive Director, St. Paul Downtown Association. 1992. Interview with author.

Frieden, Bernard J., and Lynne B. Sagalyn. 1989. *Downtown, Inc.: How America Rebuilds Cities*. Cambridge, Mass.: M.I.T. Press. Sources for the case studies appear on pp. 367–71.

Lyndon/Buchanan Associates. 1988. *Pasadena Civic Center: Master Plan*.

II
Design Review in Practice

7
Discovering Suburban Values through Design Review

Gary Hack

Massachusetts Institute of Technology

At its October 1988 meeting, the Design Review Commission of Germantown, Tennessee, reached an impasse with the Gulf Oil Company over its proposal to construct a gasoline station and small convenience outlet on a corner site on the rapidly developing eastern edge of the city. This was not the first occasion that the commission had differed with developers over its seventeen-year life, nor was it the first time the board had dealt with the troubling issues of automobile-oriented uses. However, this case came to threaten the very existence of the board.

Gulf proposed to build its standard modern prototype station in Germantown, a design that had been constructed in dozens of cities across the U.S. The company noted with some pride that the station would be identical to one they had built in the historic district of Charleston, South Carolina. Its main feature was a large metallic canopy covering the gas pumps and entrance to the convenience store (Fig. 7-1). The canopy color would be British racing green, with a stripe of green neon lighting along its edge. The supports for the canopy and the faces of the small structure housing the convenience store would be "champaign silver" metal panels. In deference to the community, the plan called for considerable landscaping around the entire perimeter of the site, a limitation on the width of curb cuts for vehicles entering and leaving the station, and a modest ground-mounted sign, well within the 24-square-feet limit prescribed by Germantown's sign ordinance.

The objection of the majority of the nine-member commission was not that the proposed station was badly designed; several members admitted that as filling stations went, this was one of the best proposals they had seen. Rather, the issue was appropriateness. As one member put it, "If the design can be put anywhere, then it isn't appropriate to Germantown." Another member suggested that the design was "completely out of character with Germantown" since "the materials do not blend with the brick, stone, wood, etc. required in Germantown." Another member expressed the view that the "color green is too shocking" and that "the slickness of the design was objectionable" to her. While the commission had no written guidelines, the several hundred proposals it had reviewed over its lifetime by now constituted a considerable body of case law on the subject of what was appropriate to the city. One member of the commission suggested to the developer that it might be useful to have the architect of the service station become familiar with the area and the "special feel of Germantown."

Other franchises that had come before the commission had ultimately bent to its will in order to gain access to the market of upper-middle-income families in this desirable suburb of Memphis. Pizza Hut had abandoned its prototypical

Figure 7-1. Gulf Prototype Station, Charleston, S.C.

red roof topped by a prominent sign and the half-timbered walls it preferred in favor of a more modest brown roof sans signage and walls of brick. McDonald's had toned down its standard prototype and set it in a lush landscape. Exxon had agreed to convert its proposed canopy into a shingled roof with domestic character, and to eliminate its typical blue and red stripes. Local residents, the commission argued, would soon discover and remember the location of these outlets without the constant reminder of their advertising conveyed by buildings identified with their company. Germantown was to be built for permanent residents, not passersby.

But the Gulf proponents seemed unwilling to bend, other than to propose that some of the landscaping around the perimeter of the site be set in brick planters and that the small "Gulf" letters be dropped from the canopy. They regarded their design as cut from whole cloth; it could not be changed with out losing its identification with Gulf, which was precisely the point of the commission's objection. To them the station was a logo as well as a building, and the commission had made a major cause of ridding the city of such evidence of commercialism. Signage should be used for identification purposes only,

not for promotion, in the commission's view. It had taken the lead in writing Germantown's sign ordinance, among the most restrictive in the nation. Not only did the ordinance restrict the size, location, and materials of signs, but it also limited the use of logos to no more than 10 percent of the total area of signs, on the grounds that logos transgressed the line of pure advertising. The commission also frowned upon the use of primary colors identified with particular businesses or products; in Germantown, earth tones that did not shout for attention were considered more appropriate. How then should the commission regard the color and materials of the proposed Gulf canopy? Green was surely an "earth color," but was this shade of green? Was the neon strip a subtle form of logo, even though it contained no letters or symbols?

The commission could see no practical way of suggesting adequate modifications to the Gulf proposal, and voted after two lengthy sessions devoted exclusively to the project to refuse the proposed application as inappropriate to the character of Germantown. Unlike earlier proponents, Gulf decided to challenge the commission. Shortly after the decision, it filed suit seeking relief from the decision, as well as damages, on the grounds that the procedures of the commission were flawed. In their court filing, they cited the absence of any written standards to guide the commission's decisions, and the arbitrary and capricious ways that decisions were made.

The court suit struck at the very heart of discretionary design review and what it is intended to accomplish. Is it fair to require developers to submit to the attitudes of a board about what is appropriate in a community without having an announced definition of community character or adopted policies? The suit also raised issues of what constitutes a reasonable scope of architectural review, and whether it is really possible to shape community character through the work of a community appearance panel. Because it has been in existence longer than most such bodies and has exercised its power vigorously, Germantown offers an ideal test case for such issues.

THE PURPOSES AND STRUCTURE OF DESIGN REVIEW

If we knew precisely how a community should look and feel, and there was genuine consensus among residents about this, a design review panel would probably be unnecessary. It would be a relatively simple task to spell the rules out in an ordinance or in a policy adopted by the local legislature, and deciding whether the rules had been followed would be a routine administrative task.

When discretionary review boards are created, there is an implicit assumption that something more than policing is required. The logic may rest on one or a combination of propositions: that creating a good environment involves weighing intangible factors and making trade-offs that are not easily spelled out in prescriptive rules; or that circumstances for building are variable and that particular sites for buildings may deserve a unique response to the context rather than holding to general rules; or that it is not possible to establish in advance all the rules that should be applied to a building decision. The first two are debatable, and probably reflect the fact that most communities do not have the capacity to make plans or debate policies for their environments. Design review becomes a real-time substitute for planning, or at least that aspect of planning that deals most directly with community appearance. The third assumption is troubling from a legal standpoint. Forcing adherence to rules that cannot be spelled out in advance is generally considered a denial of due process. And it was precisely this petard on which the Germantown Design Review Commission was hoisted.

As awkward as the notion of letting community standards evolve through case-by-case consideration of designs may be legally, it corresponds to the reality that most communities face. Knowing and agreeing upon a set of rules for building something as large and diverse as an entire community (as opposed to a single building complex or a subdivision, in which one theme is to be repeated and there are not issues of different owners with their own preferences) is an arduous task, and may only be achievable through the gradual accumulation of consensus over time. Thus, an important purpose of design review processes is that they allow a community to learn what it values, and to gradually encapsulate this understanding in formal policies.

Developing the capacity for public learning and consensus requires that a design review body be structured in a way that is both responsive to community values and stable enough to allow precedents to be considered and refreshed with each decision. Generally this is accomplished by creating a board composed of a mixture of professionals and lay persons who reflect a broad cross section of community interests. Continuity is often promoted by having lengthy (longer than the electoral cycle) and staggered terms for members, so that incumbents can pass along what has been learned from past projects to newcomers, and wholesale changes in attitudes are avoided.

Despite the widespread adoption of community appearance panels, we know little about the actual results of their work. How do they affect the quality of the built environment of a community? Do they inevitably become the captive of a professional sense of taste or an elite value system, or of the values of real estate interests or promoters of the community? Does case-by-case design review inevitably result in the lowest common denominator being applied to the screening of projects? This chapter asks these questions by examining the case record of the Germantown Design Review Commission.

IMPLICIT POLICIES FOR COMMUNITY APPEARANCE

Is it possible for a diverse group of professionals and laymen in a community to arrive at a coherent set of policies for the appearance of their community, and to enforce these consistently over a long enough time to make a difference? In historic districts, or areas with an established character, an affirmative answer is fairly clear. But what of a newly developing community? Architectural review in Germantown provides an illuminating example of the kinds of standards that can evolve in a community through a long-term effort to grapple with the intangibles of community image and character.

What follows is an attempt to generalize from case data and the examples of what got built in Germantown over a seventeen-year period. To address the awkward legal situation created by the Gulf suit—that the Design Review Commission was operating without standards—this author was asked to distill from the practice of design review the essential principles that seemed to underlie the commission's decisions. This small assignment offered a window on how members of at least one design review board thought about their task. The working method included looking at the examples identified by commission members as successful and unsuccessful developments, discussing with a circle of residents their views on community appearance, reviewing the records and minutes of commission meetings, watching the group in action, and discussing possible ways of framing their policies. As a final step, a design review manual was prepared that committed to writing the agreed upon principles and ultimately this was adopted as a policy statement.

In essence, this is an example of reverse engineering: taking apart the actual practice of design review and examining its underlying logic. Since the logic had been constructed through hundreds of decisions and actions over more than a decade,[1]

1. The Design Review Commission has jurisdiction over all construction, exterior alteration, signage, fences, curb cuts,

it also says a great deal about the kinds of attitudes that can evolve among residents of a suburban community about their environment. In a wider sense the results in Germantown may also be indicative of what many suburbanites aspire to as a self-image.

Germantown, which grew from a town of less than 8,000 to a city of almost 35,000 residents over the period that the Design Review Commission was in place. Indeed, the city now has a recognizable character, quite different from surrounding communities that operate without a design review board. The most obvious differences are to be found in the way that commercial strips stop abruptly at the city's borders, in the generosity of landscapes along major roadways, and in the restrained unity of the communities public and private buildings. But a closer look suggests that there are at least seven underlying sets of attitudes at work, each apparently widely accepted by residents of the community. These ultimately provided the basis for formal policies adopted by the commission.

1. Dominant Landscape

The fundamental guiding notion of community design that Germantown residents shared was that the natural landscape ought to be the dominant visual characteristic of the city, even in commercial areas. Buildings should be separated and surrounded by the landscape; streets should be designed as landscape corridors (Fig. 7-2). Buffers of landscape should separate one category of uses, such as residential areas, from other types of uses, such as retail complexes, or different densities of the same use from each other. Existing trees are to be vigorously protected and retained as sites are developed. As a practical matter, the taller

and landscape projects in the city, except for single-family detached residential structures. It also reviews all Planned Unit Development proposals. Its reviews occur concurrent with the Planning and Zoning Commission's review of projects in terms of their compliance with the zoning and subdivision ordinances. Both reviews are forwarded with a draft development agreement to the Board of Mayor and Aldermen for final approval of projects. Although the Board could decide to act contrary to the recommendations of the two commissions, this has happened only rarely. Thus, the Design Review Commission exerts considerable influence over the appearance of the city.

Figure 7-2. Landscape Ideal: Planned Unit Development in Germantown.

the building (although nothing had been built higher than three stories in Germantown), or the denser the use, the broader the landscape separation required.

Over the period the commission was in operation, it had never approved a project where less than 25 percent of the site was devoted to landscaped areas. This is justified not only on grounds of community character (which is the mandate of the commission), but also by the desire to reduce runoff, recharge groundwater, and retain existing vegetation. A large fraction of the commission's time is devoted to reviewing (and usually requiring additions to) landscape plans, and to drawing up agreements that insist upon irrigation and maintenance of the landscape. Almost totally absent from the decisions of the commission is the notion that there can be collections of buildings; each project is considered in terms of its own site, and is connected by green corridors to other sites.

2. Domestic Scale and Character

Germantown prides itself on the fact that, while it welcomes nonresidential uses of all kinds, it expects the buildings housing those uses to be designed so that they are "domestic" in scale and appearance. As one member of the commission put it, "Germantown is mainly a residential community, and none of the nonresidential uses should detract from that sense."

This construct has led to adoption of a style of building that clothes offices or retail uses in residential garb, complete with porticos, dormers, false attics, mansard roofs, and chimneys. It has also meant an almost total prohibition of flat-roofed structures (Fig. 7-3). The working rule seems to be that roofs should be at least at a 1:2 pitch, create a shadow line on the facade, be dark in color, and be visible from the street. Unbroken wall planes are also discouraged; the commission has generally required projects to offset facades

Figure 7-3. Domesticated offices

that are more than 75 feet in width in commercial areas and 50 feet wide in residential zones. While a few warehouses have adapted to these standards as best they could, Germantown has not had to face the issue of how large industrial structures can be domesticated.

3. Public vs. Private Domains

The commission makes a sharp distinction between front-stage areas (street facing portions or areas visible from adjacent sites) and backstage areas of sites (areas seen mainly by users or residents of the site itself), and focuses its most rigorous review on the former. In multifamily residential zones, garages and parking areas are generally prohibited from front-stage areas—the commission seems obsessed with avoiding open garage doors along the street, even in single family detached housing areas done as planned-unit developments. At the same time, it typically requires that buildings have main entrances visible from the street, rather than located in the private domain. In commercial areas where parking on the street side is generally unavoidable, it insists upon dense landscaping or berms separating these parking areas from the street. The overall intent is an orderly public environment, without the distraction of vehicles or signs of humans inhabiting the landscape.

4. Architectural Diversity

The commission makes a point of emphasizing to those who appear before it that it does not wish to prescribe a particular architectural style, and it invites applicants to respond with their interpretation of community character, rather than by simply mimicking other recent buildings. Whether it

really means it is another matter, since developers soon realize that approval is more easily gained if they instruct their architects to follow the prevailing architectural style (Fig. 7-4).

As the Gulf case demonstrates, there are limits to the tolerance of divergent approaches. Several "modern" buildings have been built in the city, notably the city hall and the post office (neither of which was reviewed in detail by the commission), and these have received mixed reviews from citizens. In both buildings, the architectural style is often dismissed as important since the buildings are predominately of brick and surrounded by generous landscape. The usual insistence that buildings be "domestic" in character rules out a host of architectural styles (decomp or postmodern, among them). As a practical matter, the commission never approves buildings that do not make substantial use of brick, stone, wood, slate, or stucco, and insists that these materials be earth tones. A widely used pale red terra-cotta-colored brick has come to be known as "Germantown brick." Primary colors are almost never permitted. In reviewing buildings, some note is taken of the style and materials of nearby buildings, particularly in approving colors and materials, but since building complexes are usually separated by extensive landscaping, there is not a need for close correspondence.

5. Restraint in Public Communications

Controlling signage occupies a disproportionate amount of time and attention of the commission. The general principle it applies is that signage should be designed for orientation and identification purposes, not to advertise products or places. No outlet should gain special advantage as a result of signage. And signage should not detract from the sense of a continuous landscape (Fig. 7-5).

Signs are strictly controlled by an ordinance and by interpretation of the committee, which is required as part of the permitting process. Primary signs (no more than 24 square feet, nor more than 6 feet high) are required to be ground-mounted, and usually set in a brick base or otherwise anchored in the landscape. Backlit signs are not allowed, and signs on the faces of buildings may protrude a maximum of 4 inches. The size of secondary signs—even the signs on gas pumps indicating the price—are strictly controlled. Bill-

Figure 7-4. Articulated facades

Figure 7-5. Domesticated commercial area

boards, temporary decorations, signs in shop windows, and even banners require special permission and are generally not permitted. The use of neon for signs or lighting is absolutely verboten. In sum, everything possible is done to make signage a minor part of the passing scene.

Occasionally, mental gymnastics are required to decide how to constrain signage to identification purposes only. The Great Wall chinese restaurant applied for permission to mount a sign on their facade consisting of the name of the restaurant in both English and Chinese. Since the commission decided that the Chinese characters could not be read by most of the public, and therefore must be a logo, they insisted that they be reduced in size to one-tenth of the overall sign area. Krogers supermarket was denied permission to place signs in their parking area reading "Kroger's Parking"; the signs were allowed when the store agreed to change them to "Grocery Parking." And after a lengthy debate over whether banners and flags constituted signs, logos, or temporary advertising, a policy was adopted restricting them to the street and only for the purposes of announcing the opening of new commercial centers.

6. Masking Utilitarian Objects

Almost as much passion is spent on ensuring that utilitarian objects are hidden from sight on or around buildings. Mechanical equipment on roofs (ventilators, exhaust outlets, air conditioners, elevator penthouses, and so forth) is not permitted to be visible from the street. Gas, water, and electric meters must be screened, and dumpsters must be enclosed on all sides.

Residential mailboxes on the street must be enclosed within brick or other "permanent" structures. Since many of these objects do not appear on typical architectural or landscape drawings, considerable meeting time is devoted to prying out of applicants how they intend to handle these functions. Loading docks or automotive service areas must be tucked around the side or rear of buildings and screened from the street. Garages and parking areas, insofar as is possible, are to be located at the rear of buildings, and where this is not possible, heavy landscaping is required to isolate them from the street. Even asphalt paving is discouraged; whenever possible the commission presses builders to substitute concrete with a sand-pebble finish or tinted to a warm color. Outdoor parking area and walkway lighting is limited to no more than 14 feet in height, and fixtures resembling park lighting are preferred. Ironically, the commission has little control over street lighting, public utility poles, and traffic signals in the public right-of-way, which are even more visible, although they do require all electric, telephone, and cable service to be placed below grade.

7. Preservation of Historic Patterns

While Germantown does not have a genuine historic district, a collection of older, modest village houses around the original Germantown train station is singled out for special attention. New structures in the area are required to follow the traditional pattern of porches, roofs running parallel to the street, and white clapboard siding. Over time this area has evolved into the one portion of the town where individual buildings comprise a district.

Taken together, these principles have resulted in an environment quite different from other suburbs of Memphis, and the city is a widely admired example of a suburb that has "maintained control over its fate," in the words of one elected official. There is considerable popular support for the work of the Design Review Commission and no shortage of people who are willing to accept appointments to serve on it (members are appointed by the mayor). Elected representatives rarely over-

turn the decisions of the commission, and when they do so they run the risk of losing political support. A recent election denied additional terms to several aldermen who were not seen as sufficiently vigilant of community character.

Ironically, the assertiveness of the lay commission, its willingness to turn down projects, and the uncertainty engendered by having (in the past) no written guidelines, places considerable power in the hands of professionals in the planning agency who serve as its staff. Wise developers meet with the staff before they advance proposals, ask for preliminary reviews to ensure that they are on the right track, and work hard at persuading the planners that they should submit a positive recommendation to the commission. The line between predicting the likely attitudes of the commission and offering personal prescriptions is hard to judge, but clearly there is advantage to having staff as advocates of a project before the commission. There is also some evidence that certain architects are more successful in getting their projects approved than others. "They know the Germantown style," was how one developer put it, and their repeated selection ensures that this style is widely duplicated. The result is considerable homogeneity in building forms. The commission has also been something of a boon to landscape architects and landscape contractors working in the area, with its insistence on extensive landscaping on every site.

ENVIRONMENTAL SYMBOLISM

In exercising its mandate, even before the commission was forced to become self-conscious about its principles, members constantly cited examples of structures that match their expectations, and drew from an equal inventory of undesirable examples, often located in Memphis and neighboring communities. This process, which John Costonis has described as the creation of "icons" and "aliens" (Costonis, 1990), has allowed the commission to operate with ill-defined principles, while providing concrete guidance about what to emulate or avoid to those who appear before it.

To the Germantown Design Review Commission the suburban environment is a powerful symbolic message system promoting the values that attract people to this developing suburb. Most people are attracted to Germantown, members of the commission argue, in search of the "estate in the country." Their icon is the porticoed mansion set in green lawns, surrounded by a white rail fence. While most new housing is confined to much smaller sites, developers in Germantown have been encouraged to at least duplicate the pastoral setting and make reference to the ideal through such details as columned entrances and winding driveways. In planned-unit development cases, the board encourages the clustering of houses to allow the scale of surrounding lawns to begin to measure up to the scale of the estate.

Images of Williamsburg, Jefferson's Monticello, the lawn at the University of Virginia, and small-town southern colleges also surface in discussions of a desired environment. Larger buildings, such as office complexes, schools, or shopping centers can sometimes emulate these icons quite directly and there are several examples in Germantown with recognizable origins. In a more widespread way, the use of brick with exposed wooden trim and shingles, and nine-over-nine-pane double-hung windows (accomplished through plastic inserts) in even quite large complexes lends an air of domesticity to nonresidential uses.

This imagery has become a new vernacular in the border states and through parts of the South. As much as Germantown prides itself as having a distinctive look and feel, similar buildings and similar approaches to the environment may be found in other suburbs for the upwardly mobile in a band of cities from Virginia to Texas. The imagery is reinforced by each issue of *House and Garden, Southern Living,* and developers' trade publications illustrating successful projects. It speaks to the desire among those who have reached a level of resources that allows them to choose where they wish to live or work to seek an environment that is ordered, comprehensible in scale, and devoted to the kind of neighboring that once supposedly existed in much smaller places. At times it seems to be life emulating political commercials.

The commission has also taken as its crusade ridding the environment of the aliens threatening this ideal of a quiet suburban life. They include commercialism, franchises, signs, and buildings (and perhaps people?) that shout for attention, unadorned modern architecture, seas of cars,

trash, evidence of decay, and temporary elements in the landscape. These are frequently summed up in a single image—the commercial strip—that embodies much of what is to be avoided. The commercial strip has acquired the approbation previously reserved for burlesque parlors, pool halls, and smoky factories. That it also seems to serve many of the needs of an automobile-oriented community has not deterred design review commissions in Germantown and elsewhere from a campaign of "civilizing the strip." Denied the key ingredients that make a conventional commercial corridor work, developers are turning to other models for how to achieve synergy among commercial outlets. The shopping village, the "collection" of shops, as well as franchise parks, with individual outlets organized around a common landscaped area are some of the responses. Thus, the design review process has had more profound impacts on the development pattern of Germantown than simply changing the appearance of buildings.

The central message of the work of Germantown's review commission is that residents and their values are dominant, rather than the development, commercial, or mercantile interests that so often shape the public environment. Newcomers, and new buildings, are judged by their conformity to the social norms of those who have an established place. This ability to control change in a rapidly developing community is critical to ideology of upward mobility of Germantown residents, and a guard against the slippery slope they have traversed to arrive where they are. As Constance Perin writes:

> Two fundamental properties of American social order, certainty and progress, stand in contradiction to one another: It must be possible to count on some things as stable, settled, and safe—but according to the American Dream and the American Creed, there is equally the imperative to improve, progress, change and evolve from lower to higher forms of living. People in motion, though, are transient and dangerous. Moving upward and onward, yet standing still (Perin, 1977, 108).

Perin suggests that, among the upwardly mobile, "the contradiction between certainty and progress is . . . resolved by putting the highest value on only the ultimate transition—single-family-detached homeownership." Hence the board's desire to enforce a domestic image on all structures, to emphasize the natural setting, and to re-create a sense of quiet landscaped streets is in service to a powerful agenda of social sympolism.

The design review commission at times resembles an ongoing seminar on community values. A central theme is how quickly the community should change, and in what direction. The debate over the Gulf station, as captured by the official minutes of meeting when it was first proposed is revealing:

> Mr. Polk noted his personal concern for the modernistic design as presented, pointing out the more traditional look the commission had required of the Exxon Station, Vickers, and other developments. Mr. Oumov felt that the City should not stay or be an old fashioned type town and gave his approval of the modernistic design. Mrs. Goodman had no problem with the colors to be used but was concerned with some of the treatment proposed, and although preferring the traditional said she could live with a more modern approach.

And so on. Where else can such issues of community identity and taste be debated and concrete decisions taken?

If there are reservations about the work of the commission, they surface only at the edges of conversations. Some residents share the concern over being an "old-fashioned town." Others regard their commercial areas as "bland" and "colorless," and report that they find other shopping malls and areas more exciting. A few residents worry that they have driven away the most interesting shops by the commission's demands that they conform to community guidelines. Some architects and landscape designers who work in the city argue that the commission's insistence on appropriateness has discouraged any real innovation or experimentation in building forms or landscapes.

A wider critique can also be made. While the city has managed to elevate the quality of individual site design, it has done little to promote the larger sense of a community as something more than a collection of individual sites. The Civic Center consists of a loose collection of individual structures, each surrounded by landscape. There are few well-used sidewalks in the city, since the enforced separation of uses makes it practically impossible to satisfy multiple purposes without an automobile. While design review has assured a comfortable, ordered environment for Germantown, it is not a substitute for imagining and planning the city.

REFERENCES

Costonis, John J. 1990. *Icons and Aliens: Law, Aesthetics and Environmental Change.* Urbana: University of Illinois Press.

Perin, Constance. 1977. *Everything in Its Place: Social Order and Land Use in America.* Princeton, N.J.: Princeton University Press.

8
Design Review Comes to Phoenix

Grady Gammage, Jr.

Gammage & Burnham, Phoenix, Arizona

Phoenix, Arizona, has recently become one of the largest cities in the United States to enact city-wide design review. This chapter examines the events leading up to the enactment and explains the procedural mechanisms used to implement the process, including a format for the design review procedures, which turns on a hierarchy of individual guidelines called "requirements," "presumptions," and "considerations."

The city of Phoenix no longer has the boomtown atmosphere it did in the mid 1980s, when new office buildings seemed to spring up on every corner and local zoning decisions drew crowds numbering in the hundreds. A severely damaged local economy has for now put the brakes on both the fast-paced development that once gripped the city, and the severe neighborhood backlash it caused. When things do start to boom again, as inevitably they will, the newly enacted design review process will hopefully insure fewer negative development impacts and a more carefully considered appearance for the city as a whole.

The Phoenix Design Review Ordinance was adopted by the city council in January 1991, as the culmination of three years of effort to bring aesthetic design regulation to a large and architecturally diverse metropolitan environment. Since the system is still new, and development has been slow, it is difficult to assess the effect of this regulation on the look of the city, but the process that led up to adoption of the ordinance and the unique system devised to implement design review in a "wild west" environment may be instructive to other municipalities.

Before the recent slowdown, large buildings were rising, like the mythical Phoenix itself, from sites that had held smaller strip commercial structures. When several four-story offices sprang up unexpectedly behind single-family homes, as a result of old cumulative zoning that permitted such construction "as of right," the shock waves created a strong pro-neighborhood reaction and resulted in emergency revisions to the zoning ordinance. But that revision alone wasn't enough to mollify growing antidevelopment sentiment. There was a feeling that more attention to project relationships and design was needed to mitigate development impact.

Much of the original impetus for imposing design review came from the current mayor, Paul Johnson, when he was a council member. Johnson, a general contractor, was a strong advocate of growth and development but found himself on a city council split between very pro-growth laissez-faire-oriented council members and members who were strong advocates of neighborhood protection and preservation. He also felt that the visual appearance of the city of Phoenix was negative compared with some of its neighboring suburbs (most notably, Scottsdale and Tempe), which have long engaged in rigorous design review programs. He advocated design review, therefore, as a way to make development better, rather than slower, and to create potential compromises between development and neighborhood interests.

The process began with the appointment of a task force to consider whether or not design review was appropriate in Phoenix. The task force worked for about a year and recommended that Phoenix should attempt to implement a design review program, but that it should not be open-ended, discretionary, "style-oriented" review, such as was conducted in the smaller suburban communities. Rather, it should be made as objective and predictable as possible.

The city council ultimately concurred with that decision and adopted an ordinance authorizing design review. That ordinance provided three critical directives that thereafter shaped the process. First, the ordinance established two citizen committees to draft the program. The Design Review Standards Committee (DRSC) was charged with adopting the standards to be applied. The Design Review Appeals Board (with the extraordinarily unfortunate acronym DRAB) would hear specific project appeals. Second, the ordinance directed that DRAB decisions would not be appealable to the city council, so as to hopefully insulate them from political pressure. The only appeal would be to superior court. Third, the program was directed to be designed to operate city-wide, as a "base-level" design process, applying to all new construction other than single-family homes, which were excluded because of the overwhelming workload their review would present and because of the political risks inherent in reviewing house design.

PHOENIX PRINCIPLES OF DESIGN

The DRSC began its work in August 1989. This eighteen-member group was made up of neighborhood advocates, design professionals, developers, and attorneys. Almost all of them had some development-related experience, and the lawyers and architects even managed to get along. The DRSC met for over a year and ultimately proposed the *Phoenix Development Review Manual* to the council. Its provisions are the direct result of the committee members working with city staff, without any outside consultants being used.

The committee met as a whole and discussed the daunting task that lay before it. Phoenix is the ninth-largest U.S. city in population (1,012,273), and covers the third-largest land area (427.8 square miles). In 1987 approximately 9,000 permits were obtained that would fall within the program's scope. There was also no clear community consensus formed around any particular architectural appearance. The city grew so quickly that it had no real chance to develop a "Phoenix style." In 1940, the city had only 65,000 people. Contrast, for example, one hundred years of growth a relatively similar western city, Denver:

	1890	*1990*
Denver	107,000	505,790
Phoenix	3,200	981,000

This growth was mostly postwar, and therefore postautomobile. As a result, Phoenix may be the most clearly realized vision of Reyner Banham's utopia. Its average developed density is less than one-third that of Los Angeles. The city is linear, heterogeneous, and new: a fabric of detached single-family homes with walled backyards, commercial strips, and neighborhood shopping centers. Its buildings are also extraordinarily visible, as a result of the absence of dense landscape material. So what was the committee to do to bring an aesthetic order?

The city council had provided no guidance to this question. The politicians apparently wanted a process that didn't unnecessarily impede development and didn't land too much controversy in their lap, but made the city look "nicer".

The DRSC concluded that it was undesirable to attempt the creation of any artificial style or theme and enforce it city-wide. Rather, it suggested that a second-tier review process could later be added dealing with subareas and seeking to impose a particular style in that narrower context. This conclusion was consistent with the Phoenix general plan, which organizes the city into distinct "urban villages" centered around "cores."

On a city-wide basis, the committee felt the process should address design quality in its broadest sense: responsiveness to climate, relationships between individual uses, appropriateness to surrounding context. In furtherance of this conclusion, a subcommittee wrote a section of broad

KENDLE

Figure 8-1. Contextualism: This new building fits comfortably within the scale and rhythm of the Roosevelt Historic District, an area made up of bungalows converted into small office buildings.

urban design statements called the "Phoenix Principles of Design," each of which has an accompanying illustration. Following are examples of the "Phoenix Principles."

1. *Contextualism*

   Every development has a relationship to its setting. Positive relations can be achieved by examining the next largest (and smallest) context of the site. Ignoring the context can often assure poor relationships.

   The size, character, and setting of proposed projects should relate to their specific contexts and functions of adjacent streets and pedestrian networks. Buildings should be oriented to public rights-of-way as well as additional internal circulation systems (Fig. 8-1).

   The natural environment of the desert context contains critical extremes. The opportunity of a harmonious response exists when these factors are understood and addressed in the design. Those projects that acknowledge this tend to thrive; those that ignore this fact tend to be foolish.

2. *Amenity/Comfort*

   Settlements in the desert generally occur in an "oasis" setting, which is a respite from the extreme of the larger arid context. A development in an arid setting requires design features to aid human comfort. It is important to understand that urban conditions such as paved areas and buildings generating reflected heat create aridity and require mitigating design features that enhance habitability (Fig. 8-2).

   Shaded areas, courtyards, colonnades, and other areas should be provided as site amenities to promote human comfort. Protection from the sun and heat is a priority between late April and September, while access to the sun is a priority from October to mid-April.

3. *Visual Interest*

   An environment that contains a harmonious balance of various forms and materials can be visually interesting. Too much variety or too much uniformity can lack visual interest. New development should seek to preserve and enhance this basic human need.

   Promote a diversity of architectural styles. When a project occurs in a visually rich context, its form, materials, orientation, and detailing should incorporate the assets offered by its setting.

4. *Views*

   City dwellers and visitors alike appreciate be-

Figure 8-2. Amenity and comfort: Architectural elements can create outdoor places that are functional and comfortable.

ing reminded of the beauty of their environment. Protecting views of it assist in fostering appreciation of our environment, as well as allowing the environment to aid in orienting people spatially within Phoenix.

Protect major vistas and panoramas that give special emphasis to open space, mountains, and special manmade or natural landmarks. Promote the creation of views both from within a project and from the adjacent streets and neighborhoods into the projects. Consider the access to views of both the project users and the general public (Fig. 8-3).

5. *Cultural History*
Our city is a crossroads for various cultures that can thrive together or be ignored completely. While Phoenix may appear to be a very new city, there are many layers of history upon which this valley has been built. These remnants contribute to our heritage and to the vitality of this city. Honoring this heritage enriches our community. To ignore this decreases the opportunity and significance of the development.

Enhance and promote the historical and cultural qualities that are inherent and distinctive to the area. Identify and incorporate as much as possible the particular history of each site. Whenever possible, historically significant buildings and their related landscape setting should be retained and restored, or put to adaptive reuse with respect to their cultural value, and their connection with the city's heritage.

The DRSC hotly debated these principles, but ultimately formed a consensus that they represented a coherent expression of design philosophy that would make Phoenix a better city. But next, the committee faced the task where so many design review systems fail, the challenge of communicating expectations—telling builders and designers what they are "supposed to do."

THE HIERARCHY OF DESIGN GUIDELINES

Since from the outset it was decreed that the Phoenix Design Review process was to operate objectively and at a staff level, the statement of broad design principles was obviously inadequate. Additionally, the Phoenix city attorney's office was concerned about the enforceability of any set of vague, open-ended design criteria, and consistently urged that the criteria be made as objective and as quantifiable as possible.

In designing any review process, an overriding tension exists between strict measurable design standards that may be clear, but are also rigid, inflexible, and can lead to "straitjacketing" the designer, and, on the other hand, vaguely communicated, lofty goals that are interpreted only by a subjective panel long after the initial project design has been done and when likely to lead to the maximum disagreement.

Additionally, a series of subsidiary questions arise when attempting to structure the design communication. Should the guidelines be organized by building type? By land use or zoning category? By size of project? By design characteristic? And how are the different criteria weighted? Are they all of equivalent importance? Do those administering the process have equal flexibility in enforcing or relaxing a given standard? Should an individual project accumulate "points" by complying

Figure 8-3. Views: Care should be taken to enhance views for new development, as well as preserving existing view corridors of neighboring properties.

with some of the standards such that it can avoid complying with others?

The Phoenix DRSC discussed all these questions, but initially concluded that it could not answer any of them until more specific objective guidelines were written. The committee was therefore organized into a series of subcommittees dealing with aspects of project design. At that point, there appeared to be a fairly clear community consensus that the process should not deal with architectural style per se. Because these were the city-wide standards and because Phoenix is a large community of heterogeneous design, an enforced style is not appropriate for the community as a whole. Since this was also Phoenix's first venture into widespread design control, the committee also felt it was appropriate to stay away from issues of color and specific architectural design. As a result, six subcommittees were appointed: site plan, subdivision design, architecture, landscape architecture, traffic and circulation, and signage.

While each of these committees attempted to construct a series of design guidelines operating within its jurisdiction, a seventh subcommittee (dubbed the "format" subcommittee) was to dis-

cuss and wrestle with the problem of structuring and formatting the individual design guidelines. The format subcommittee, made up of three lawyers, immediately proceeded to "grab turf" and assert its right to review and word individual guidelines coming from any of the other subcommittees.

As the dialogue over individual guidelines began, it quickly seemed that the guidelines being generated fell into three broad categories. First, there was a category of issues where virtually everyone agreed that certain past design practices were detrimental and should simply be ruled out except in the most extraordinary of circumstances. These issues dealt with such things as mechanical equipment on the roofs of buildings that were visible from street level; "back-on" subdivision treatment leaving bleak canyons of unlandscaped areas against major arterial streets, the need for handicap accessibility to buildings (this was prior to the Americans with Disabilities Act); and, perhaps most significantly, the context a design proponent should address in considering his project. As to this last issue, it was the widespread feeling of the DRSC that many of the perceived design problems and controversies of the early 1980s had been caused by developers and designers viewing their site in isolation and ignoring the surrounding development patterns. And indeed, the city's permitting process did not require the submittal of any documents viewing the site in its context.

With regard to the "context" review, the design guidelines being discussed were viewed as indispensable to reviewing any project. But as the committee worked further, it became clear that the specific subcommittees had a relatively small number of such absolute "requirements" they sought to impose on applicants, and that many of these were procedural in character, such as a requirement to file a "context plan."

At the opposite end of the spectrum, the specific subcommittees were also producing a large number of design issues they wanted applicants simply to "think about" in some formal way. They felt there was a demand for a document highlighting a number of design "considerations" that any good designer should review and consider in connection with his or her project, but of which only a limited number might ultimately be incorporated. These "considerations" would simply be things the city would suggest designers take into account in designing buildings for Phoenix, but which would not otherwise be enforced in any regulatory framework.

Between these two extremes—on the one hand, of *requirements* every designer would have to meet absent extraordinary circumstances, and on the other, of *considerations* every designer would only have to read and think about—were those design characteristics the City would like to see incorporated into most of the projects coming through the process. Yet any given project might incorporate some, but not all, of these design characteristics and there might be a good reason why particular characteristics were more important than others. These characteristics needed clarity or flexibility. The format committee, ever true to its legal roots, quickly dubbed this middle range of design guidelines "presumptions."

In legal parlance, a "presumption" shifts the burden of proof. For example, if one's blood alcohol level is over the specified limit he is "presumed" to be intoxicated, unless he can, by other evidence, prove that he is not, thereby "overcoming" the presumption. As a practical matter, this format simplifies the discussion of responsibility between parties by establishing clear priorities

and presumptive results if all other factors are equal.

The Phoenix Development Review Manual evolved, therefore, into a hierarchy of design guidelines called "requirements" (R's), "presumptions" (P's), and "considerations (C's)." As finally adopted, the manual includes seven "R's", fifty-nine "P's," and thirty-one "C's". Each guideline also has its own rationale.

A "requirement" is a design standard that has the force of an ordinance: it must be followed unless a variance is received through an elaborate and expensive hearing process. These are kept to a minimum because of their rigid character. Examples include:

- All roof-top equipment and satellite dishes must be screened to the height of the tallest equipment and/or integrated with the building design (R).
- Five percent of the surface parking lot, exclusive perimeter landscaping and front setback, must be landscaped. Landscaping shall be dispersed throughout the parking area (R) (Fig. 8-4).

A "consideration," on the other hand, is simply something for the designer to think about in connection with a project—something he or she might choose to incorporate:

- The proposed site plan should enhance the street context and take into account the view corridor along the street as well as the opportunity for pedestrian interaction at street level (C) (Fig. 8-5).
- Materials and colors in the context area should be considered when selecting the materials and colors used in the project (C).
- The building facade should be designed to provide a sense of human scale at ground level (C).

While the considerations have no legal force, they can serve as a testing ground for future presumptions or requirements. That is, if a "C" seems useful and workable, it may be upgraded to a "P" or an "R" in future revisions to the guidelines.

The real meat of the design review regulatory process is played out in "presumptions." These are

Figure 8-4. Clarity and convenience: Expressing the entry and access areas can easily guide people to their destination.

Figure 8-5. Character and distinctiveness: The unique details of a project create character and distinctiveness.

design standards that a project *should* incorporate, such as:

- Overhangs and canopies should be integrated in the building design along all pedestrian thoroughfares (P).
- Where open space appears on a site plan, it should be designed to be accessible and usable by people (P).
- The proposed building orientation should respect climatic conditions by minimizing heat gain and considering the impact of shade or adjacent land uses and areas (P).
- For office and retail projects, every parking space should be no greater than 150 feet from a sidewalk leading to the building or from a building entrance, and unshaded segments of walking should not exceed 15 feet except at driveway crossings (P).

If an applicant or designer can convince the staff that there are good reasons, grounded in the

"Phoenix Principles of Design," for "overcoming a presumption," he can escape from its requirement. Since the guidelines have been developed to suggest a performance basis rather than to mandate an explicit design solution, considerable flexibility is intended in administering the presumptions. Examples of reasons for overcoming presumptions can be a potential conflict with another presumption, a demonstration of a preferable alternative solution, or a showing that certain "considerations" will be furthered by not applying the presumption. The reasons must be grounded in a better design solution, however, not in cost savings.

If the city staff agrees with the applicant, the applicant can escape from the presumption's impact. If the staff disagrees, however, the applicant may seek relief through an appeal to the Design Review Appeals Board. From that board, the only remedy is to go to superior court.

In order to implement the new Design Review Process, the *Phoenix Development Review Manual* requires the filing of more detailed site plans and landscaping plans than had previously been required. Additionally, two new documents must be included. The first, the "context plan," is designed to show both the applicant and the city staff the larger context surrounding the proposal. The second, a "shading plan," is designed to demonstrate how shade is being incorporated into the project to enhance the pedestrian environment in the harsh desert climate of Phoenix.

On either the set of plans that are filed or in a separate narrative, the applicant is asked to address each of the requirements and presumptions applicable to the project. As to the presumptions, the applicant must either explain how they are met or offer an explanation for why that particular "P" should not be applied.

AREA SPECIFIC DESIGN GUIDELINES

In addition to the city-wide design review process, the Phoenix system allows specific areas of towns to adopt design guidelines applicable only within that particular geographic area. Through the use of a specific plan process such guidelines may add to or modify the city-wide standards. The first such effort dealt with the Camelback East

Core Specific Plan. This location is identified as one of the "village cores" of increased intensity around which the city's future growth is to be organized. Originally a suburban shopping and office location, the "East Camelback Village Core" became in the mid-1980s a fashionable midrise office location. The residents of that area were very concerned about the impact of this development on high-quality surrounding residential neighborhoods and upon the views to Camelback Mountain.

In developing a specific plan to deal with this problem, the "Village Planning Committee" worked with a subcommittee chaired by a local planning and design consultant to develop a set of design guidelines specifically applicable only to the East Camelback Village Core area. These guidelines go far beyond the city-wide design review standards in seeking to create a particular design theme. This theme is implemented principally through streetscape and landscaping plans and is intended to evoke an imagery similar to the nearby Frank Lloyd Wright–inspired Arizona Biltmore Hotel.

Because these guidelines deal with a "high-intensity" (for Phoenix) village core area, the guidelines are more specifically oriented toward creating a pedestrian environment in an urban setting. The specific plan guidelines also add to R's, P's, and C's an additional designation: "I," for "incentive," indicating that appropriate handling of the guideline may be eligible for bonuses of height and intensity.

Examples of the East Camelback guidelines include:

- A strong and relatively continuous building frontage should be provided along the public right-of-way. A minimum 30 percent of the lot frontage should include buildings at the setback line of each lot along the public right-of-way of all major streets. (P) (Fig. 8-6).
- Active, pedestrian outdoor public spaces (a plaza, courtyard, garden, "outdoor room," or a promenade) should be provided within private development (P).
- Provision of a destination space (large destination plaza, park, and so on) in the core may qualify for a bonus (I).
- A continuous pathway system should be cre-

Figure 8-6. Definition of space: Functional pedestrian space is defined by architectural and landscape features.

ated, particularly midblock between Camelback Road and Highland Avenue from the Squaw Peak Parkway to 26th Street (C).

- Provision of an easement to provide a corridor in which the pedestrian spine can operate may qualify for a bonus (I) (Fig. 8-7).
- Buildings should be designed so they do not extend closer to the street than a line drawn at 60 degrees from the front property line (plus or minus 5 percent or 3 degrees) on Camelback Road, 24th Street, 20th Street, and 22nd Street (P).

IMPLEMENTATION OF THE PROCESS

The initial phase of design review began operating on March 1, 1991. At that time, the process was applied only to newer commercial zoning districts that had previously required site plan review or to individual projects that might have been stipulated to site plan review at the time of a rezoning case.

In the first fourteen months of the program, approximately 74 projects were reviewed under the new process. Because development has been so slow, the majority of these projects were small and noncontroversial. In fact, the two largest projects to face the process were the city's new city hall and public library. The inclusion of city projects in the process had initially been resisted by the city staff charged with their construction, who said it would delay projects and increase their cost. The hypocrisy of this position was not lost on private-sector interests, who repeatedly pointed out to the city council that it was unfair to impose the new procedures on everyone but the city. The council had little political option but to agree.

Two appeals have been pursued to the DRAB as of this writing. One was brought by the developer of a single-family subdivision seeking to modify the twelve-foot landscape buffer presumption where individual yards would back up to an arterial street. The board upheld application of the presumption with slight modification. The second appeal dealt with a three-foot parking-screen wall

Figure 8-7. Scale and pattern: Detailing should be of scale and respectful of those utilizing the space.

in front of a large drugstore. The applicant sought relief from this presumption because of the already limited visibility of the building. Again, the appeals board accepted a compromise wall and hedge combination that the staff had previously indicated was acceptable but which the applicant had resisted until he came before the board.

Starting in March 1992, the second phase of implementation was to move forward. Originally this phase was to subject all nonsingle-family developments to the full scope of design review. Because of severe budgetary constraints, however, the city staff proposed an abbreviated form of second-phase implementation. That abbreviated form would apply design review only to projects with major impact either on highly visible arterial streets or close proximity to single-family neighborhoods. This abbreviated second phase was approved by the city council on March 17, 1992, and is now moving forward.

CONCLUSION

Phoenix's effort is a bold move to impose citywide design review. The standards themselves reflect the fact that Phoenix is not seeking to create or protect a particular style, but rather only to codify quality design elements that cut across various styles. The process proposed by the DRSC for applying "presumptions" presents a different and novel framework that might be used by other jurisdictions.

Despite the limited experience to date, the system has been effective in structuring the design dialogue. The R/P/C format is becoming a newly ingrained part of development language and has proved useful to other groups and committees throughout the community. Designers and developers are getting used to the process and so far seem to believe it is relatively fair. We hope the next few years give us the opportunity to see if the aesthetic quality of our built environment is also improved.

9
Santa Fe Styles and Townscapes: The Search for Authenticity

Harry Moul

Planner, City of Santa Fe

PRESERVATIONIST PLANNING

Beginning around 1912, historic preservation and the promotion of a regional architecture have been parallel efforts to maintain and encourage a unique appearance to the city of Santa Fe, New Mexico.

The report of the Santa Fe City Planning Board to the city council on December 3, 1912, states clearly what were to become tenets of preservationist belief:

> It is the opinion of this Board that the preservation of the ancient streets, roads and structures in and about the city is of the first importance and that these monuments should be preserved intact at almost any cost . . . and that it should be the duty of all city officials to guard the old streets against any change that will affect their appearance or alter their character such as widening or straightening.

And as if in anticipation of the Historical District Ordinance:

> We further recommend that no building permits be issued to any person intending to build on any of the streets . . . indicated on the map as old or ancient streets until proper assurance is given that the architecture will conform exteriorly with the Santa Fe style.

This is a remarkable statement of contextual design review for its emphasis on streets and architecture taken together.

In a statement that has proven to be prophetic the Board urged that "everything should be done to create a public sentiment so strong that the Santa Fe style will always predominate."[1] From 1912 on, public and private buildings in Santa Fe were increasingly constructed in variations of Santa Fe revival architectural style (Figs. 9-1, 9-2).

Interest in this regional revival architecture coincided with interest in Pueblo Indian and Spanish Colonial architecture and the desire to promote tourism[2]. It was a reaction to the eclecticism of architectural styles that had been imported from the East during the period of 1846–1912,[3] an importation that accelerated with the construction of railroads in New Mexico in the 1880s.

To put the Santa Fe revival architecture into a

---

1. Report of the Santa Fe City Planning Board, December 3, 1912.

2. Nicholas C. Markovich, "Santa Fe Renaissance: City Planning and Stylistic Preservation, 1912," in *Pueblo Style and Regional Architecture,* ed. Markovich, Preiser, and Sturm (New York: Van Nostrand Reinhold, 1990). Professor Markovich sees the concurrence on Santa Fe style as an "agreeable compromise" between conservative factions interested in protecting Santa Fe's heritage and progressive factions of the community: "new growth should proceed . . . but remain within the construct of Santa Fe's indigenous architectural heritage."

3. John P. Conron, "A Glossary of Architectural Styles," in *Design and Preservation in Santa Fe: A Pluralistic Approach* (Santa Fe: Planning Department, January 1977).

Figure 9-1. La Fonda Hotel, Pueblo Revival Style. Rapp, Rapp and Hendrickson, Architects, 1920. (Photo: T. Harmon Parkhurst; courtesy Museum of New Mexico, Neg. no. 10692.)

Figure 9-2. Museum of Fine Arts, Pueblo Revival Style. Rapp and Rapp Architects, 1916. (Photo: Conron & Lent, Architects.)

rough historical perspective the following summary is offered. During the Spanish and Mexican periods (1692–1846), a regional style of architecture was developed utilizing the methods and materials of the Pueblo Indians. Pueblo Spanish (Fig. 9-3) refers to the architecture surviving from this period.

Territorial Style (Fig. 9-4) refers to the architecture developed after the American military occupied Santa Fe in 1846. Fired brick, milled lumber, and metal material roofing changed the building technology and permitted the addition of wood frames and lintels, *portales,* and brick capping to adobe buildings.

Toward the end of the Territorial period, between the coming of the railroad in the 1880s and statehood in 1912, a proliferation of architectural styles were imported as Santa Fe strove to achieve the appearance of a contemporary American city.

Thus, Santa Fe Style was both a reaction to the immediate past and an inventive evocation of an earlier pre-Anglo regional architecture.

The dominance of Santa Fe revival architecture, first as a romantic ideal and after 1957 as a design standard, created some problems. Victorian-era buildings from the late 1800s were remodeled to conform to the Santa Fe Style (Figs. 9-5, 9-6). This not only represented a lack of respect for the original architectural style of the building, but created a kind of architectural ambiguity with respect to the history and context of the building. Also, in numerous instances authentic buildings from the Spanish and Mexican periods were demolished to make way for new Santa Fe Style replacements (Figs. 9-7, 9-8). However, it was the threat of postwar "modern" architecture that led directly to the drafting of the Historical District Ordinance (Fig. 9-9).

Figure 9-3. "Pueblo Spanish" house on Manhattan. (Photo 1912: Jesse L. Nusbaum; courtesy Museum of New Mexico, Neg. no. 11183.)

Figure 9-4. Tully House, restored Territorial style with painted brick pattern on adobe walls, 1851. (Photo: Courtesy Planning Division, City of Santa Fe.)

Figure 9-5. Staab House.

HISTORICAL DISTRICT AND HISTORICAL STYLE COMMITTEE

The Santa Fe Historical District was adopted by the city council in 1957 with the following statement of purpose:

> In order to promote the economic, cultural and general welfare of the people of the city . . . it is deemed essential by the city council that the qualities relating

to the history of Santa Fe . . . be preserved; some of these qualities being: The continued existence and preservation of historical areas and buildings; continued construction of buildings in the historic styles, and a general harmony as to style, form, color, proportion, texture and material between buildings of historic design and those of more modern design.[4]

---

4. Santa Fe City Ord. No. 1957–18.

Figure 9-6. La Posada, Staab House remodeled in Pueblo Revival Style. (Photo: Carol Schneider.)

At the same time, a Historical Style Committee was established. Chief among its powers and duties was that the committee "shall review and approve or deny all applications for new construction, exterior alteration and demolition of structures . . . in the Historical District."

With the creation of the Historical District Ordinance, the two basic styles were recognized: Old Santa Fe Style and Recent Santa Fe Style. Old Santa Fe Style, considered to have evolved in Santa Fe from 1600 onward, was characterized by construction in adobe and included the so-called Pueblo, Pueblo-Spanish or Spanish-Indian, and Territorial styles. Recent Santa Fe Style was considered an elaboration of the Old Santa Fe Style but built with different materials and with added decoration.

In 1964, the Supreme Court of New Mexico held that regulations in the ordinance pertaining to size of windows in construction or alteration of buildings within the historic area of Santa Fe as part of the preservation of the Old Santa Fe Style of architecture was a valid exercise of the police power granted to the city, and that the preservation of historical areas and buildings was within the term "general welfare" used in municipal zoning enabling legislation. The court found that "Santa Fe is known throughout the whole country for its historic features and culture. Many of our laws have their origin in that early culture. It must be obvious that the general welfare of the community and of the State is enhanced thereby."[5]

As the concepts of historic preservation and contextual design expanded, it became evident that not all concerns for design and preservation in Santa Fe were being addressed. For example,

5. 389 Pacific Reporter, 2nd Series, p. 18.

Figure 9-7. Old convent on Cathedral Place. (Photo: Courtesy Museum of New Mexico, Neg. no. 14109, c. 1912.)

Figure 9-8. U.S. Post Office, 1921, on site of former Convent; James A. Wetmore, Supervising Architect. (Photo: Courtesy Planning Division, City of Santa Fe.)

Figure 9-9. Desert Inn, a postwar "modern" motel on the Old Santa Fe Trail, c. 1955. (Photo: Joyce Bond.)

Figure 9-10. Lincoln Avenue Officers' Houses. (Photo: U.S. Army Signal Corps Collections; courtesy Museum of New Mexico, Neg. no. 30827.)

HISTORIC TOWNSCAPES

In 1975, with the assistance of a grant from the National Endowment for the Arts, a study was made of the historic development of city structure and townscape.[6] Among other things, architectural styles were correlated with the period of development of the various sections of the city. The idea was that if the building styles and planning features of each district were placed in their historic context, the sense of history would be clarified for the contemporary observer. It was felt that this approach would also tend to emphasize the uniqueness of the Spanish, Mexican, and early Territorial period townscapes through contrast with districts developed at a later date.

Along with building style, "townscape" features such as building height, placement, and massing, and the presence or absence of landscap-

ing, walls, and *portales*[7] were identified for each district. The clearest example is the sudden change in planning principles that occurred after the occupation of Santa Fe by the U.S. Army in 1846. The Americans brought town planning practices from the eastern United States, where traditional planning included free-standing buildings set well back from broad tree-lined avenues with front yards and picket fences (Fig. 9-10). This tradition was directly in contrast to Spanish Colonial town planning principles codified in the Laws of the Indies.

Characteristics of Pre-1846 Townscape	*Characteristics of Post-1846 Townscape*
Narrow streets	Wide avenues
Houses front on street	Yards separate houses from street
High walls	Picket fences
No plantings in public right-of-way	Street trees in parkways
Portales over sidewalks	Front porches
Plantings confined to interior courtyards.	Front lawns

---

6. "Historic Structure and Townscape Study," supported by a grant from the National Endowment for the Arts.

7. A *portal* is a long porch or portico with roof supported

The notion that meaningful subdistricts could be defined each with its own design principles was further developed by William Weismantel, then a professor at the University of New Mexico.[8]

The two observations—the existence of unique and multiple subdistricts and the diversity of architectural styles—supported the need for regulations to complement those in the Historical Ordinance. Also, many projects, while incorporating details of Santa Fe Style consistent with the written standards, were nevertheless out of harmony and scale with adjacent buildings.

SOME DIFFICULTIES WITH PRESERVATION AND DESIGN REVIEW

Streetscape

While the Historical Style Committee had been empowered to deny a permit for the demolition of a structure on the basis of its importance as an example of Old Santa Fe Style, the application of this power has been subject to appeal. One instance when the Historical Style Committee's decision to deny a demolition was overturned by the planning commission in 1979 involved a request for demolition of two small, late Territorial period brick houses on Marcy Street in order to permit use of the property as a parking lot (Fig. 9-11). These houses did not meet the criteria of Old Santa Fe Style in that they were brick, not adobe, and were built with pitched, not flat, roofs; and although they dated from the turn of the century, they were not considered to be "architectural specimens" of any sort. Interestingly, the Committee defended its position in terms of contextual factors. The chairman noted that Marcy Street "has a very distinct streetscape" and that "by demolishing two of the buildings on the corner, and just leveling it, you're destroying the whole feeling of the neighborhood." One member objected to putting a parking lot in place of a building

Figure 9-11. Small brick bungalows on Marcy Street, demolished in 1979. (Photo: Conron & Lent, Architects.)

and another member in favor of preserving the homes noted: "Those houses are part of a streetscape in Santa Fe which is vanishing. . . . They are part of the history of Santa Fe, even though they are not 'historic.' " The state historian described the homes as "a little piece of the fabric of Santa Fe at the turn of the century."[9]

Amid criticism that the committee had acted "subjectively" in interpreting the ordinance, the planning commission voted to overturn the committee and to permit the demolition. However, the chairman of the commission called the prospect of a parking lot on the property "pretty darned repulsive."[10]

In retrospect, two issues are illustrated in this case. First, by 1979, buildings from the turn of the century had become "historic" and were valued as such despite not qualifying for protection from demolition under the ordinance. Second, the character of older neighborhoods depends on the preservation of the qualities of the streetscape. Although the committee was unsuccessful in their attempt to bring these concerns under the umbrella of the ordinance, these issues were subsequently addressed by new city legislation.

Pitched Roofs vs. Flat Roofs: An Ambiguity

According to the *Santa Fe Reporter,* the top story of 1980 was the controversy over whether or not a pitched roof would be permitted on a house on

---

by vertical posts. Typically, in the downtown area, *portales* cover sidewalks within the public right-of-way.

8. William Weismantel, "Visual History: Townscapes and Evaluair," in *Design and Preservation in Santa Fe: A Pluralistic Approach* (Santa Fe: Planning Department, January 1977).

9. *New Mexican,* June 3, 1979.
10. *New Mexican,* June 9, 1979.

the corner of Acequia Madre and Garcia Street. The controversy centered on the intent of the Historic Styles Ordinance with respect to flat roofs.

The request to construct a pitched tin roof was submitted to the Historical Styles Committee for a house being remodeled by builder Betty Stewart. After approval by the committee, the decision was appealed to the planning commission by the neighborhood on the basis that the pitched tin roof was "contrary to the intent" of the ordinance. The planning commission upheld the decision of the committee and a permit was issued. The neighborhood then appealed the case to the city council, which, faced with a roomful of angry neighbors who didn't want to see a pitched roof in their historic area, overturned the decisions of the Historical Styles Committee and planning commission.[11]

Although the ordinance, in discussing Old Santa Fe Style, states that "roofs are flat," the ordinances stop short of prohibiting pitched roofs. Philosophically, opponents of pitched roofs argued that although pitched roofs dating from the late nineteenth and early twentieth centuries are found in the neighborhood, these had been "grandfathered" in when the Historical District Ordinance was passed,[12] and that it was "to preserve and extend the pre-Anglo, indigenous character of the city that the ordinance was designed."[13] Placed in context, most of the neighborhood was developed during the early 1900s. Pitched tin roofs are common even on older buildings (Fig. 9-12).

The city attorney interpreted the ordinance as "being vague enough on the subject as to allow the Historical Styles Committee latitude in judging whether the roof is in harmony with the surrounding neighborhood's architecture."[14] The case was subsequently appealed to district court where the judge found the appeal to the city council to be defective and ordered that Stewart be permitted to complete the remodeling. However, the judge did not rule on the question of whether

Figure 9-12. House with pitched roof on E. DeVargas Street. (Photo: Conron & Lent, Architects.)

pitched roofs may be permitted within the Historical District.[15]

Saving a Wrought-Iron Fence

In another instance where the committee invoked the concept of streetscape, the committee denied the owner of the inn at Loretto permission to demolish the crumbling sandstone wall and wrought-iron fencing in front of the Loretto Chapel (Fig. 9-13). Committee member and historian Tom Chavez commented that "Part of Santa Fe is that wall, to me," and that he "didn't think historical integrity meant returning everything to its original state."[16]

EXPANSION OF DESIGN REVIEW WITHIN AND WITHOUT THE HISTORICAL DISTRICT

As a result of controversial decisions by the Historical Style Committee and especially the growing awareness of the importance of context in maintaining the character of Santa Fe, a resolution and two ordinances were adopted by the City Council during 1982 and 1983.

11. *New Mexican,* December 18, 1980.

12. *New Mexican,* letters to the editor, November 20, 1980. Anita Gonzales Thomas, Executive Board of the Historic Neighborhood Association.

13. Sylvia Loomis, *Santa Fe Reporter,* February 19, 1981.

14. *New Mexican,* December 18, 1980.

15. Dale Zinn, architect and former member of the Historic Design Review Board, has pointed out to me that in the report of the Committee on Preservation of the Santa Fe Character to the Planning Commission (c. 1956), gabled roofs were to be allowed in Territorial period buildings "in which cases the roof is not steep" and "the roof is carried out to form a portal." Writer Oliver LaFarge and architect Irene von Horvath coauthored this report.

16. *Albuquerque Journal,* July 13, 1982.

Figure 9-13. Loretto Chapel with wrought iron fence, 1878. (Photo: Conron & Lent, Architects.)

Figure 9-14. An 1880s house in Santa Fe Vernacular style. (Photo: Courtesy Planning Division, City of Santa Fe.)

Harmony with Adjacent Buildings

In 1982, planning staff drafted guidelines to the Historical District Ordinance to aid the board in interpretation of the phrase, present in the original ordinance, that "The board shall *judge any proposed alteration or new structure for harmony with adjacent buildings*."[17] Specifically, the guidelines, adopted by resolution, provided criteria relating to scale, continuity of streetscape, spatial quality of street sections, and roofs. Under the latter criteria a building may have a pitched roof if evidence is provided showing the existence of pitched roofs within the related streetscape prior to the date of the resolution and that the proposed pitched roof meets the criteria for scale and continuity of streetscape.

Not-So-Historic Districts

In 1983, three new historic districts were created. These districts—Westside-Guadalupe, Historic Transition, and Don Gaspar—included older parts of the city that had developed during the late 1800s and early 1900s. In each of these districts, prevalent styles either did not conform to the definitions of Santa Fe Style in the 1957 ordinance or included many other styles in addition to Santa Fe Style.

17. Resolution No. 1982–88.

Figure 9-15. *Portales* on Palace Avenue. (Photo: Courtesy Planning Division, City of Santa Fe.)

PLAZA/SAN FRANCISCO
SUBDISTRICT

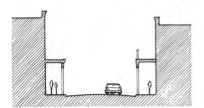

PLAZA/SAN FRANCISCO SUBDISTRICT

CHARACTERISTIC STREETSCAPE

Looking east on San Francisco Street

PHYSICAL DESCRIPTION

BUILDING TYPES
— primarily 2 story on narrow, deep lots with common side walls

ARCHITECTURAL STYLES
— Pueblo Spanish
— Territorial

BLOCK FORM
— continuous
— 2 story building mass at front property line

STREET SECTION
— narrow streets
— no yards or planting between building and street
— portales over sidewalks

CHARACTERISTIC BUILDINGS
— Sena Plaza
— buildings on the south side of San Francisco Street from the Plaza to Galisteo Street

HISTORY

This portion of town, laid out in 1610 by Spanish Governor Pedro de Peralta, exhibits Spanish colonial planning principles as set forth in "The Laws of the Indies". The original plaza and rectilinear street pattern, both defined by closely spaced buildings, remain substantially intact to this day.

Figure 9-16. Plaza/San Francisco Subdistrict; pp. 5, 6, Business Capitol District Handbook. (Layout and artwork: Wayne Thowless)

For example, the term "Santa Fe Vernacular" was coined to classify buildings that, although sometimes derived from Spanish Pueblo and Territorial styles, are owner-built structures designed to personal taste (Fig. 9-14).

Design Review Outside the Historic Districts

In the interest of promoting the general harmony between buildings in the historical districts and

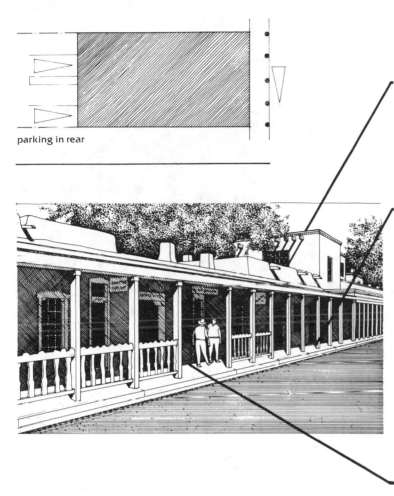

parking in rear

DESIGN STANDARDS

(Ordinance Sections
14-26.107—14-26.115)

MAXIMUM BUILDING HEIGHT
— 36 feet

MAXIMUM LOT COVERAGE
— no requirement
— 100% lot coverage permitted

BUILDING PLACEMENT AND SETBACKS
— buildings fronting San Francisco Street between Sandoval and Cathedral Place <u>shall</u> be built to the front property line.
— elsewhere, buildings <u>should</u> be built to the front property line.
— where buildings are set back from the front property line, a solid wall is required at the front property line <u>or</u> the front yard shall be 80% paved and designated for public use.

MINIMUM OPEN SPACE
— no requirements

LANDSCAPE TREATMENT
— no requirements

HEIGHT OF WALLS AND FENCES
— where walls are required, walls shall be stuccoed masonry between 6 and 8 feet in height.

PLACEMENT OF PARKING
— parking shall be located off-site or in rear yard with access from rear.

PORTALES
— portales are permitted within public right-of-way.
— City review, fee, and Council approval are required.

DESIGN OBJECTIVES

(Ordinance Section 14-26.106)
— maintain narrow streets and continuous street facades
— encourage additional portales for pedestrian use and to provide continuity of building mass
— limit building height to heights characteristic of existing buildings
— encourage high walls to separate open or vacant areas from public right-of-way and to provide continuity of street facade
— except for the Plaza and Cathedral areas, confine landscaping to walled courtyards.
— emphasize the verticality of facades on San Francisco Street

those of recent construction outside the districts, the city has applied architectural design review standards to new construction, except single-family residences, throughout the city. More pointedly, the demand for such standards was prompted by the rapid influx of franchises and franchise architecture during the 1970s. Because of opposition to design control outside of the historical districts, guidelines with voluntary compliance were first adopted in 1982. These were replaced by ordinance in 1988. Drafted with the assistance of the Santa Fe chapter of the American Institute of Architects, the ordinance consists of a point system based on the qualities and characteristics of Santa Fe architecture. Primary among these are massing, roof form, material, texture, and color. This approach has gained acceptance because of its flexibility and because it does not mandate any particular architectural style.

TOWNSCAPE

Also in 1983, within the downtown area of Santa Fe, the city council adopted development standards for fifteen separate townscape subdistricts. Each subdistrict is described by a set of physical characteristics that distinguish it from all other subdistricts. Typically these include block form; street section; architectural style; maximum building height; building placement and setbacks; minimum open space; landscape treatment; walls and fences; and placement of parking and *portales*—in short, the usual categories of zoning but related to the design objectives of each subdistrict. For example, along sections of San Francisco Street, buildings are required to be built to the front property line and *portales* are encouraged within the public right-of-way for pedestrian use and to provide continuity of building mass (Fig. 9-15).

Maximum building heights were lowered from 65 feet to 36 feet around the plaza and on the streets leading to the plaza. This limitation addressed an area of ambiguity in the Historical District Ordinance that would have allowed buildings taller than three stories provided that certain criteria of style and scale were met.[18] Design objectives and standards for the Plaza/San Francisco Subdistrict are illustrated in Fig. 9-16.

Portales and Parkways

Two buildings on Lincoln Avenue, one new and one a renovation, illustrate the concern for townscape. Lincoln Avenue is the prototypical "American" avenue from the second half of the nineteenth century (Fig. 9-17)—wide and lined with street trees and a curbside parkway strip. It is also strategic with respect to city structure running between the northwest corner of the plaza and the

18. The 1957 ordinance said that "with rare exceptions [Old Santa Fe Style] buildings are of one story, few have three stories, and the characteristic effect is that the buildings are long and low." However, the ordinance did not prohibit outright the construction of taller buildings in recent Santa Fe Style, "provided that the facade shall include projecting or recessed portales, setbacks or other design elements."

Figure 9-17. Looking at Lincoln Avenue from Santa Fe Plaza. (Photo: Courtesy Museum of New Mexico, Neg. no. 14120, c. 1917.)

U.S. Federal Courthouse two blocks north of the plaza (Fig. 9-18).

In both cases, architects initially proposed *portales* within the public right-of-way and in both cases were denied. Subsequent designs included an arcade outside of the public right-of-way on the First Interstate Building and awnings on the Lincoln Place Building (Figs. 9-19, 9-20). In both examples street trees were either kept, or replaced, or newly planted (Figs. 9-21, 9-22). Although neither building provides a front yard, the "American" streetscape is maintained and encroachment of *portales* prevented.

Washington Avenue: A Clash of Revival Styles

The Santa Fe Public Library, designed by John Gaw Meem as the Santa Fe Municipal Building in 1936 (Fig. 9-23), is characteristic of many buildings within the subdistrict. It underwent a sensitive partial reconstruction in 1986 that preserved its original two-story Territorial Revival *portal*, brick coping, and front yard.

On a former parking lot next to the library, the architects who were responsible for the remodeling of the library designed the Hotel Plaza Real in Territorial Revival Style in harmony with the library and other buildings on the block. At the same time, architects from Aspen remodeled the

Figure 9-18. U.S. Courthouse at terminus of Lincoln Avenue, 1850–89. (Photo: Courtesy Planning Division, City of Santa Fe.)

Figure 9-19. Sears Building, John Gaw Meem, Architect, 1948. (Photo: Courtesy Planning Division, City of Santa Fe, c. 1975.)

Figure 9-20. Remodeled Sears Building, now Lincoln Place, Dorman & Breen, Architects, 1991. (Photo: Carol Schneider.)

former State Securities Building next door in a Pueblo Spanish Revival Style (Fig. 9-24). City staff unsuccessfully urged the two architectural teams to coordinate their designs in the interest of creating a "harmonious" streetscape. Even allowing for the eclectic architecture of the Marcy subdistrict, this is an instance where the section of the ordinance directing the board to "judge any proposed alteration or new structure for harmony with

Figure 9-21. East side of Lincoln Avenue. (Photo: Courtesy Planning Division, City of Santa Fe, c. 1975.)

Figure 9-23. Santa Fe Public Library, John Gaw Meem, Architect, 1936. (Photo: Carol Schneider.)

Figure 9-24. Hotel Plaza Real, Duty and Germanas, Architects, 1991; and Inn of the Anasazi, Aspen Design Group, architects, 1991. (Photo: Carol Schneider.)

Figure 9-22. First Interstate Building, Phase 2, Lincoln Avenue, McHugh, Lloyd, Architects, 1984. (Photo: Carol Schneider.)

adjacent buildings" might have been invoked in the interest of achieving a more uniform streetscape. Stylistic harmony within the block would have been achieved through adherence to the Territorial Revival Style. However, greater streetscape consistency might have been realized through a less literal application of either revival style.

Redevelopment of the Railway Yards

Design objectives and standards were not adopted for the railway yards because the area was judged to not be sufficiently developed to qualify as an established townscape. Instead, the area was designated as a redevelopment subdistrict with the stipulation that design standards would be established as part of any plan for redevelopment.

Although the site does not lie within a historic

Figure 9-25. Santa Fe Railway Depot, c. 1909. (Photo: Jesse L. Nusbaum; Courtesy Museum of New Mexico, Neg. no. 66658.)

Figure 9-26. Gross, Kelly Warehouse, Rapp & Rapp, Architects, 1914. (Photo: Conron & Lent, Architects.)

Figure 9-27. Stone warehouse, c. 1885. (Photo: Courtesy Planning Division, City of Santa Fe.)

district, the northern part of the site lies between the Westside-Guadalupe and Historic Transition districts. Within the northern site there are four or five important historic buildings, including the Denver and Rio Grande Depot (c. 1906), the Santa Fe Railway Depot (c. 1909), and the Gross, Kelly Warehouse (c. 1914) (Figs. 9-25, 9-26). The latter structure, modeled after a Pueblo Spanish mission church, was designed by the same architects who designed the Fine Arts Museum in 1917. Although these structures are small in scale to be considered as centerpiece buildings, they are important in establishing the design theme of the area. Also important are several warehouses within and adjacent to the northern end of the site that have been converted to shops and restaurants (Fig. 9-27). By referencing the railroad and mercantile themes from the turn of the century, there exists the possibility of broadening the definition of Santa Fe Style within a regional and historic context.

CONCLUSION

The promotion of Santa Fe Style as a regional architecture has existed as a movement since 1912 and as official policy since the adoption of the Historical Styles Ordinance in 1957. However, in the enthusiasm for Santa Fe Style, objectives of historic preservation have frequently been secondary. In the thirty-five years since the adoption of the ordinance, and the eighty or so years since the beginnings of the Santa Fe Style, many other buildings of a variety of styles have come to be considered historic. Indeed, recent legislation adopted by the city would protect any structure approximately fifty years old or older that helps to establish and maintain the character of a historic district against demolition, excessive remodeling, or additions out of character or scale.

The proliferation of Pueblo Spanish Revival architecture has resulted in an overall sense of harmony; however, particular characteristics important to the sense of the historic development of subdistricts in Santa Fe have been weakened. Based on the experience in Santa Fe, design review within a historical context can be most effective if regulation of architectural style is combined with zoning and landscape design standards that have also been crafted to reflect the characteristic qualities of the district. Townscape standards reinforce the characteristics of subdistricts while maintaining distinctions among the different historic townscapes.

The continued appropriateness of revival architectural styles needs to be questioned. The revival styles are now "dated" between 1912 and the present. There is a need for a "postrevival" architecture that is contemporary while remaining in harmony with buildings of historic design.

10
Transforming Suburbia: The Case Study of Bellevue, Washington

Mark L. Hinshaw

Urban Design Consultant, Bellevue, Washington

Design review has not commonly been used in suburban communities. However, the city of Bellevue, Washington, instituted a complex approach to design review in the early 1980s that has, in the subsequent years, fundamentally altered the form and organization of its downtown. Previously a collection of one-story strip retail malls, Bellevue's downtown is now not only a major center in its region for shopping and employment, but for dense residential as well. Furthermore, it is acquiring a setting that is conducive to transit and pedestrian movement.

BACKGROUND

Fifteen years ago, Bellevue was a nondescript bedroom suburb of Seattle. Located about ten miles east of downtown Seattle, on the east side of Lake Washington, Bellevue was not unlike hundreds of other largely single-family communities scattered around North American metropolitan centers. A small agricultural village during the first half of the century, with a four-block-long main street and dirt roads, Bellevue exploded in the decades following World War II. With a current population of over 90,000, it is now the center of a subregion of 350,000. Within the state, Bellevue is second only to Seattle in quantity and concentration of commercial activity.

For more than thirty years, Bellevue had a typical suburban development pattern: one-story retail strips, vast subdivisions, and arterial streets lined with signs, gas stations, and fast food places. By the late 1970s, office parks and shopping centers were beginning to crop up along freeway corridors, invading nearby neighborhoods. The city had no real center, just a confluence of wider streets with variously sized shopping malls and a handful of anonymous office buildings surrounded by huge parking lots. Walking was virtually unheard of; the police would stop pedestrians to see if they might be indigent.

FORCES OF CHANGE

By the end of the 1970s, three forces converged to produce a radically new direction for Bellevue. First, the location and intensity of commercial development was seen, both by citizens and elected representatives, as being out of control. The principal symbol of this absence of direction was a proposal for a huge, superregional shopping center on a wooded site just outside the city limits. The city decided to oppose the center and eventually persuaded the county not to issue permits for it.[1] In taking this action, the city declared that regionally oriented retail was not appropriate in

---

1. The site of the rejected shopping center was later developed into the world headquarters of the Microsoft Corporation.

the hinterlands of the community, but should be part of a more central location.

Second, neighborhood groups had formed and were starting to clamor for protection from invasive commercial zoning and the subsequent development of office complexes. In response, the city adopted neighborhood plans that called for no further commercial rezones and established a floor-area ratio ceiling of .5 for existing commercial zoning districts. The sole exception to this was the "downtown" district, for which neither a plan nor any special zoning had yet been devised. In addition, while single-family development still dominated the city, multiple-family zones were established, often in areas that might have otherwise been viewed as prime for commercial use.[2]

Third, around 1980, land-use studies had identified a twelve-block square area, adjacent to the original townsite, that could be transformed into a true downtown. Economic analyses projected that this area would likely support several million square feet of commercial development.[3] A policy plan for downtown Bellevue was adopted that called for a whole host of public and private investments, transit service, additional freeway access, and tailor-made regulatory techniques.

THE DOWNTOWN CONTEXT

Declaring an area to be a downtown by drawing lines on a map is one thing, what was actually there was quite another. Cheaply built wood-frame buildings of no particular character lined almost every street. The zoning code required huge setbacks and high parking ratios. Providing for the movement and storage of the automobile was paramount. Some streets did not even have sidewalks; what sidewalks did exist were only meager, six-foot-wide strips of concrete, next to multiple lanes of fast-moving traffic. Within downtown, there were no public spaces, no parks, and no civic buildings. There was no sense at all

of any "public realm." A common joke during Seattle cocktail parties involved the mention of Bellevue's "downtown."

In fact, despite good intentions, the city did not have the tools to bring about its vision. It had a weak, general-purpose zoning ordinance. Design review had only been experimented with in a few outlying locations, as a condition of rezoning. And the staff had virtually no experience with "cutting-edge" forms of development regulations.

NEW TOOLS

In 1982, the city threw out the old zoning ordinance that governed property within the area designated as downtown and replaced it with a entirely new set of regulations. Three key sets of strategies were employed.

Land-use strategies stressed the role of retail in serving both the region and the surrounding neighborhoods, compressed new office development into a tight "core," and provided zoning incentives for housing. Ground-floor retail uses were required in certain locations and were exempt from FAR limits. The core, an area six blocks by eight blocks, was established as the only location where true high-rise commercial buildings would be allowed,[4] in order to create a "critical mass" of intensity that would support transit and encourage pedestrian activity. Surrounding the core, several urban residential districts were established that would, over time, fill in with buildings ranging from five stories around the perimeter to twenty stories toward the core[5] (Fig. 10-1).

Transportation strategies centered around emphasizing public transportation and limiting the use of single-occupant automobiles. The new parking regulations set *maximum* ratios, as well as

2. In the thirteen years following the establishment of multiple-family districts, the majority of residential development has been in that category, to the extent that now almost half of the city's housing stock is multiple-family.

3. During the 1980s, commercial development proceeded much more vigorously than predicted, such that the downtown area now has over 5 million square feet of office space and over 3 million square feet of retail space.

4. Commercial buildings within the core can be in the range of twenty to thirty-five stories, while outside the core, heights step down from nine stories near the core to three stories around the perimeter of downtown. Of the sixteen new commercial buildings built since the code was adopted, all but five are in the core.

5. In all downtown zoning districts, residential buildings have an "as of right" greater height and larger floor-area ratio, to encourage residential use. Some districts allow only residential (above ground-floor retail).

Figure 10-1. The "stair-stepped" zoning envelope has begun to fill in, with the core highly visible in the skyline.

Figure 10-2. Recent buildings, set to the sidewalk, have begun to frame certain street corridors.

minimums. The maximums were set substantially below what the market seemed to want. And new, free-standing commercial parking lots were prohibited. By constricting the supply of parking as additional office space was occupied, prices would rise to the point that public transportation and ride-sharing would be seen as economically attractive alternatives. To further enhance the appeal of transit, the regional bus authority built a new transit center precisely in the center of the core, in accordance with city design criteria that make it seem like a natural part of the streetscape. New standards for sidewalks called for widths of twelve to sixteen feet, with large-caliper street trees. These new "urban" sidewalks would be built both as part of new development as well as along with the numerous street improvement projects by the city's Public Works Department.

The land-use strategies created a destination, while the transportation strategies created multiple ways to get into and around the downtown. But urban design strategies intended to produce a diverse, comfortable and lively environment were critically important. Urban design strategies emphasized pedestrian movement, public spaces, and design quality. While many of the design strategies were to be accomplished through public works (streets, public buildings, and parks), design review criteria and processes were established to ensure a dramatic redirection in the form and appearance of all new development, public and private.

MULTIPLE TECHNIQUES

Various aspects of Bellevue's multifaceted approach to design review have been cited in articles and books.[6] Bellevue's use of design review has been marked by the employment of many approaches in combination.

First, conventional zoning standards play a major role in setting "baseline" conditions at a higher level than that typically found, especially in communities that have evolved in postwar decades. One of the simplest devices, but one with the most dramatic effect, has been the use of "set-to" lines. In sharp contrast to the form of development produced by setbacks in which buildings are detached from the street envelope, the set-to lines in downtown Bellevue have reintroduced the notion of the street wall, framing and engaging the sidewalks. Figure 10-2 is an example of one of the new buildings that are set to the sidewalk. Buildings can incorporate setback areas, but only to provide for public spaces in specific locations established by the new code. As a corollary to the set-to lines, parking and access drives cannot be placed between a building and the sidewalk.[7] And, furthermore, on most of the streets within the core, retail uses must be included along the ground level of any new building.

Second, a complex set of incentives encourage a mixture of uses, public amenities, and cultural features. A menu of bonusable items is set forth for each of the six downtown districts. While many of these are commonly encouraged in other

6. Allen; Kay; Hartshorn; Lassar; Miles and Hinshaw; Peirce; Shirvani; and Whyte.

7. If a project has multiple phases, temporary surface parking is allowed on the site of a future building, but the lot has to meet extensive landscaping standards.

Figure 10-3. A number of public places, with water features and ample seating, are now found throughout the downtown.

Figure 10-4. The downtown transit center contains a unisex public restroom that is monitored, with the result that it is clean and safe.

cities that make use of incentive zoning, Bellevue's code offers floor-area ratio bonuses for unusual features like public restrooms, art, theaters, and underground parking. Each proposed feature is evaluated during the design process to determine if it meets specific design criteria and if it provides a real public benefit. It is not uncommon for proposed features to be rejected or redesigned. Figure 10-3 is an example of one of the many public spaces throughout downtown that have been created as a result of the incentive system.

Third, design overlay districts have been used to address particular issues in three parts of the downtown. Each has its own set of design guidelines. The Core Design District emphasizes the provision of pedestrian spaces and the connections between them. The location, configuration, and detailing of public places and corridors are thoroughly scrutinized to ensure that they encourage opportunities for walking, sitting, outdoor dining, and summertime musical performances. Midblock pedestrian connections to the transit center (Fig. 10-4) must be especially safe, convenient, and attractive.

The Perimeter Design District ensures that newer, more intensive development is accomplished in a manner that fits with the existing low-rise residential areas surrounding downtown. Design guidelines for this district call for physical elements such as sloped roofs, terraced building forms, bay windows, more subtle signage, and certain uses such as neighborhood services and child care. In addition, specific uses that could benefit both downtown residents and those in

Figure 10-5. Bellevue's code offers incentives for museums, among other uses; a new, privately funded museum is being completed.

areas surrounding downtown are exempt from floor-area ratio limits. These uses include schools, churches, libraries, museums, drugstores, and supermarkets.[8] In the past few years, a library, a museum (Fig. 10-5), and a large supermarket complex have been built within the perimeter district.

The Civic Center Design District applies to a sector of the downtown within which a series of public assembly buildings will be developed. The first phase, recently completed, includes a small convention center and performing arts theatre (Fig. 10-6). The guidelines for this district seek to mitigate the usual massive, deadening

8. Several projects have taken advantage of this provision, including an expanded supermarket, a new county library, and a museum of doll art.

Figure 10-6. Currently under construction, the convention center and performing arts theatre are the first phase of a civic center.

character of this type of building by calling for offsets, recesses, terraced massing, and decorative roof forms, as well as retail shops and services, water features, and awnings along the sidewalk. The intent of these provisions, though to be applied for the most part to public buildings, is to suggest that such large, otherwise windowless structures also have an obligation to contribute to street life.

Fourth, Bellevue's design review process is administrative, in contrast to many that make use of appointed boards or commissions. Projects are reviewed by staff trained and experienced in architecture and landscape architecture. The process does not require public hearings or meetings, but extensive notification is mailed to surrounding property owners and tenants. In addition, a 4' × 8' sign (Fig. 10-7) is erected at the site. Information on the board describes the proposal and whom to contact in the city. Citizens can review plans and write letters of comment that are addressed in the staff report.

The design review decision is issued by the director of the Design and Development Department, with a written analysis of the project that includes conditions of approval and requirements to mitigate any identified adverse impacts. This

Figure 10-7. The public notice sign for an impending design review decision is placed in a prominent location on each site.

decision can be appealed to the city council and, ultimately, to the courts, though few projects have been appealed. Only one downtown project has ever been denied as the result of an appeal, suggesting that the design review process is well supported and viewed as producing positive results by the city council.[9]

SPECIAL TOOLS

When Bellevue first initiated its Administrative Design Review process in the early 1980s, project proponents would frequently show up in city hall with finished drawings and models. The staff would then only be able to react to a design. Clearly, the proponent and the design professionals involved would already have an investment in the project and would be loath to consider any changes.

This was a painful and frustrating learning experience. For the city to have any meaningful influence on the evolution of a project, it would have to become a participant earlier. In the mid-1980s, a technique was added: the preapplication conference. Proponents of projects are now encouraged to sit down with city staff when they first begin putting the project together. No drawings, except very conceptual ones, are required. And the preapplication meeting includes representatives from every city department, so that there can be an interchange. Preapplication meetings can help identify any issues so that they can be resolved before becoming conflicts. And all participants feel that they are collaborating on a project rather than being adversaries.

Bellevue's approach to design review relies heavily on the use of design guidelines. In addition to the guidelines associated with the overlay districts described above, there are two documents that govern very specific conditions in the downtown.

One document addresses the design and management of a pedestrian corridor and associated public open spaces along the central "spine" of the downtown core. The Major Pedestrian Corridor links the downtown shopping center on the west

Figure 10-8. Initial segments of the Pedestrian Corridor have been completed.

end of the core with the emerging civic center on the east end. The corridor is being built in segments, each part of individual development projects but complying with city-enforced design guidelines. One of the initial segments is shown in Figure 10-8. The guidelines address such subjects as alignment, width, adjacent uses, connections, edge treatment, paving, planting, lighting, and furniture. The guidelines are meant to encourage a variety of design responses within an overall framework of desirable characteristics.

A second set of guidelines applies to the entire downtown and addresses the relationship between buildings and sidewalks. This document has most directly shaped the form of downtown development in a manner strikingly different than most other suburban centers. Ironically, the guidelines merely recall the classic, time-tested rules of thumb that have been used in building cities for hundreds of years.

First, the sidewalk level of a building should contain shops and services. Second, there should be a relatively continuous street wall abutting the sidewalk. Third, the street-level facade must not be blank; it must have glass that people can see through. Fourth, there must be multiple entrance points, not just a single doorway into a lobby. Fifth, the ground level must contain interesting materials and details that can be appreciated by people on foot. Because of the rainy but mild climate of the region, a sixth guideline was added calling for awnings, canopies, or arcades over the sidewalk. A complex of buildings completed three years ago illustrates these basic principles (Fig.

---

9. The denied project, a twenty-story residential tower on the edge of downtown, was eventually appealed to the State Supreme Court by the developer. The court affirmed the city council's decision, agreeing that the building, despite having a commendable design, was out of scale with nearby buildings. The case is considered to be a landmark decision in Washington State.

Figure 10-9. New buildings must help create a street wall and incorporate shops and services.

Figure 10-10. The 35-story tower designed by Kohn Person Fox exhibits the ground-level detailing called for by the code.

10-9), and a proposed tower is to be built in the next few years (Fig. 10-10).

While these are seemingly simple, almost commonsense in nature, they have had a profound impact on the form of development in downtown Bellevue, as developers and their design teams have had to rethink their typical buildings. The guidelines shift the emphasis away from freestanding "products" toward building designs that contribute to the public realm.

Finally, another special technique, also seemingly basic, is used in the review of proposed buildings. Bellevue's submittal requirements include elevation drawings of the ground level of a building at $\frac{1}{4}'' = 1'$. By depicting this level at a larger scale than is usually done, architects automatically detect a need to embellish surfaces and detail corners and joints more elegantly. The buildings that have resulted present a wide variety of materials, finishes, and details where they can be most appreciated by the public.

IMPACT OF BELLEVUE'S PROCESS

In the decade since Bellevue first instituted an aggressive design review process, at least five effects have become apparent.

First, new buildings are externally oriented, in sharp contrast to pre–design review buildings that were often inwardly focused. Because of this there is a public realm that is beginning to be shaped that did not previously exist. Buildings incorporate features that reflect the fact that they are part of a larger whole and they connect to other buildings and public places.

Second, the presence of retail shops, services, and restaurants along the street has made a difference in the development of a sense of street life. And very little retail was needed to do this. In contrast to the deadening effect produced by banks and offices, not to mention blank walls, these uses send out a powerful message. People see that they can walk down the street to buy a book, grab a cup of coffee, or join up with a friend for lunch. The effect is that distances between destinations are perceived to be less when there are other things to do, to look at, or enjoy, like trees or a fountain. With the availability of transit, perceived walking distances are extended even further.

Third, Bellevue has established that the ground level—the street level—is to be the critical connection between buildings. Skybridges and tunnels are not allowed to usurp the activity on the street. Virtually no city, even much larger ones, has enough pedestrian activity to support two levels of movement. The street level is also the easiest, most cost-effective method of circulation; no elevators or escalators are necessary. Few signs or maps are even needed, as most people simply understand how to use ordinary streets.

Fourth, design review has had a practical effect on strengthening the downtown economy. It is, in one sense, a form of insurance for good developers, who are thus assured that their competition cannot throw up a cheap building. This encourages better and better projects over time, as investors seek a development setting that reinforces their own efforts. Developers of property, both private companies and development agencies, have tended to use the best of design talent in the Pacific Northwest. In recent years, downtown Bellevue has also benefited from the talent of architects from outside the region.[10]

Finally, an unexpected effect has been the increased public consciousness about design. It is the subject of newspaper articles, meetings of civic associations, and public hearings. The city has sponsored two design competitions, the first of which lead to the development of a seventeen-acre downtown park that was opened two years ago. And several recent buildings have been featured in the architectural press.

10. Kohn Pederson Fox of New York City has two projects in downtown Bellevue: the convention center/performing arts theater and a thirty-five story office tower. Both will be landmark structures.

REFERENCES

Allen, J. Linn. 1991. "It's a Big Step: Seattle Suburb Driven to Change to a More Walking-Oriented City." *Chicago Tribune,* May 28.

City of Bellevue. *Land-Use Code,* 1981, Amended 1983, 1985, 1986.

———. *Design Guidelines for Building/Sidewalk Relationships,* 1983.

———. *Pedestrian Corridor and Major Public Open Space Design Guidelines,* 1981, Amended 1983, 1985.

Egan, Timothy. 1986. "Bellevue, Washington: Bringing Back the Pedestrian." *New York Times,* September 7, section 8, p. 1.

Kay, Jane Holtz. 1991. "Building a There There." *Planning Magazine* 57 (1) :4–8.

Hartshorn, Truman Asa. 1992. *Interpreting the City: An Urban Geography,* pp. 468–469. New York: John Wiley and Sons, Inc.

Hinshaw, Mark L. 1989. "Transforming a Suburb." In *Proceedings of the Tenth Annual International Pedestrian Conference* (Boulder, Colorado), pp. 81–91.

Lassar, Terry Jill. 1989. *Carrots and Sticks: New Zoning Downtown.* Washington D.C.: Urban Land Institute.

Lorenzen, Leo. 1986. "New Land-Use Policies Transform Bellevue." *Zoning News* (American Planning Association), August.

Miles, Don C., and Mark L. Hinshaw. 1987. "Bellevue's New Approach to Pedestrian Planning and Design." In *Public Streets for Public Use,* ed. Anne Vernez Moudon, pp. 221–31. New York: Van Nostrand Reinhold.

Peirce, Neal. 1985–86. Washington Post Writers Group, nationally syndicated column, variously titled.

Shirvani, Hamid. 1985. *The Urban Design Process,* pp. 169–170. New York: Van Nostrand Reinhold.

Whyte, William H. 1988. *City: Rediscovering the Center,* pp. 307–9. New York: Doubleday.

11
Discretionary Design Review: Shaping Downtown Cincinnati

Hayden May

Miami University of Ohio

The city of Cincinnati has a long history of urban design review. The city began review of important projects in the mid-1960s, when Fountain Square was developed in the heart of the city. The Urban Design Review Board is composed of three design professionals and one community business leader appointed by the city manager on the recommendation of the director of the Department of Economic Development. The board has enjoyed a relatively stable membership since its initiation. David Niland, Professor of Architecture at the University of Cincinnati, has been one of the design professionals on the board since its inception. Fred Lazarus, respected community business leader, has served as chair of the board for twenty-two years. The other current design professionals are Jayanta Chatterjee, Dean of the College of Design, Art, Architecture and Planning, University of Cincinnati, and Hayden May, Dean of the School of Fine Arts, Miami University.

The board considers the merits of various building proposals in Cincinnati, specifically those in the Central Business and Central Riverfront Districts, and determines whether these proposals conform to the city's Urban Design Plan. More specifically, in the contract for services, the city of Cincinnati charges board members with determining whether development proposals "relate properly to their immediate surroundings in terms of the best available urban design criteria," and whether the "architecture is

of a quality commensurate with the City's aspirations in the CBD." In actual practice, the Urban Design Plan offers little guidance. It consists of a few general guidelines, part of the *Cincinnati 2000 Plan,* and more fully developed studies for several isolated sections of the city. When necessary, the board has reviewed projects against abstract principles rather than thoughtful guidelines or plans.

Typically, the board reviews and approves projects during the schematic design and design development stages. Projects before the board include public ones initiated by the city and built on public land. Others are reviewed because they require assistance from the city in assembling property, or in negotiating variances from applicable codes and regulations, whether or not the issue is one of design.

There is a third category. The new zoning code for downtown development includes incentive zoning. Building owners are encouraged to provide certain amenities—such as space for public gathering, gardens, or recognized art work—or public services—such as day-care centers or sheltered bus stops. In return, they are permitted to increase the density of development on that site. One way for owners to achieve this bonus is to have their building design approved by the Urban Design Review Board (City of Cincinnati, 1987).

There are many downtown buildings that do not fall under the board's jurisdiction, but for those that do, the board assumes the role of design critic. Practitioners and educators are well aware that the act of presenting one's work and receiving criticism is fundamental in the education of designers. Obviously, this learning doesn't stop with a college degree or license. Critical thinking continues in professional practice. In every office there is some mechanism for internal criticism. Cincinnati's urban design review is best understood as a similar process with equal opportunity and benefit.

The board adopts a pluralistic attitude regarding basic parti and visual character. The criticism of the various board members does not stem from a singular, unified attitude about what constitutes good architecture and urban design. It is not based on the grounds that the board knows what is right and others don't. Rather, as it strives to insure a physical environment of the highest quality, the board endorses the concept that different solutions from different architects may be equally good. By the time the board is consulted, a significant amount of work on schematic design has already occurred. The board begins by accepting that direction, and proceeds through criticism to sharpen and elevate its actualization. The process of review is flexible enough that there are working sessions where board members offer direct assistance by demonstrating alternatives, very similar to teaching design in an academic setting. However, the more normal procedure is to respond to alternative studies presented by the architect, and to assist in identifying strengths and weaknesses, leading to a mutual agreement about the preferred solution. At its best, it is a critique of work in process at a point where critical dialogue is timely and useful.

Again, a reference to teaching design is pertinent. In most design programs today, the faculty is quite diverse. The prevailing attitude is that students should explore various design ideologies, and that it is the responsibility of the program to help them do that. In some cases this occurs through exposure to faculty with an appreciation for the pluralistic attitudes observed in architecture the last twenty years. In other cases, it occurs through opportunities for students to select studios directed by faculty who are much more prescriptive. In either case, educators and critics maintain it is possible to evaluate the quality of the work generated. What has the student set out to do?

Figure 11-1. Chemed Center: view from northeast. (Photo: H. May.)

How well was it accomplished? The work of the board transfers this same attitude to working with professionals in its belief that the potential for work of the highest quality exists independently of the design ideology.

This pluralism that serves so well in teaching is equally important for the design critic in the professional world. It is the essential characteristic that enables dialogue to be constructive rather than restrictive or arbitrary. The board supports and advocates good design regardless of the style or idiom. Recent projects approved by the Urban Design Review Board verify the diverse visual vocabulary that results.

CHEMED CENTER

The second phase of a Central Trust office complex, now named the Chemed Center, is located on the west side of Sycamore, between Fourth and Fifth Streets (Fig. 11-1). Diagonally northeast of the site is the large and important urban plaza providing the frontal viewing area for Procter & Gamble's corporate headquarters. Across the street to the north is the Chiquita building, and across Sycamore to the east are Taft Auditorium and Christ Church. On the south side of Fourth Street one finds both new and older office buildings.

Prior to this second-phase development, the approved master plan for this city block located small office towers at three corners. The first phase of the project was built several years ago. A revised master plan, prepared by David Childs of the New York office of SOM Architects, is a radical departure. It combines the remaining floor area in one building along Sycamore. The building has a five-floor base to the sidewalk line, generally corresponding in height to the Taft, and a twenty-five-story office tower above. This type of slab building, with primary facades facing east and west, is quite unusual in Cincinnati. Cincinnati's downtown buildings tend to be corner buildings, occupying quarter blocks, as intended in the initial master plan for this development. Nevertheless, this change was accepted because the board was confident of the architect's abilities and persuaded by his thorough study of the varied implications of this revision.

As the project developed, several troublesome issues developed, two of which dominated discussion. First is the location of the tower. David Childs proposed centering the tower along Sycamore Street. The board questioned whether this location responded appropriately to the varied conditions of the surrounding environment, in particular the significant open plaza of Procter & Gamble, the different direction of vehicular traffic on Fourth Street and Fifth Street, and the lower historic buildings to the East (Urban Design Review Board, June 13, 1988, and June 27, 1988a).

Childs argued strongly for the central location of the tower. Existing conditions provided some justification, but there were two more demanding reasons. The owners wanted a Fifth Street address, but locating the tower toward Fourth Street, as the board suggested, made a Fifth Street entrance more complicated and unnatural. In addition, Childs believed there was a quality of goodness, a correctness inherent in symmetry. He believed that only under extraordinary situations should one depart from the principle of a facade balanced through symmetry. The designers on the board were opposed.

The board also questioned the visual appearance of Childs's proposal. Childs intends it to be

Figure 11-2. Chemed Center: corner of Fourth and Sycamore looking north along Sycamore. (Photo: H. May.)

seen in reference to the Carew Tower, the city's tallest building, built in 1929–31 and designed by architect Walter Ahlschlager of Chicago with Delano and Aldrich, Associate Architects. In doing so, Childs minimizes Chemed Center's reference to the more mechanical, cellular appearance of the first phase of this project occupying the same block. This was also a concern. The board started with the knowledge this was the second phase of a master planned project, and expected more visual continuity (Urban Design Review Board, October 28, 1987).

David Childs prevailed in each of these issues. In retrospect, with regard to visual character, Childs demonstrates the value of departing from the vocabulary of the earlier tower. It is a welcome relief to the overwhelming cellular nature of the first-phase project and other adjacent buildings. But the board was correct on the other two issues. The lack of presence of the tower on Fourth Street (Fig. 11-2) detracts from the sense of entering the city, an event that could have been pronounced because the preceding experience of entering town from the east sets the stage—the smaller scale of the historic Lytle Park further preceded by the

Figure 11-3. 312 Walnut Street: Third Street facade. (Photo: H. May.)

open views of the river along Columbia Parkway. Nothing appears to be gained by the symmetrical Sycamore facade. Because of the proximity of adjacent structures, it is almost impossible to perceive the symmetry.

If there had been an urban design plan for this part of town, it would most certainly have specified the importance of the Fourth Street entrance to the downtown. The architect would have understood this objective at the beginning of the project. The board's position would have been enforceable.

312 WALNUT STREET

The new office building located at Third and Walnut Streets in Cincinnati offers different lessons (Fig. 11-3). The Third Street facade is most important since it is so prominent as one approaches the city from the south. It is also a corner site, adjacent on Walnut Street to a very satisfactory, unpretentious, fourteen-story building, designed by architect Daniel Burnham and built in 1903. The 312 Walnut building is about thirty-eight stories tall on the Third Street facade, a thirty-story

office tower over about an eight-story parking-garage base.

The architect for 312 Walnut is Norm Hoover, 3D International, Houston, Texas, in association with Glaser Associates, Cincinnati. In the early schemes for the proposed building, the board had a number of concerns. The traditional tripartite facade—base, body, and top—was abandoned in favor of a difficult four-part solution. Large arches were proposed for the base and top referring to the popular image of Union Terminal, Cincinnati's Art Deco train station. The design difficulties in accommodating an existing pedestrian bridge from the stadium over Third Street were underestimated. Early schemes for the building treated all four facades differently, which seemed unjustified to the Board (Urban Design Review Board, February 18, 1988).

The primary issue became the Third Street facade. Unfortunately there is no overall urban design plan for Third street. The existing street facade resulted from incremental decisions over a long span of time, with no concern for unity. Third Street didn't exist as an important facade in the city until everything between it and the river was torn down in the 1960s. It is now possible to see this city facade, and for the first time, significant development interest exists. The *Cincinnati 2000 Plan* establishes this area as the location for buildings of twenty-five to thirty stories, the intention to emphasize taller buildings in the center of the city, and to provide views of the Ohio River (Gale, 1986, 47–48). There is no clear direction-setting urban design plan for this important city facade.

A primary feature of Hoover's design is the curved facade of the south wall of the office portion of the building, about thirty stories tall. This facade is composed of several curved sections with different radii. These curves are a response to the river view and the significance of that southern orientation.

The board endorsed this concept in principle, and refinement proceeded well until the design development review, when recommendations for specific materials were presented. At that point, Hoover presented several alternatives for the glass of the curved curtain wall, and recommended that mirror glass be used in combination with granite and precast concrete in the base and walls.

Members of the board objected to the mirror glass (Urban Design Review Board, June 27, 1988b, and November 14, 1988). Hoover suggested that the board members become more familiar with the specific glass he recommended by visiting buildings in Indianapolis and Chicago. He argued that several factors dampened the reflective quality of the mirrored glass. He contended the pewter mirror glass he recommended would reflect a satiny rather than sharp image. Secondly, he suggested the faceted facade, following the curve, distorted the reflection in an interesting way.

The concerned board members continued to object on several grounds. One simply didn't believe that mirror glass was appropriate in Cincinnati. Another objected because the building would look so different during the day and night. Still another board member argued that one should be able to look into the building and see people, a serious contradiction of the architect's desire. A specific provision in the design guidelines of the *Cincinnati 2000 Plan* states that "new buildings as viewed in the skyline should provide a 'solid' surface appearance complementing the city's tradition of masonry buildings" (Gale, 1986, 49).

In the final analysis, compromise on both sides was necessary. The poured-in-place concrete structure was well along the way when several full-sized samples of reflective glass were brought to the site and hoisted to a position along the south facade. Members of the board and representatives of the developer and the city of Cincinnati considered the samples. A slightly less reflective pewter-backed glass was selected for the main facade, and a different glass for the center crease (Urban Design Review Board, March 28, 1989).

There was a time when it appeared the dilemma would be solved in a different way. This project was before the board for one reason. The developer wished to receive a significant floor-area bonus, more than 68,000 square feet, by submitting it for the board's review and approval. There were other things they could do to receive floor-area bonuses that do not require approval of the board (City of Cincinnati, 1987, 7–16). In the last meeting prior to the decision about the glass, a day-care center appeared on the ground-floor plan. The board suspected it was an alternative to neutralize the board's position on the mirror glass.

In fact, it was a serious proposal, and the daycare center is an important part of the existing project.

The board's critical dialogue with Norm Hoover certainly led to identifiable building design improvements. However, one must question whether the more fundamental decisions of building height and mass were subject to the same careful attention. It appears the floor-area bonuses available in the downtown zoning code resulted in a much taller building than envisioned in the *Cincinnati 2000 Plan*. One could argue that extended dialogue about reflective glass or other materials is only useful when the critical urbanistic decisions are equally grounded.

ADAMS LANDING HOUSING

The Adams Landing Housing project, at the base of Mt. Adams along the Ohio River, illustrates different issues. The project is a rather extensive development of housing, mostly luxury units, with convenience retail space to support the residents, some unrelated office structures, parking and open space, and pedestrian links to Mt. Adams and the public park along the river. The project architect was Bill Turnbull, a well-respected architect with experience in housing and a reputation for sensitive design, working in collaboration with KZF Architects in Cincinnati.

Prior to Turnbull's involvement with the Adams Landing Housing Project, proposals for this site provoked considerable concern in the community. There were three dominant issues: protection of the views of the Ohio River valley from Mt. Adams and Columbia Parkway, construction stability at the base of Mount Adams, and varying opinions regarding the desired visual character of the development.

With regard to the views, the city incorporated this statement of Design Covenants and Deed Restrictions. "The design of the project should contain a number of breaks in the massing of the total complex in order to provide significant and appropriate views from the parkway for motorists traveling in both directions and for the residents of Mt. Adams, consistent with the character and concepts of the Master Plan."

The city also agreed to hire an independent

Figure 11-4. Mt. Adams Hillside. (Photo: H. May.)

engineering firm to review all geological studies and their impact on the schematic and preliminary design as well as on construction.

Turnbull responded to the visual appearance issue by developing a design vocabulary that reflects the individual building images one associates with Mt. Adams and the riverfront (Fig. 11-4). In his terms:

> The character of the north-facing (uphill) side will be one of a solid masonry wall with windows treated as punched openings, creating a visual link to the old brick buildings which are found throughout the riverfront districts of the city. The elevation will have extensive planting of vines to add a vertical landscape element to the structure. On the south facing street facade the brick wall will recede in prominence as the glazed openings become larger, often enfronting balconies whose lacy metalwork railings and supports will recall riverboat imagery. The overall effect will be one of layered surfaces of varying degrees of transparency (Turnbull, June 29, 1987).

Turnbull contends that continuity of visual image is a response that is particularly appropriate for this site lying between Mt. Adams and the Ohio River.

This project illustrates the advantages of having more clearly identified the concerns about the relationship of this project to its surroundings. Selecting an architect who has demonstrated sensitivity to those issues allows a stronger collaborative effort between all parties. Representatives of the Mt. Adams Community Association and the more broadly based Hillside Trust closely monitored all Urban Design Review Board reviews of this project. They encouraged special sensitivity to preserving views and to maintaining geological stability.

However, there remains a question of the success of this project. A succession of developers and financiers and the necessity to face economic realities forced numerous delays and considerable modification in the first phase of the project. The initial phase is one of the denser sections of this linear riverside development. In its realized form it presents two almost identical towers separated so slightly that they appear as one massive block building (Fig. 11-5). They are not so tall that they restrict the view from the top of Mt. Adams, but one must concede they block the view from the lower residential section and from Columbia Parkway. It is fortunate to have an approved master plan to modulate the height of subsequent devel-

Figure 11-5. Adams Landing Housing: view from the Ohio River. (Photo: H. May.)

opment and to protect views between this first phase and subsequent building.

There was another important change. The variety of unit plans and the resulting visual richness were diminished considerably. Again, this was probably a matter of economic necessity, but it illustrates the importance of changes in design that occur after the board has given its approval to schematic design and design development. There are numerous instances where the realized building deviates substantially from the design approved by the board. This is a matter of considerable concern.

There was an attempt to follow Turnbull's recommendations regarding materials. The predominant brick is not so much warranted by the context of Mt. Adams as it is appropriate for this location at the base of the hill. The copper roofs add their statement of visual quality from the river as well as the hill. It is unfortunate that the roof-mounted mechanical equipment is so visually prominent.

FOUNTAIN SQUARE WEST

Fountain Square West is a mixed-use development on the west side of Fountain Square, Cincinnati's urban living room. This project is not yet built, but it is critical to the city of Cincinnati and illustrates additional aspects about the Urban Design Review Board's process.

After a previous unsuccessful attempt on this site with JMB/Federated as developer and Bill Pederson of Kohn-Pederson-Fox as architect, the city of Cincinnati engaged John Galbraith as de-

Figure 11-6. Fountain Square West: Rendering of Helmut Jahn design. (Reprinted with permission of Helmut Jahn Associates.)

veloper and Helmut Jahn as architect. A 50–60-story building is envisioned, the tallest in the city, including 600,000 square feet of office space, 175,000 square feet of retail space, a 250-room hotel, and a 750-car garage (Harrington, June 24, 1990).

When Galbraith and Jahn presented their building design, Jahn stressed the site-specific nature of his proposal (Fig. 11-6). He emphasized the multiple roles: fronting on Fountain Square to the east, facing the historically and symbolically

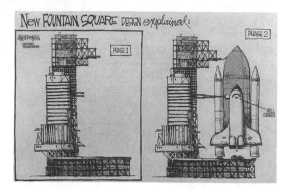

Figure 11-7. "New Fountain Square Design Explained," cartoon by Jim Borgman. (Reprinted with special permission of King Features Syndicate.)

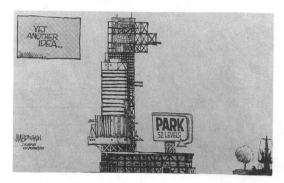

Figure 11-8. "Yet Another Idea," cartoon by Jim Borgman. (Reprinted with special permission of King Features Syndicate.)

important Carew Tower to the south, and extending and anchoring the central city retail functions along Race Street. The difficult integration of multiple functions was accomplished by locating the office tower entrance at the corner of Fifth and Vine, and the hotel entrance midblock along Fifth Street. The thin office tower, Jahn said, creates "breathing room" from the adjacent Ameritrust Center, while the upper terraces make an overture toward Fountain Square at the same time they make reference to the adjacent Carew Tower. Besides these important site-specific considerations, Jahn emphasized the building's visual character: "I hope it will become a symbol for Cincinnati in the 1990s and toward the turn of the century." The building's fragmentation and deliberately differentiated facade was explained as an expression of the various and diverse functions of the building (Harrington, June 30, 1990).

In contrast to the normal experience of the board, the presentation of schematic design took place in a televised public forum before the city council, which assumed a greater degree of oversight because of the project's significance to the economic well-being of the city. Because this more public presentation was anticipated, the board reviewed Jahn's progress in a working session in Chicago previously.

Jahn's design proved controversial and difficult for the layman to understand, and prompted considerable criticism, letters to newspaper editors, and cartoons emphasizing the building's mechanical and industrial character (Fig. 11-7). "It's ugly, it's going to stick out like a sore thumb," was characteristic of reactions. Fifty-six percent

of the respondents disapproved but others rose to defend the design. "We will be entering the 21st century soon, and there will be a whole new way of looking at things then. This building is unique, and we've got to move along with the times" (Thomas, July 1, 1990).

Members of the city council were divided in their opinion, as was the architectural community, in spite of a firm endorsement from the Urban Design Review Board. "If Helmut Jahn had produced a building now that duplicated . . . what went before, he would have missed a glorious opportunity," board member Niland said, adding that "the design was the 'most promising' ever to be presented to the board." The city council had questions about the adequacy of the garage, the smallish size of the lobby atrium, and the pattern of shadows cast on Fountain Square, but approved the preliminary design with one dissenting vote (Harrington, August 1, 1990).

Subsequently, doubt arose regarding the economic feasibility of the project. In February 1991 Galbraith bowed out of the developer's role. Various suggestions of alternatives were forwarded, some reducing the scope and size of the building, some eliminating the hotel function from the desired mixed use, others suggesting that expansion of Fountain Square was a more appropriate and achievable objective for this prime site. City Manager Newfarmer recommended demolition of the existing buildings, long vacant, and development of a temporary parking lot (Fig. 11-8).

The Urban Design Review Board was asked to conduct hearings to review these conflicting proposals, and to make recommendations to City Council. They concluded and recommended the following: 1) Fountain Square should not be enlarged; 2) the retail function should be increased to 240,000 square feet to make it more viable for an anchor store; 3) the broadest possible mix of uses should be pursued but the hotel should be dropped, if necessary, rather than delay the project; 4) the project should be built at one time, because it is more difficult to control the design quality of a phased project; and 5) the city should be more concerned with the quality of the project than its size (Green, May 4, 1991).

More than a year later, economic conditions have not improved. The city has not found developers interested in the full project as recommended by the board. In June 1992 Lazarus department store, the intended retail anchor, announced that it must move into Fountain Square West within three years, or it would close shop in its present location. The immediate response was that Fountain Square West was too valuable to remain parking forever (editorial, June 21, 1992). Public attention to this important project continues. The role of the Urban Design Review Board is more critical in mediating conflicting interests.

OHIO CENTER FOR THE ARTS

The Ohio Center for the Arts includes a 2700-seat theater acoustically suitable for symphonic performances, a 350-seat theater, a rehearsal hall, and exhibition spaces. The center is located one block away from Fountain Square, on the block bounded by Sixth and Seventh Streets between Walnut and Main. Most buildings along Sixth and Main streets will remain. It is an extremely important project financed by the state of Ohio, the city of Cincinnati, and private enterprise.

The architect is Cesar Pelli in association with GBBN Architects in Cincinnati. Pelli and GBBN were selected through a national competition. The committee responsible for Pelli's selection was impressed by his other work, especially the similar arts center in Charlotte, North Carolina. Coming on the heels of continuing controversy about Fountain Square West, the public announcement of Pelli's selection emphasized his international reputation and his sensitivity to local values:

Cincinnatians are proud and protective of their downtown, and proposals for eccentric buildings, such as Helmut Jahn's proposed skyscraper for Fountain Square West, are frequently met with a flood of protest. But Cincinnatians need not fear that Pelli's design for the Ohio Center for the Performing Arts will stun their sensibilities. Pelli is famous for his ability to create exciting buildings that win praise from the design community and satisfy the needs and wants of the populace as well (Findsen, December 1, 1991).

Similar to Fountain Square West, the Ohio Center for the Arts commanded public attention. Pelli presented initial design concepts to the city council and the Urban Design Review Board before television cameras, and fully developed schematic design to the council and the board in council chambers before a large audience.

The basic organizational concept placed both theater entrances along Walnut Street. An internal street parallel to Sixth Street links the entrances and ticket offices to two outside plazas at the corners of Sixth and Seventh streets, plazas that theater audiences could spill onto after performances. The exhibition and rehearsal functions were lined along Seventh Street with offices above, an effort to enliven that street and mask the usual large blank side wall of the main theater. Existing buildings along Sixth Street and Main Street were carefully maintained in the overall scheme.

The visual character of the complex is dominated by massive brick walls on both sides of each theater (Fig. 11-9). These are seen in contrast to transparent glass lobby facades, and curtain wall construction elsewhere. The initial public presentation occurred about halfway through schematic design. The board approved the project with minor recommendations. The center should enliven adjacent sidewalks. The simplicity of the schematic design demanded greater emphasis on detailing and selection of materials during design development. Consistency in detailing the glass lobby facades was important. The board's response was understated but genuine (Urban Design Review Board, April 2, 1992).

Six months later, at the time fully developed schematic designs were presented, the concept remained the same. Most of the design development was internal, insuring the functional adequacy of both theaters and related support functions. The board was disappointed in the development of the exterior and responded with

Figure 11-9. Ohio Center for the Arts: schematic model, Walnut Street facade. (Reprinted with permission of Cesar Pelli Associates.)

more pointed suggestions, approving the schematic design with the provision that Pelli resolve a number of points: enliven the lobbies and facades of the two theaters, expressing the two facades as variations of one concept; demonstrate the solar conditions on the two west facing lobby facades; study and refine the relationship of the extensive pallet of exterior materials; establish continuity of curtain wall design; define the public and private zones of the public plazas; design the portion of the center on Main Street so that it is compatible in mass and vertical orientation with the buildings in that historic district; present graphics and exterior signs for board review (Urban Design Review Board, December 9, 1991).

The board approved the schematic design because it was convinced the functional placement decisions were justified, and it believed that Pelli's strength as a designer was most often realized in careful design development. The board understood it had the opportunity to continue working design meetings with Pelli so it could participate in this process. The board was also very aware of the highly political character of the project and a developing split within the arts community about the center's appropriateness. Some feared the center would diminish current symphony and ballet programs at Music Hall. Others advocated renovation of existing buildings like Emery Hall or Taft Auditorium rather than a new center. Opponent's efforts were successful in placing the center on the ballot for a fall election so that citizens could indicate whether it should proceed (Harrington, July 30, 1992).

At some point in this process, it became clear that review by the Urban Design Review Board was taking on greater importance. It would be much to the advantage of the project if the board could take an unequivocal stand in support of the center's quality of design because this would eliminate one further point of controversy. With this in mind, the board engaged in several working sessions with Pelli and his staff, some in New Haven at Pelli's office, others in Cincinnati. For the most part, there was agreement on design objectives. Specific issues about the way the building met the sky, and the size and configuration of the side entrances through the masonry walls, for example, were quickly and easily engaged.

Figure 11-10. Ohio Center for the Arts: design development model, Walnut and Seventh Street facades. (Photo: Kenneth Champlin and Associates.)

However, two instances arose where significant differences in design objectives became clear. The board desired a sense of coherence in the entire design. Pelli advocated a design solution that emphasized differentiation of the various components of the center. Secondly, the board advocated an approach to the design of the theater lobbies that took advantage of the activity of the various levels and movement between them as a way of enlivening the lobby, utilizing the full depth and the lobby facade transparency. This concept was consistent with Pelli's early schematics, but during design development, he proposed a change that placed an optical barrier separating the interior street from the congregating areas closer to the various levels of seating. The optical barrier contained openings for people to see through, but the overall objective was to mask the visual clutter of the stairs. Through a series of working sessions, both of these issues were resolved to the satisfaction of Pelli and the board. The rendering presented in November 1992 illustrates these refinements, especially the balance between continuity and contrast, the careful articulation of the various curtain walls, the enhanced condition of the brick piers meeting the sky, and the consistency in design of the two theater facades (Fig. 11-10). This is a clear illustration of the value of design criticism and interchange between professionals.

There remained one unresolved issue. From the beginning, the board disagreed with Pelli's proposed third corner plaza at Main and Seventh. They believed it was inconsistent with the conservation guidelines of the Main Street Historic District, which specified a three- to four-story building with zero setback to maintain the continuity of street facade. Chris Cain, the Urban Conservator, represented the Historic Conservation Office of the Department of City Planning at all presentations and agreed with this interpretation. Pelli maintained the building program did not accommodate Ohio Center for the Arts uses at that location. Attempts were made to incorporate the design of a future retail building on that corner, but the board eventually realized it was unrealistic to assume such a private market initiative. In November 1992 that corner of the project was redesigned, with a more prominent Main Street entrance to the rehearsal hall used as a rationale for the setback, the first time this plaza seemed justified.

This is a case where clear guidelines did exist. However, they were based on an assumption that buildings on Main Street would continue the existing pattern of residential or office functions over ground-floor retail. The Ohio Center for the Arts presented a function that had not been anticipated. Even though the board endorsed the Main Street Historic District guidelines, they recommended approval of the setback entrance plaza to the rehearsal hall as the solution best serving the project and the neighborhood.

CONCLUSIONS

What conclusion can be drawn from these experiences of the board? Each of these projects is quite different. The architects had distinct attitudes about design. Does the board have a consistent posture or position about design quality? What is it, if it isn't a preference for a particular visual character?

At a very basic level, the board searches only for a sense of specialness, for the assurance that the design challenge was understood, that it was not treated casually; rather, that demonstrable care was taken, and that a resulting quality can be seen in the results. The board is presented with buildings that attempt distinctive visual character.

Chemed Center turns its back on the tempting pyramidal roofs of Procter & Gamble in favor of the flat viewing platforms of the Carew Tower, and risks this imagery with the belief that no other new building in Cincinnati will attempt the same.

The office at Third and Walnut is exhibitionist in its imagery. Even with careful attempts to relate the base of the building, the primary visual impression of this building will come from the dominating reflectance of the faceted, curved facade.

The Adams Landing housing is intentional in its use of brick masonry and the massing and articulation of the buildings as it seeks an appropriate vocabulary for riverfront development.

Helmut Jahn's Fountain Square West, because of its absolute central position in the city, was conceived as a symbol for Cincinnati at the turn of the century, pointing to the future rather than the past, just as the adjacent Carew Tower had in a previous era.

The Ohio Center for the Arts differentiates its major components as it weaves them carefully into a city block, but the visual character speaks to the technology of our time.

None of these projects is indistinct or anonymous. They make strong design statements, but are they appropriate? In order for visual distinctiveness to be a positive attribute, it must be based on something perceivable and understandable. In the case of these projects reviewed by the Urban Design Review Board, the underlying principle is drawn from the city's charge to the board: do these buildings relate properly to their immediate surroundings and do they convey a quality of design commensurate with the city's aspirations? The board has taken a very strong position advocating site-specific solutions.

The environment surrounding the building site is the most obvious consideration of context. The primary arguments with the board revolve around this issue. Did Chemed respond effectively and sensitively to the differences between Fourth Street and Fifth Street, to the open space of the Procter & Gamble plaza? Was the office building at Third and Walnut leading the city in the proper direction in establishing this front entrance to the city? Does the Adams Landing housing preserve the valued river views? Is its design compatible with the backdrop of housing on Mt. Adams? Does Fountain Square West recognize its important location adjacent to the city's central outdoor space? Does it maintain the continuity of retail activity at ground level that is essential in this location? Is the Ohio Center for the Arts designed for this location in Cincinnati, or is it a variation of the Charlotte center? The board concluded that these are all projects demonstrating site-specific

design. If these projects were located elsewhere, they would respond to a different context, and one should expect a different solution. Realizing the opportunity for rational, understandable, site-specific solutions is one of the most significant responsibilities of contemporary design. It is a primary criterion for establishing specialness, and for determining quality.

A regional definition of context is also evident. There are many qualities of geographic regions that influence building design. The most obvious are variations in local building materials, topography, and climate. Although in our worldwide community, use of local building materials has lessened, as have distinctions in regional populations, a regional environmental character, developed over a long period of time, is still identifiable. Such considerations are seen clearly in design objectives and the board's response in Adams Landing, 312 Walnut, and the Ohio Center for the Arts.

Thirdly, each site has a particular history. If that history is important to us today, as it seems to be, should not contemporary environments be designed to reflect this history? An example is the current development of the Internationnale Bauaustellung in Berlin. In this area, leveled by bombing and demolition, the context established for redevelopment is the Berlin that existed once before. The history of a site can also be an important context for design. To this point, projects in Cincinnati do not address this potential.

And in balance, "the spirit of our time" must also be part of the context for design. This is a much more illusive concept, and much more arguable. What is the essence of our time? How do you know it when you are part of it? It's possible to look back as little as twenty years and get some sense of the distinguishing character of that period. It's much more difficult to grasp the essence of our own time, but clearly projects like Fountain Square West reach for this sense of context and appropriateness. It is interesting that the extensive public debate about Fountain Square West, reported in the newspapers, centered around this issue. This has been a principal way we understand and explain the character of physical environments throughout history. Some of the appropriateness of the architecture of our past has been based on the technologies available at the time, but cultural values and intellectual postures have affected design as well.

Consideration of context has influenced the board's discussions. The character of the environment surrounding specific sites, context defined by a concept of the future, appropriateness of visual character for our time have all formed the board's opinions. Sensitive response to context is essential to attaining environmental quality in this pluralistic time.

However, as illustrated in the previous examples, there are four general conditions that constrain the effectiveness of the board. First, not all buildings in downtown Cincinnati fall within the board's jurisdiction.

Second, most of the board's critique is constrained to comments about the visual character of the exterior and public spaces. Yet other factors are often more critical—for example, the mix of functions in Fountain Square West, the geologic stability of Adams Landing, the overall size and mass of 312 Walnut. In many cases, the most critical variables fall outside the board's jurisdiction, governed by the zoning code or determined by economic feasibility.

The board's effectiveness is also restrained by its limited period of involvement in the design and construction process. At the beginning of the process, the basic design concept is often established before the board has an opportunity for input, resulting in a process that is reactionary and remedial rather than participatory. The board's involvement ends with approval of design development documents. There are numerous instances where the realized project departs in some important detail from the scheme approved by the board.

But the most critical limitation is the inadequacy of the city's urban design plan. There are very few cases where there is a detailed urban design plan, like the plan for Garfield Place. The city has developed very useful guidelines for various environmental quality districts, principally for hillside development and for several historic districts. Beyond these, the only guidelines are those contained in the city's *Cincinnati 2000 Plan* (Working Review Committee, 1979) and its update (Plan Review Committee, 1990). This plan encompasses the area bound by the expressways on the east and west and Central Parkway and the Ohio River on the north and south.

The *Cincinnati 2000 Plan* and its update contain four principal ideas in the section on environmental quality and urban design. First, the dominating objective is to maintain the city skyline with its pyramidal shape peaking at Fountain Square. Second, in parallel with this primary concept, the height of new buildings should be limited to protect the views of the river from existing buildings. Third, the downtown's historic character should be preserved in designated areas— Fourth Street, Lytle Park, Northframe, Main Street from Sixth to Central Parkway, as well as specific individual buildings along Fourth Street. Fourth, pedestrian amenities, paving patterns, pedestrian scale lighting, seating, and so on should be emphasized to create a pleasing city.

It is clear these are not adequate to guide the deliberations of the board. The example of Fountain Square West should suffice. The only principle that appears to effect consideration of Fountain Square West at the point of schematic design is the concept of the pyramidal shape peaking at Fountain Square. The others are important concepts but they do not inform fundamental design direction. Elsewhere in the *Cincinnati 2000 Plan* there is another important objective: the prescription for a mixed-use building at Fountain Square West, a building that would include retailing, office, and hotel functions in a manner appreciated over the years in the Carew Tower. Do these two ideas in the *Cincinnati 2000 Plan*—tall and mixed—offer sufficient guidance regarding Fountain Square West? One must conclude they do not.

In their review of the *Cincinnati 2000 Plan*, the Plan Review Committee continued to endorse the pyramidal concept, although they recognized that it has already been compromised by recent development (Plan Review Committee, 1990). The pyramid no longer exists. Because of the height of the Chemed Center and other office structures to the east, and the prominent 312 Walnut to the south, the visual impression now is a city of buildings of rather uniform height in the entire central area. Only the corporate headquarters of Procter & Gamble contributes to the desirably dense but lower-rise concept that was necessary in peripheral development to sustain the pyramid.

It is precisely the inability of the pyramid concept to give direction to development on Third Street, or Broadway Commons, or the eastern edge of the frame that has led to this dilemma. Nevertheless, the vision of a pyramid still has a dominating influence on the Fountain Square West debate. Its persistence derives from its congruence with our society's dedication to achieving the maximum economic potential of any site. Many conclude this is the prime site remaining in the downtown area and thus justifies, even demands, the tallest building in town. This appears to be the singular argument against a smaller, more economically viable project. In this case, however, that position may be encouraging a level of functional concentration at Fountain Square that exacerbates the difficulties in transportation and parking cited elsewhere in the plan. Finally, regarding the pyramid, one must observe that height has little to do with quality. The objective of pyramidal form wasn't very compelling to begin with, and certainly shouldn't guide the city now.

Reexamination of the urban design concept for this location should conclude that it is more important for this building to be well designed than to be a tall building, because that quality will speak more positively about Cincinnati. Also, it is more important for Fountain Square West to house an appropriately complex mix of mutually supporting uses than it is to build something quickly in response to public criticism or the city's sense of frustration. Surely, bigness and quickness are not the right objectives. Rather, good planning, thoughtful urban design, and challenging architectural design are.

In spite of the limitations of inadequate guidelines and limited jurisdiction, the Urban Design Review Board has been effective over a long period of time. In the projects they review, they challenge architects to provide their highest quality of professional service. Incrementally and collectively, over the years, the board has improved the quality of environment in Cincinnati, with a special emphasis on design distinguished by its site-specific quality. Most architects have indicated their appreciation for the board's efforts and contributions to this process.

REFERENCES

City of Cincinnati City Planning Commission. 1987. "Downtown Development." Chapter 24 of the Zoning Code, September 11.

Editorial. 1992. "Downtown." *Cincinnati Enquirer*, June 21.

Findsen, Owen. 1991. "Cesar Pelli Has Designs on the Arts." *Cincinnati Enquirer*, December 1.

Gale, Oliver M., ed. 1986. *Cincinnati 2000 Plan: A Comprehensive Development Plan for Downtown*, prepared by the Working Review Committee, November 3.

———. 1990. *Cincinnati 2000 Plan Review Committee*. Report to the City Planning Commission and City Council, December.

Green, Rick. 1991. "City Urged to Revive Square-Project Idea." *Cincinnati Enquirer*, May 4.

Harrington, Jeff. 1990. "Lending Squeeze May Slow Square." *Cincinnati Enquirer*, June 24.

———. 1990. "Scraping the Cincinnati Sky." *Cincinnati Enquirer*, June 30.

———. 1990. "Panel OKs Tower Design." *Cincinnati Enquirer*, August 1.

———. 1992. "Art-Center Foes Take the Stage." *Cincinnati Enquirer*, July 30.

Thomas, Scipio. 1990. "Building's Design Unpopular." *Cincinnati Enquirer*, July 1.

Turnbull, William. 1987. Statement of Design Intent Schematic Design Phase, June 29.

Urban Design Review Board. October 28, 1987. Minutes of October 20 board meeting.

———. February 18, 1988. Minutes of February 11 board meeting.

———. June 13, 1988. Minutes of May 31 board meeting.

———. June 27, 1988a. Minutes of June 15 board meeting.

———. June 27, 1988b. Minutes of June 20 board meeting.

———. November 14, 1988. Minutes of November 10 board meeting.

———. March 28, 1989. Minutes of March 27 board meeting.

———. December 9, 1991. Minutes of December 5 board meeting.

———. April 2, 1992. Minutes of March 31 board meeting.

12
The New England Life: Design Review in Boston

Allan Wallis

University of Colorado at Denver

The design review process surrounding Phillip Johnson's proposal for the New England Life Insurance Company's new headquarters in Boston's Back Bay marks a transition. Under the administration of Mayor Kevin White, citizen input in the design review process had been achieved through the ad hoc use of citizen advisory committees. The committee appointed for the New England Life project worked hard to win modifications of Johnson's design. It felt that it had met community concerns only to find itself caught in the middle of intense criticism from neighborhood interests and the Boston Society of Architects.

When Ray Flynn subsequently assumed the office of mayor he appointed Stephen Coyle as new director of the Boston Redevelopment Authority (BRA). Coyle wanted to revamp the design review process significantly, but before he could do that he had to deal with $3 billion in new office construction in the "pipeline." One of Coyle's most pressing challenges was to achieve an effective resolution to the controversy surrounding the design of the New England Life. This case discusses transformation of Johnson's design for the New England Life as it reflects evolution of the design review process in Boston.[1]

---

1. This case was originally developed under the auspicies of the Taubman Center for State and Local Government at the Kennedy School of Government, Harvard. A longer version of

DESIGN REVIEW IN BOSTON UNDER MAYOR WHITE

On December 8, 1983, the BRA—the city's planning and redevelopment agency—issued a news release announcing that its board had voted initial approval of the sale of the St. James Avenue parking garage. The prospective owner—the New England Life Insurance Company—planned to construct twin towers containing a total of 1.2 million square feet of office space and a 1,000-space underground garage. The design, by the firm of Phillip Johnson and John Burgee, would rise about 350 feet in height, standing adjacent to the Back Bay neighborhood's architectural jewel, Henry Richardson's Trinty Church.

The BRA's news release emphasized benefits to the city. Sale of the property alone would yield $7.7 million. The proposed development would produce approximately $8 million a year in property taxes, and a total of $6 million for the city's affordable housing fund. The project would create 3,000 construction jobs and 4,000 permanent jobs. To a financially strapped city facing a $40 million budget deficit, the garage sale was a huge success.

Mayor Kevin White expressed his support for

---

this case is available from the Case Program at the Kennedy School.

the BRA's vote: "It's gratifying to know that one of our major corporations is expanding its Boston headquarters." He went on to "commend New England Life and the representatives of nearby neighborhoods involved in extensive review of the development proposal. It is this kind of public input which helps the city retain its distinctive character while experiencing vigorous economic growth."

Ten months after the BRA's optimistic news release the proposal for the St. James Avenue garage site was deeply embroiled in controversy. Several members of the Citizen Advisory Committee (CAC) eventually resigned in protest. By March 1985, as the BRA was ready to vote on final approval of the design, neighborhood activists were saying "It's dumb. A building like that has no place in the Back Bay." A lawsuit to halt the approval process was in the works.

The BRA's new director, Stephen Coyle, was faced with the challenge of trying to resolve the controversy so that the project could move ahead while, at the same time, appeasing neighborhood concerns. He was not impressed with the CAC review, but this project was already well along in the review process. Major development interests in Boston were anxiously waiting to see how Coyle would resolve the impasse.

The review of major building projects in Boston is controlled by the BRA, which serves as a combined city planning department and redevelopment agency. The BRA reviews projects at each stage of development, beginning with schematic plans and ending with final working drawings. Despite the thoroughness of the review process, through the mid-1980s the BRA was guided by no specific criteria.[2] Rather, guidelines were developed individually for each project.

The agency's urban design staff meets frequently with project architects and developers. Together they determine the kind of project acceptable to all interests. The process offers significantly more flexibility to both sides than traditional, as-of-right zoning. This flexibility allows the city to adjust to market demand. When the real estate market is strong, the city can negotiate for additional benefits from developers. In a weak market the city can offer developers more incentives.

The BRA's highly descretionary review process had no specific requirements for citizen review outside of a few public hearings, usually occurring well into the final design stage. But experience with projects, especially in the late 1970s, fostered significant reforms in this aspect of the process. In particular, design review for a project at Copley Square became a major turning point in the treatment of citizen review. The proposed office, hotel, and retail complex was opposed by neighborhood activists who feared that it would generate major negative impacts while returning few benefits to existing residents. In order to mollify protest, the Citizen Advisory Committee (CAC) was appointed.[3] Working directly with the developer and project architects, the CAC was able to win consessions in the project's program and design that made it acceptable to the neighborhoods. Although the use of CACs was never formally endorsed as a component of BRA design review, it became standard practice for large projects likely to provoke controversy.

The St. James garage site is not far from Copley Place. Because of the scale and character of the project that New England Life proposed for the site, there was little doubt that a CAC was needed. The project was also potentially sensitive because it would loom over Trinity Church, which already sat in the shadow of Boston's tallest building, the 700-foot-high Hancock Tower designed by I. M. Pei (1975). Moreover, the Back Bay neighborhood was extremely sensitive about its architectural heritage. The neighborhood's streets, lined with Victorian town houses and punctuated by the green esplanade of Commonwealth Avenue, made it one of the city's most attractive communities. Influential professionals made it their home, and would defend it against adjacent development that threatened to alter their skyline and suffuse local streets with additional traffic.

Shortly after the BRA accepted New England

---

2. For a description of the design review process as it existed in Boston in the late 1970s and early 1980s, see H. Shirvani, *Urban Design Review* (Washington, D.C.: American Planning Association Press, 1981), especially chapters 3 and 9.

3. For a description of the Copley Place project, see "Citizen Participation at Copley Place" (Cambridge, Mass.: Harvard University, John F. Kennedy School of Government Case Program), case number C14-83-552.

Life's bid for the garage site, Director Ryan invited Spencer Rice, Rector of Trinity Church, to chair the St. James CAC. The committee's eleven other members included representatives from two Back Bay residents associations, the Ellis Neighborhood Association, neighborhood business associations, the Boston Society of Architects, Trinity Church, and the area's state legislator. In all, four committee members were architects. Two BRA staff attended CAC meetings, along with three representatives of the developers. Aside from meetings with the CAC, BRA staff met frequently with the developers and their designers.

Formally, the CAC was under contract with the BRA. Technically, its role was advisory. But politically, its function was to represent neighborhood interests to the BRA, and to assure the neighborhood that the BRA and the developers were listening and being responsive. If the CAC worked effectively, when the project was presented for public hearing local interests would feel that their concerns had been met.

The Client and the Architect

Beginning in the mid-1970s, New England Life Mutual Insurance Company (NEL) started acquiring properties on the northern side of the Berkeley/Claredon block, across the street from its existing headquarters, with the objective of building new headquarters (Fig. 12-1). The south half of the block was occupied by the city-owned St. James Avenue Garage. When the city announced that it would be selling the facility, NEL joint ventured with Houston-based developer Gerald D. Hines to bid on the property.

The as-of-right density allowed on the site was defined by a floor-area ratio (FAR) of 8.[4] In their bid proposal the developers requested a FAR of 11.45, which they argued was necessary to make the project profitable and justify their price offered for the garage. At that density, the building would contain almost 1.6 million square feet.

After placing their successful bid, the developers began interviewing architects for the project. One candidate was the firm of Phillip Johnson

and John Burgee. Johnson was no stranger to Boston. He had studied architecture at Harvard. His addition to the Boston Public Library had won wide praised for its sensitive massing, which was modern yet sympathetic with the Renaissance style of the original structure. At their interview Johnson and Burgee talked about how they intended to make their design for NEL fit in with the area. The developers felt confident that the firm could provide a design that was distinctive yet responsive to neighborhood concerns about maintaining the area's architectural character.

Preliminary Design

Johnson and Burgee completed their preliminary design in February 1983. The proposal featured twin barrel-vault-crowned towers. One tower would be occupied primarily by NEL offices, and the other leased. The towers would sit atop a ninety-foot base covering the entire block and punctuated by symmetrical courtyards. The arches, attached pilasters, and column details were meant to recall structures found elsewhere in the Back Bay.

The architects had met many times with BRA urban design staff in bringing their proposal to its present level of development. Now, in March 1983, it was the CAC's chance to comment on the proposal. The charge of the CAC was to act as a conduit for community concerns. Although it had no formal power in the review process, the BRA would report the CAC's recommendations to the city council and the Zoning Board of Appeals when those bodies prepared to vote on project approval. In addition, the BRA agreed that it would not make changes in the project without affording the CAC an opportunity to "advise" on such changes.

When the CAC saw the mass of the proposed project and the bold symmetry of the twin towers, its members realized that they had their work cut out for them. That impression was confirmed a month later when the *Boston Globe* published renderings of Johnson and Burgee's design. CAC members began hearing from their constituents that the design was unacceptable and out of keeping with the Back Bay. The Boston Society of Architects (BSA) characterized the design as "a reactionary neo-Classical or neo-Renaissance object . . . not expressive of the dynamic vitality

---

4. FAR is the ratio of build floor area to site area. For example, on a site with an area of 1,000 square feet and an FAR of 8, the maximum building area would be 8,000 square feet.

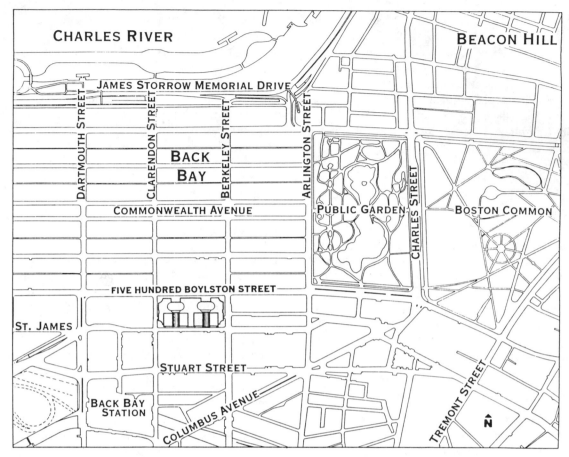

Figure 12-1. Context map of the Back Bay; the New England Life buildings is shown as Five Hundred Boylston Street

of the City and the modern, imaginative insurance corporation today. The intent of the modeling [massing] and plan form, as expressed, are commendable and desirable. However, the conglomerate stylistic abstractions of historic and architectural paraphernalia do not seem appropriate for this place and time" (Boston Society of Architects, 1983).

For CAC members there were two issues to be addressed: the scale and massing of the building, including its program (e.g., number of parking spaces, and the percentage that would be available to the public), and the design or style of the building.

Since it had no specific guidelines, the committee debated the degree to which it should tackle aesthetic issues. Passing judgment about the effects of shadows and the distribution of parking was one thing, evaluating the stylistic choices of a prominent designer was quite another. Most

CAC members, including architect Ken Gritter from the Ellis Neighborhood, felt that at a certain level the style of the building was an issue between architect and developer. "The developers have a right to build a silly building. I'm just concerned about the size of it, and the effect it will have on traffic in my neighborhood."

With regard to nonaesthetic aspects of the proposal, however, the committee felt more comfortable about suggesting changes. In particular, it was concerned about building setbacks (i.e., the distance from curb to building) and FAR. Johnson and Burgee's original proposal provided for only a narrow, eight-foot setback on St. James Street, where the building would rise up as a straight wall. For the Boylston Street side the proposed setback was fifteen feet. The CAC felt that both setbacks were inadequate. On the St. James side the narrow sidewalk would "canyonize" the street. On Boylston, members wanted to preserve sight lines toward Trinity Church and Copley Square. The CAC voted to recommend a setback of twenty-five feet on Boylston, and sixteen feet on St. James.

Although the setback issue might seem minor, it is directly related to a more substantive concern of developers—FAR. The greater the setback, the taller the building must be in order to preserve the same FAR (i.e., amount of floor area). If a building is further limited in height, it may not even be possible to reach the economically desired floor area. The developers wanted an FAR of 11.45, insisting that it was required to make the building economically feasible. They made clear that their generous bid on the garage site was predicated on a building of that volume. Zoning for the site permitted an FAR of 8.0, so the difference between the two was the area of negotiation.

Even before the CAC formed, the neighborhood association of the Back Bay had written BRA director Ryan requesting that he delay any recommendation for an FAR exceeding 8.0 until more was known about the building being proposed. After the preliminary design was unveiled the Urban Design Committee of the Boston Society of Architects urged maintaining an FAR of 8.0, even though it acknowledged that the building's economics might require greater density. However, CAC members from the Back Bay Association and the Newbury Street League, representing commercial interests in the neighborhood, supported the developer's position.

Part of the debate over FAR concerned trade-offs that might be negotiated as a condition for endorsing higher density. These trade-offs related not only to what the neighborhood wanted from the developer, but to what it hoped to secure from the city. Among the benefits CAC members hoped to win from the developer was a higher percentage of short-term parking in the new garage, and payment for improvements to Copley Square, onto which Trinity Church opens. From the city, the CAC hoped to secure agreement that part of the "linkage" funds exacted from the developer for affordable housing would be designated for use in the Back Bay and South End. But the most significant trade-off considered by the CAC was to secure a guarantee from the BRA that if NEL got its requested density, then the BRA would down-zone the rest of Boylston Street. If, as many CAC members suspected, the BRA had already

agreed to the higher FAR in principle, then the CAC could at least win assurances that the overall development of Boylston, where several other major developments were being proposed, would be limited.

In August, after six months of meetings, the CAC sent its recommendations to the BRA. At the top of its list was the request for an FAR of 8.0.

Compromising on FAR

All of the CACs recommendations were acceptable to the developers, but not the FAR of 8.0. They continued to insist that project economics necessitated higher density. When it met again in November, the CAC requested an economic analysis to determine the project's break-even density. That study concluded that the project could be supported with an FAR of 9.5. BRA chairman Ryan offered that option as a compromise between the CAC and the developer. It was accepted.

The CAC voted its approval so that the matter could be taken up by the BRA's board at its December meeting. The board's vote formally designated NEL and Hines as developers, indirectly accepting their preliminary design. Most CAC members felt that they had won significant concessions. Although they avoided direct recommendations or aesthetic aspects of the building, they informed the BRA that at subsequent reviews they felt free to revisit consideration of such matters. The next meeting of the CAC was not scheduled

Summary of Design Changes

	Conceptual Design (2/83)	Preliminary Design (11/83)
Building height to top of parapets	396'	344'
Number of stories	29	26
Distance between office towers	40'	50'
FAR	11.45	9.5
Square footage	1,572,458	1,300,000
First-floor setbacks		
Boylston Street	15'	25'
St. James Street	8'	15'
Parking		
Short-term	250	315
Public monthly	0	310
Tenant	750	375

until May. At that time Phillip Johnson would give a public presentation of his refined design at the Trinty Church Parish Hall.

The Presentation at the Parish Hall

Even before Phillip Johnson got up to present his design for the NEL, Boston's architectural community was up in arms against him. They had already seen his preliminary design published more than a year before, but they were also concerned about another project.

Johnson had won the commission to design a development for one of the city's other six surplused garage sites, this one at the edge of the financial district. Preliminary designs for the project, called International Place—a 1.6-million-square-foot complex of cylinders and slabs—were opposed by the Boston Society of Architects' Urban Design Committee. To critics, both of Johnson's massive projects were indifferent to the city's architectural heritage.

The public presentation at the Parish Hall began the next phase of CAC review: bringing the project from preliminary through schematic design, and bringing the proposal for approval of the sale of the garage site. But when the committee met at the end of the month, its members objected that the developers had not met all of their previous concerns (specifically with regard to recommended setbacks). CAC members also realized that they needed to address aesthetic concerns directly.

Oscar Padjen, representing the Boston Society of Architects on the CAC, declared that his organization found Johnson's design "unacceptable," objecting to "the regressive style of the project" and the "towers dwarfing Trinity Church." David Johnson, of the Back Bay Architectural Commission, questioned the scale of the project and the aesthetics of its elevation.

At the next meeting of the CAC, on June 28, Robert Kroin, the BRA representative to the committee, reported that his agency liked the NEL project and wanted to see it go ahead. Nevertheless, the BRA hoped to see improvements made to the building's massing, treatment of the courtyard, and elevation details.

On July 2, with the clock running out on the review period and with an extensive set of project drawings before it, the CAC met to consider approval of the schematic design. Gritter, Johnson, and Padjen, the three remaining architects on the CAC, presented a detailed memorandum outlining design concerns. Despite their many reservations, the committee voted unanimously to approve the schematic design (Fig. 12-2). In July the BRA Board voted unanimously to approve the schematic design for NEL.

CHANGING ADMINISTRATION: KEVIN WHITE AND STEPHEN COYLE

The BRA's July Board meeting was the last Ryan attended as director. A new mayor had taken office in January and his appointment of a BRA director was about to assume his duties. After sixteen years in office Kevin White was succeeded by Ray Flynn. Whereas White was identified with Boston's tony Beacon Hill, Flynn was a native of the South Side, an Irish working-class neighborhood. Critics of White felt that his attention to the city's economic development favored downtown interests while ignoring Boston's neighborhoods. By contrast, Flynn campaigned on a platform of placing neighborhood needs first, promising to protect neighborhoods from the adverse effects of new development.

Six months after taking office Flynn nominated Boston-born Stephen Coyle as BRA director. Coyle was no stranger to the urban development process, having just stepped down as executive vice president for management of the huge San Francisco design and planning office of John Carl Warnecke.

Coyle wanted to establish a new design review process, one that was less discretionary and more predictable. Part of that predictability would come from a new master plan, with district plans addressing the distinctive character of special areas of the city (e.g., the midtown theater district). CACs would still be utilized, but the aesthetic dimensions of urban design would be addressed by a Civic Design Commission. The new BRA director believed that the project review process could be used, not only to assure high-quality development, but also to regulate the pace of development so that the market did not overbuild and fall into a slump.

In moving toward implementation of these

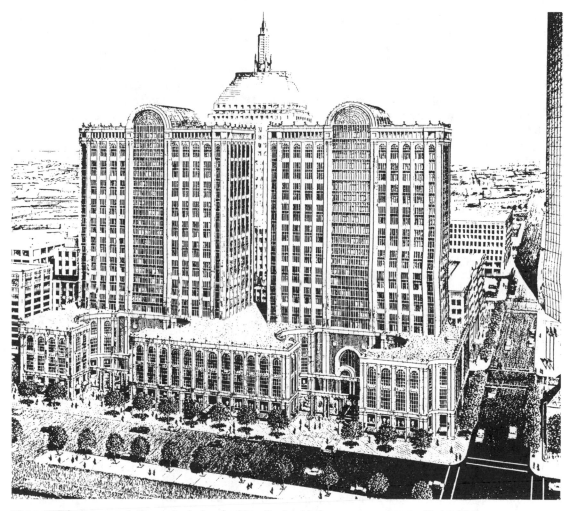

Figure 12-2. Johnson & Burgee's design for New England Life as presented at the Parish Hall

ideas, however, Coyle was faced with a huge inherited backlog of projects. There were $1.5 billion in projects under construction and an equal amount making its way through the approval process. The new director's challenge was to get a different review process established while simultaneously taking care of projects already in the works.

One month after becoming BRA director, Coyle announced that there would be a "pipeline review" of all projects currently under consideration. He hoped to use the review to reassure developers and neighborhood groups regarding the approach he would be taking toward development proposals in the future. But when the report—*Downtown Projects: Opportunities for Boston*—was released in October, it showed only

modest changes in the NEL proposal. The height of the twin towers would be reduced by one story, but the FAR remained the same. The report largely sidestepped the issue of neighborhood design compatibility.

New and Old Neighborhood Voices

A month after the pipeline review appeared, and a day after the Boston City Council unanimously approved a resolution supporting the NEL project, a group calling itself Citizens for a Better New England Life (CBNEL) was formed. Acting chairman Robert Manning conceded to the neighborhood paper, the *TAB*, that "we're late in the game . . . [but] a lot of us thought the various civic organizations reviewing the project [CAC] would be more effective in getting modifications." He added, "We're not talking about strangling the city's need and desire for growth . . . we just want to know if it is necessary to be as massive as this seems to be."

The size of the proposed development was a common concern uniting the opposition. Organizers felt that yet another overscaled project was being thrust on the Back Bay with no comprehensive plan in sight. Some of CBNEL's founding members, however, were particularly incensed by the style of the building. Robert Sturgis, former chair of the Boston Society of Architects' Urban Design Committee objected that "the building as proposed is a massive symmetrical type thing." He further observed that "Symmetry like that asks for a grand mall down the river" (*TAB*, November 13, 1984).

After its vote to approve the schematic designs in July 1984, the CAC had virtually dissolved. With its membership demoralized, the city simply stopped working with the CAC, preferring direct discussions with community interests, including CBNEL. CAC member Fritz Casselman conceded, "We felt we got the best deal we could. . . . In hindsight maybe we could have held out longer" (*Boston Globe*, January 6, 1985).

Opponents felt that the failure of the CAC to achieve more was a result of the identification of several of its members with development interests. Cambridge developer E. Jackson Hall, who represented Trinity Church on the CAC, found himself in an awkward position when three hundred members of church signed a petition supporting the goals of CBNEL. "I'm not a proponent or opponent," Hall replied, "I just want to make sure the church's interests are protected" (*Boston Globe*, January 6, 1985). Church rector and CAC chair Spencer Rice found himself in a similar position, with scores of members threatening to leave the church. Eventually, one hundred resigned in protest.

Final Approvals

When the BRA board met in March to approve the NEL site as a Planned Development Area (PDA)—a designation that would legally permit consideration of a higher FAR than permitted as-of-right—opposition was well organized and the hearing room was packed. Despite strong testi-

mony against the project, the board voted unanimously for project approval. Late the following August (1985), when the matter came before the Zoning Commission, the hearing room for which it was originally scheduled was so crowded that the session had to be moved to larger chambers. After eight grueling hours of testimony, the ten-member commission voted unanimously for approval with an FAR of 9.5. Approval by the Zoning Board of Appeals followed shortly.

Reporting on the Zoning Commission hearing, *Boston Globe* columnist Otile McManus observed:

> What is striking about the case [NEL] is how thoroughly the Flynn administration has failed to calculate the depth of frustration that residents in the Back Bay and adjacent city blocks feel about architect Philip Johnson's ungainly granite and glass building, and the degree to which they believe their concerns about its impacts have not been heard. . . . Flynn, a self-styled man of the people and champion of the underdog, the mayor for whom splinter groups are the meat and potatoes of everyday politics, has seemed to ignore the concerns of this old and honorable section of Boston (September 1, 1985, 1).

With the developer now in possession of all approvals needed to begin demolition of buildings on the site, CBNEL prepared to file suit against the BRA and the two regulatory boards that had approved the project. The basis of their suit was adverse neighborhood impact, especially due to traffic. According to CBNEL's Robert Manning, Coyle was unmoved by the pleas of opponents. Mayor Flynn "met with us, and wanted to hear us out, but Coyle was far less accommodating. When we mentioned our intention of filing a law suit, he simply told us—see you in court." CBNEL filed its lawsuit on September 11.

Eleventh-Hour Negotiations

His statements to CBNEL notwithstanding, Coyle had been working behind the scenes since early November trying to negotiate a compromise that would satisfy opponents of the project without alienating the developers and the development community. One rumored alternative was to scale down the development; another would allow the developer to build the first phase while redesigning the second. The developers, however, had already made a huge investment in the project. They had met all the requirements of a citizen review process, and had twice before agreed to scale down the project (once for the CAC, and again in the pipeline review). A further reduction, they said, might jeopardize the financial feasibility of the project.

Coyle and NEL representative Joe O'Conner met on November 13 to discuss potential alternatives, but after the meeting O'Conner would only reveal that "we need some breathing room." Five days later, Martin Nolan, editorial page editor for the *Boston Globe,* wrote an article entitled "Good Enough for Tysons Corner, Not Good Enough for Boston" (November 18, 1985, 15). The story featured the now-familiar rendering of the twin towers of NEL, but juxtaposed next to it was a three-tower proposal, also by Johnson and Burgee, for an office project in Tysons Corner, Virginia. Nolan wrote:

In the twilight of his career Philip Johnson has defined post-modernism by emptying his attic—bric-a-brac for Dallas, a Chippendale knick-knack for New York, a curio for Denver and Mansard geegaws for San Francisco. In busy garage sales, the same item can be sold twice. Boston was supposed to get the matched set of two giant Philco radios from the 1930s. Instead a suburb of Washington is about to inherit three of these strikingly familiar towers. . . . Mimosa Drive in Tysons Corner may be the right address for this sort of architecture. Boylston Street in the Back Bay is not.

The project at Tysons Corner was not a revelation to the developers, but Nolan's article in the *Boston Globe* embarrassed the developers, who from the beginning had professed the desire to deliver a project reflective of Boston and the Back Bay. The day after Thanksgiving, Coyle and O'Conner met again to discuss the fate of the NEL proposal. On December 1, the *Boston Globe* reported that "in a refreshingly statesmanlike decision the New England Mutual Life Insurance Company has done what few large real estate developers do. It has said it might have been wrong (*Boston Globe,* 1985)." The company stated that it would go ahead with construction of one of Johnson's towers, but that it would hire a new architect to design a scaled-down second tower.

Joe O'Conner, in a guest article for the *TAB,* portrayed the motivation of the developer as one of good citizenship.

Some fellow developers in the city have criticized our willingness to offer such a major compromise so late in the game. After all, we meticulously followed a three year approval process that included more community involvement than any previous construction project. All that separated us from going ahead was one final design approval [the traffic study] that generally had been granted automatically. That decision to make this major concession literally may cost us several millions in lost design costs, yet we're willing to make that sacrifice. As an involved corporate citizen of long standing, our compromise recognized the continuing concerns of still critical community activists and responded to them, even though we were under no requirement to do so (O'Conner, 1985).

O'Conner stated that the developers were willing to take a completely open look at Phase 2 as to use, massing, style, size, and all other issues. In return Coyle would recommend to the BRA board that it approve construction of Phase 1 to begin early next year.

Despite O'Conner's characterization, senior BRA staff close to the negotiations portray the situation as somewhat less than voluntary. Although the developers could have chosen to hold out for their current proposal, relying on the momentum of the review process to carry them through, in private meetings Coyle apparently made it clear that in following such a strategy they risked the potential of further delays that could cause them to miss the current peak in the real estate market. By accepting Coyle's compromises the developers could rapidly begin construction on Phase 1 and start preleasing space.

Coyle also asked CBNEL if it would drop its suit in light of the agreement reached with the developers. But the organization remained adamant. In March 1986, CBNEL's suit came before Judge Marilyn Sullivan in the Massachusets Land Court. On May 5 Judge Sullivan ruled against the plaintiffs. In her opinion, Sullivan suggested that "this building should not be held hostage to whatever weaknesses there may be in the city's solution to its general [traffic] problems. So far as the contextual relationship of the proposed building to its surroundings, that appears to be a matter of taste on which opinions vary. . . . So far as the public welfare is concerned . . . nothing in the Developer's development plan is injurious to the neighborhood or otherwise detrimental to the public welfare, and so I find and rule" (*Manning et al. v. BRA,* 30).

CASE DISCUSSION

Design review is fundamentally the exercise of political power in an attempt to direct the development process. As such it is an activity that helps define the boundary between public and private interests in the city. Where this boundary is set reflects a balancing of interests operating in different policy arenas.[5] In one arena elected officials adopt policies to make their city's market competitive with other cities. They want to attract new development and high-income residents. To the extent that they can facilitate the development process—working cooperatively with developers and creating a predictable review process—they may create a comparative advantage.

Although elected officials must concern themselves with market competition, in another policy arena they must be mindful of the pluralistic interests of the electorate, especially in responding to neighborhood concerns.[6] These interests typically press for redistributive considerations (i.e., park improvements, affordable housing allocations, and so forth). Neighborhood leaders argue that if their residents are to suffer from the adverse impacts of new development in order to enhance the city's overall economic base, they should receive some of the benefits, as well as have a say regarding acceptable levels of impact.

The challenge for city officials and administrators is to balance concern for economic development with preservation of community quality as desired by residents. While these interests are not mutually exclusive, they often compete. The design review process provides one mechanism through which the balance of competing interests can be played out.

---

5. On the notion of balancing competing interests in the city see J. R. Logan and H. L. Molotch, *Urban Fortunes: The Political Economy of Place* (Berkeley: University of California Press, 1987).

6. See, for example, D. Kantor. *The Dependent City* (Glenview, Ill.: Scott, Foresman, 1988).

The NEL case unfolds at a time when the balance of interests is shifting toward greater public control and, more significantly, toward greater empowerment of neighborhood interests. At the same time, Boston was in tight financial straits. It wanted to maximize new development in order to enhance its tax base and reduce a significant deficit. The developers played to this interest by offering to keep NEL employees in Boston and by proposing a major new office development. Under the White administration the balance of interests clearly favored the new development as proposed. Even so, the BRA had to appoint a CAC that could facilitate the project with respect to mollifying potential community objections. It seemed to have done its job well until late in the process when some CAC members began to waffle in their support of the project. Assuming that White had remained in office, it is likely that he would have toughed out the opposition, allowing the project to proceed as planned.

When Flynn became mayor it was not clear how the city would address the balance of development with neighborhood interests. Unlike White, Flynn had little interest in retaining strong control over the BRA. Flynn's campaign contained a lot of proneighborhood rhetoric, but would he significantly pare down development projects if that meant reducing potential tax benefits?

Flynn's appointment of Coyle was pivotal. It signaled the development community that someone was being placed in charge of the BRA with working experience on the developers' side of the process, and hence someone who could be understanding if not necessarily sympathetic to their interests. At the same time, Coyle wanted to assure neighborhood interests that development decisions would be made within the context of more comprehensive district plans, which he proposed to develop. He also wanted to establish a standing review board capable of dealing with sensitive aesthetic issues.

A first order of business for the new BRA director was to offer reassurance to developers that Boston was still a good town to invest in. One assurance that Coyle could provide was that projects already in the pipeline could proceed in an orderly fashion. However, if Coyle appeared to be rubber-stamping decisions made by the previous administration, the concerns of neighborhood interest groups could become organized against him and his mayor. He made a calculated guess as to how much reduction in scale of pipeline projects would be acceptable to both sides. For the most part the calculation worked, but not in the case of NEL.

The CAC established for the NEL had lost its credibility and Coyle saw little value in investing in it as an agent of compromise. Instead he chose to show CBNEL an uncompromising position while trying to negotiate with the developers to offer a solution that would meet the neighborhood objections. In short, Coyle made full use of his discretionary powers as BRA director to affect an acceptable compromise, and thereby cleared the decks for implementing his own review process.

If Coyle is the tacit hero of this case—the figure who understands changing political interests and is able to strike the necessary new balance—is there a presumptive villain? Clearly one candidate for that role is the architect, Phillip Johnson. He was portrayed by the press, much through his own actions, as arrogant and indifferent to local aesthetic concerns.

In retrospect it is not clear that objections raised over the twin tower proposal were genuinely grounded in aesthetic concerns, or if their real energy came from tensions between the city and its neighborhoods over the issue of who should determine the distribution and balance of impacts and benefits generated by a major new development. Was the neighborhood genuinely offended by the design, by the project's size, or both?

Looking back on Johnson's design two years after construction, CBNEL's Herbert Gleason concedes that that "the pinkish granite is friendly. From a distance the arched window of the roof is distinctive, a landmark especially when lighted at night." Robert A. M. Stern, who was selected as architect to redesign the second NEL tower, confesses that he had a honeymoon with the community in part because his commission came on the heels of Johnson's. He hopes that history will be as kind to his design.

REFERENCES

Boston Society of Architects. 1983. "Preliminary Architectural and Urban Design Review." Memorandum from the BSA to the CAC, p. 2.

TAB. November 13, 1984, 1.

Boston Globe. "A Decision for the Back Bay." December 1, 1985, p. 26.

O'Conner, Joe. 1985. "A Corporate Compromise." *TAB*, December 3, p. 1.

III
Critical Perspectives
of Design Review

13
Place-Making and Design Review

Michael Hough

York University, Toronto

There's an often-quoted and well-worn adage that the camel is an animal designed by committee. This is clearly a poor description of this beast since it is not only homocentric, but lacks what should be a central ingredient of the design process—organic growth and evolutionary change. From this perspective the (Arabian) camel may be seen to be a creature of elegant design, superbly adapted through evolutionary time to dry desert environments, capable of traveling at speeds of eight to ten miles per hour for eighteen hours, able to go without food or water for weeks, and to flourish on the coarsest of vegetation. Thus, if the design review process could design cities as well as nature has designed the camel, with the same elegance and sense of environmental fit that make for livable urban places with a clear sense of regional identity, then cities would be the ideal places they should be to work and play in. Since this does not seem to be the case, the question of design review requires some examination.

Design review committees come in various forms. There are committees appointed to national or provincial capitals to review proposals for planning, architecture, landscape, and art, for federal lands with jurisdiction over the quality of the built environment. The National Capital Commission in Ottawa, the Wascana Authority in Regina Saskatchewan, and Washington, D.C., are examples where a design review process has been the basis for implementing an overall conceptual plan for these capital cities. And there are the review processes of local authorities responsible for municipal development. Each of these bodies employ a variety of approaches to the review process, ranging from panels of experts that meet periodically as a committee, to the formal review process where municipal and government agencies check proponent plans to ensure their compliance with local and regional regulations. It is this latter end of the design review spectrum that is the focus of this chapter, since what happens at the municipal planning level has by far the greatest impact on environment, place, and how we shape our cities.

What has become known as urban sprawl has, arguably, produced some of the most placeless, environmentally destructive, and energy-consuming human habitats of modern times (Fig. 13-1). Yet, all too frequently, these have been achieved not through a lack of planning, or a laissez-faire attitude to the approvals process, but by the all-too-stringent application of zoning, density, and bylaw requirements that dictate how they should be built and how people should live their lives. Bylaw requirements in most Ontario municipalities dictate such things as the width of street, building setback requirements, the height of backyard fences, the location of garages, landscaping, location of services, lot coverage, and the uses that may be permitted.

A host of restrictive codes conspire to inhibit the natural evolution that makes for diverse neigh-

Figure 13-1. This suburban development could be anywhere in North America. Urban sprawl has all too frequently been achieved not from a lack of planning, but by its all too stringent application. (Photo: Royal Commission on the Future of the Toronto Waterfront.)

borhoods, and where corner stores, mixed uses, and street life can flourish. There are well-known physical problems too. New development continues to be built without regard to topography, woodlots, streams, and wetlands, or the historic cultural patterns of the land. Conventional storm-drainage systems short-circuit the hydrological cycle at the cost of degraded rivers and aquatic life. While there are many planning, economic, and political issues driving the development process, much of the problem can be attributed to three or four.

First, there are regulatory frameworks that are characterized by overlap and duplication by different levels of government (Fig. 13-2). Such frameworks are fragmented and often conflicting in their objectives.[1] For an example of the complexity of jurisdictional frameworks, one can invoke the issue of surface water on the Toronto waterfront. Federal, provincial, Conservation Authority, metropolitan, and local municipal agencies all are responsible in one way or another for its management. A variety of federal departments have jurisdiction over navigation, shipping, harbor activities, fisheries, and transboundary waters. At the provincial level, the primary responsibility for protecting water falls on the Environ-

ment Ministry; wetlands and fisheries are the responsibility of the Natural Resources Ministry; municipal planning is overseen by the Ministry of Municipal Affairs. The reduction of erosion and riverine flooding belong to the Metro Toronto and Region Conservation Authority that also implements an environment program for controlling the quality of soil used for lake filling. The Municipality of Metro Toronto manages water supply and sewage systems and operates the Main Sewage Treatment Plant, while various municipalities own and maintain the sanitary and storm sewers that flow into the sewage plant and Lake Ontario. In addition, a citizen initiative to restore Toronto's most polluted river, through efforts by the "Task Force to Bring Back the Don," depend on concerted action by jurisdictions throughout the watershed, since the Task Force mandate is limited to only six of the thirty-eight kilometres of the river's length. Similar problems affect municipalities as a whole. The planning decisions made in one municipality are made at the expense of another downstream; a condition that arises when political boundaries take precedence over watershed boundaries. The Royal Commission for the Future of the Toronto Waterfront, a body appointed in 1987 to examine environmental, economic, and political issues of the waterfront, recently commented: "Through a maze of laws, policies, and guidelines, those agencies regulate the use of surface waters; the use of the harbour

1. Suzanne Barrett and Joanna Kidd, *Pathways: Towards an Ecosystem Approach*. (Toronto: Royal Commission on the Future of the Toronto Waterfront, April 1991).

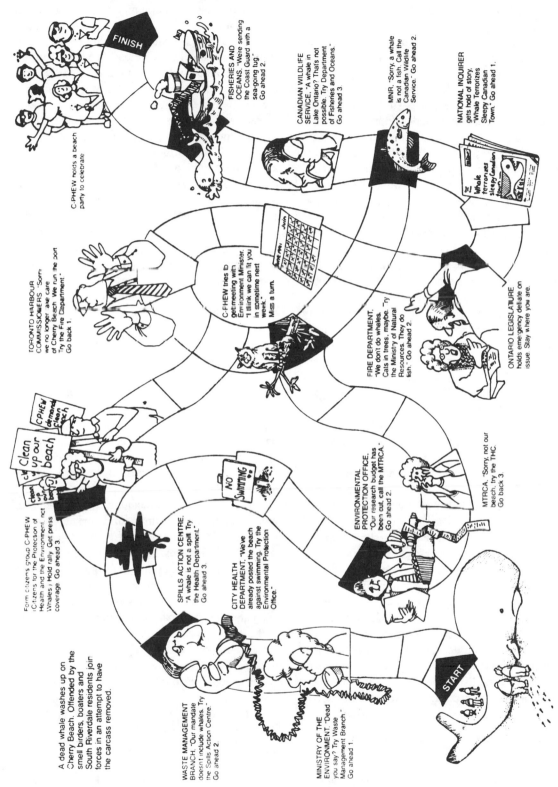

Figure 13-2. In the complex and often conflicting jurisdictional framework of government, the question arises, who is in charge? (Figure: Royal Commission on the Future of the Toronto Waterfront.)

and Lake Ontario for shipping and navigation, for industrial cooling and process needs, as wildlife habitat, for drinking water, for recreational activities, and for receiving stormwater and treated sewage."[2]

Second, there is a lack of context within which specific decisions are made—the absence of a larger ecosystem's view of development that integrates nature, people and economy in a larger bioregional perspective. To understand why this is so requires, on a philosophical plain, an examination of an environmental set of values that have traditionally regarded cities as "unnatural," or at best, disconnected from natural processes. In a world increasingly concerned with the problems of a deteriorating environment, be they energy, pollution, vanishing plants, animals, or productive landscapes, there has been a marked propensity to bypass the environment most people live in. Over the last twenty years, however, society has begun to recognize that global or local environmental sustainability will be determined largely by our cities. Such a goal will be dependent on finding ways to regenerate urban ecosystems, and by adopting more sustainable urban life-styles. From a more pragmatic point of view, the realities of unswimmable beaches, undrinkable water, rivers without fish, cleared woodlands, and drained wetlands are no longer an acceptable basis for achieving economic prosperity. The piecemeal management of human activities, that treats the economy as a separate issue from social issues or the environment, must be replaced by one that sees them as interrelated, where decisions made on one area affect all others.[3]

Third, there is an inbuilt bureaucratic inertia in much municipal planning that maintains a rigid adherence to development standards. With the rule books in place, it is much easier to do things the way they have always been done. Municipal design review and approval of new development is a process that works within the safety net of well-worn established procedures. It shies away from innovation or departures from the norm, and consequently acts to inhibit what is essentially an organic process of community building, a natural process of change that can only evolve over time.

Fourth, there is little recognition of the multicultural makeup of most cities.[4] In Metro Toronto there is an ongoing shift of culturally diverse communities to the suburbs, which is not only changing but greatly enriching their physical and social character and environment. The fact that changes to buildings and properties may often take place in contradiction to local bylaws or zoning is an indication that the regulatory process is not geared to respond to these cultural needs and realities. It is paradoxical that while much of the environment experienced in daily life appears to be moving toward an increasing physical homogeneity, the social makeup of most cities is shifting in the opposite direction, to an increasing heterogeneity and social complexity.

These issues raise fundamental philosophical questions about current perceptions of the design process. The forces that are creating these environments that many see as the increasingly placelessness of the urban edge seem to derive, at least in part, from fixed visions of the world that have little to do with the nature of the processes that govern life. Conceptually, they may be seen to represent the imposition of an authoritarian view on biophysical and human processes that militates against regional diversity, identity, and place. Patrick Geddes once compared the term *utopia,* derived from the Greek word meaning "no place," with the word *eutopia,* meaning "good place." In doing so he summed up a fundamental tenet of the regional imperative, that it makes sense to design with the forms, and cultural and ecological processes, already present in a location rather than trying to force an idealized, preconceived plan upon a site.[5] Thus, eutopia is assured when culture and nature become part of design thinking; utopia is the consequence of ignoring them.[6] It can be argued, in fact, that nothing could be more fatal to society than to achieve its utopian ideals.

One would be hard pressed, however, to as-

---

2. Ibid.

3. Royal Commission on the Future of the Toronto Waterfront, *Regeneration.* (Toronto: Minister of Supply and Services Canada, 1992).

4. Brenda C. Lightner, "Design Review: A Critical Evaluation," *Cities* 9 (November).

5. Philip Boardman, *The Worlds of Patrick Geddes.* (London: Routledge and Kegan Paul, 1978).

6. Michael Hough, *Out of Place, Restoring Identity to the Regional Landscape* (New Haven: Yale University Press, 1990).

cribe utopian ideals or motives to the array of rigid and often baffling controls and bylaws imposed on human habitats. But even the most meaningless regulations of today have their roots in past history. The visionary proposals for planned cities, particularly those of the first half of the twentieth century, were an inevitable reaction to the social and environmental degradation of the nineteenth-century industrial city, and the perceived need to right past social and environmental wrongs. It was felt that nothing less than total change based on doctrines of social betterment, fresh air, and opportunities for a healthy life-style could solve the problems of the city. The utopian cities proposed by Wright, Le Corbusier, and Ebenezer Howard were plainly unworkable. Yet their ideas, grossly distorted through the passage of time, have survived in the contemporary built landscape. The traditions of intellectual dogma have been passed on by generations of planners, designers, and decision makers who see their role as determining the future of society, and maintaining a built form and systems of controls that are now loosing their relevance to the issues facing cities today.

The results of this view were demonstrated in Alice Coleman's exhaustive study of high-rise housing in Britain. She showed how the postwar visions of ideal housing environments have in fact resulted in squalor, vandalism, and social breakdown—the very opposite of what they were intended to be, and a huge waste of public and private money. On trial was the utopian view, through the medium of design control, about how people should live.[7] As Coleman observes, such deeply embedded ideals have had a lasting impact on the social and physical environment. But all that remains of the past ideals are the restrictive conventions of municipal planning and approvals processes—the residue left around the coffee cup long after its contents have been drained.

The problem of the design review process may lie, in part, in established aesthetic criteria. What is aesthetically appropriate and what is not for streetscapes, front yards, or building facades? What kind of landscaping may be permitted? How do we ensure a nicely uniform street? In the light of the evolutionary processes at work in natural

and urban environments, such questions are not useful or even relevant. Aesthetic criteria, conceived in the absence of environmental and cultural imperatives, and the sensory stimuli that derive from the vitality of a lively neighborhood, have little meaning. Ultimately, though, the goal of much of the design review process, particularly at the municipal level, lies in the need for maintaining control, a process that is almost guaranteed to produce the least desired results for the greatest effort made; in effect, the opposite of what should be.

But whatever the reasons for the inadequacy of the review process, it can certainly be argued that successful, diverse, and livable places often occur not through strict design control, but by a policy of minimal intervention; and that the recipe for homogeneity, sensory deprivation, and lack of environmental or social identity may well come from too much control, not too little. There is some observational evidence that lends weight to this notion of minimal intervention. Most diverse and interesting communities with a strong sense of identity arise out of a combination of natural evolution and the structure imposed by authority, what J. B. Jackson has called the "Political Landscape."[8] They have a complex mix of small-scale commercial, industrial, and residential uses, new and old buildings, small industries, vegetable and flower gardens, houses with new additions, a vibrant street life. Their stamp of identity or sense of place has been permitted to evolve within an established structure of streets and houses, while a minimum but appropriate level of planning control protects it from massive and destructive changes in land use. Their aesthetic appeal stems from their history and the functions they perform, from the sights, smells, crowding, and languages of lived-in multicultural places. An observer of Toronto's places, John Bentley Mayes, describes the Kensington Market as being "no neat, antiseptic theme park or museum. The Saturday morning bustle and shove of shoppers is as tough to elbow your way through as it was generations ago. Every wave of immigration in the past century—Jewish, Portuguese, Italian, Chinese, Vietnamese—has left its mark here, its particular trace, in the jumble

7. Ibid.

8. J. B. Jackson, *Discovering the Vernacular Landscape*. (New Haven: Yale University Press, 1984).

of shops and cafes on Nassau and Augusta and St. Andrews. The rich stench of fish and a hundred kinds of cheese is as dense and exhilarating as ever."[9] None of this would be permitted in the new suburbs being built on the edges of the city.

The same goes for the regenerative power of nonhuman nature. Evidence of this dynamic force can be found in the unbuilt places one finds in abandoned parts of town that are evolving into a richly complex community without the help of the maintenance man. Such places are often much more diverse, and more indicative of the local region, than the ones that have been purposefully created.[10] There are, in fact, persuasive parallels between the inherent forces that shape interesting and diverse human communities and those that shape naturally succeeding landscapes. None of these places have been "designed" in the formalistic tradition, or shaped by design committees. But they often represent the best in livability, emotional investment in home and locality, in diversity, and vitality, and with the aesthetic that is the consequence of such evolutionary processes. They have just those qualities of place that are admired but cannot be replicated by fixed design standards. With this in mind, I would suggest some general principles that might help create a framework for a more effective approach to design review.

AN ECOSYSTEM VIEW

There is a need to focus on the meaning of the term *ecosystem* when we are dealing with urban regions. As I have already suggested, an ecosystem view uses a broad definition of the environment that involves the links and relationships between land, water, and living organisms, and social, cultural, and economic processes (Fig. 13-3). In its practical application to the replanning of the Toronto waterfront, the bioregion has become the planning unit, since the entire system of aquifer recharge areas and rivers, residential and industrial development, and recreation, are all linked to the lake. The disparity between the

political boundaries within which planning decisions are currently made and the continuity of natural processes has been addressed by the Royal Commission on the Future of the Toronto Waterfront. The commission adopted this ecosystem approach as a way of solving previously insoluble problems by looking at them as a whole and in context; by developing links or partnerships between different levels of government, the private sector, and the public; and by finding common goals and objectives that everyone can agree on through a continuing series of round-table discussions.

KNOWING THE PLACE

Knowing the place involves familiarity with the natural and human history of a place—those influences that shaped it and made it what it is. Thus, a place's identity has to do with two fundamental criteria: first, with the natural processes or a region or locality—what nature has put there; second, with social processes—what people have put there. In Central Park, Manhattan's underlying geology is visible as surface granite boulders and emergent formations, which helps explain New York's skyline. Olmsted put the humanized landscape there, and New York citizens have established its patterns of uses and places and made it their own. It's necessary to understand through direct observation, as well as through maps and statistics, what is there and how it works. Jane Jacobs's observations on the social life of cities emphasized the need to understand places for what they are and how they work in real life, rather than relying on theories and predetermined ideas about how they should.[11] To invoke the Scottish planner Patrick Geddes's dictum: before attempting to change a place, one must seek out its essential character on foot in order to understand its patterns of movement, its social dynamics, history, and traditions, its environmental possibilities.[12] Thus the review process should be cognizant of the three-dimensional environments and contexts of design submissions, and should base their critical evaluation on such determinants.

9. John Bentley Mays, Curbing a Passion for Street Life, *Toronto Globe and Mail,* November 4, 1992.

10. M. Hough, "City Form and Natural Process. (London: Routledge, 1984).

11. Jane Jacobs, *The Death and Life of Great American Cities* (New York: Random House, 1961).

12. Philip Boardman, *The Worlds of Patrick Geddes.* (London: Routledge and Kegan Paul, 1978).

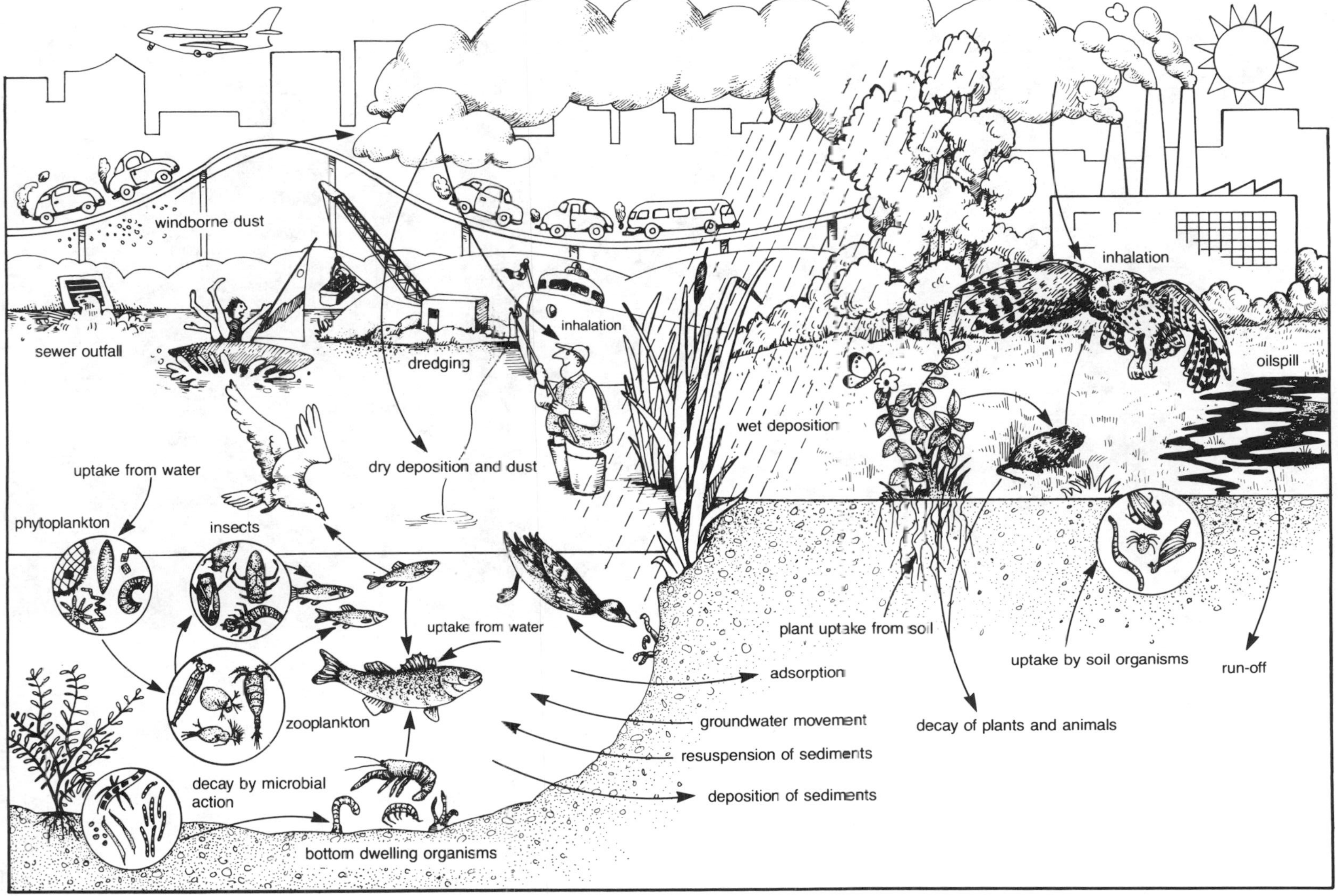
windborne dust
sewer outfall
dredging
inhalation
inhalation
oilspill
wet deposition
dry deposition and dust
uptake from water
phytoplankton
insects
uptake from water
plant uptake from soil
uptake by soil organisms
run-off
adsorption
zooplankton
groundwater movement
decay of plants and animals
resuspension of sediments
decay by microbial action
deposition of sediments
bottom dwelling organisms

Figure 13-3. Ecosystem pathways, Port Industrial Area, Toronto. An ecosystem view in planning links biophysical, cultural, and economic processes. (Figure: Royal Commission on the Future of the Toronto Waterfront.)

Figures 13-4, 13-5, 13-6.
Three faces of Toronto. The
sense of place in these neighborhoods derives from people
creating their own social and
physical environments within
a framework of minimal planning intervention. (Photos:
Michael Hough.)

Figure 13-4. The Kensington
Neighbourhood, famous for its
street market.

Figure 13-5. The Greek
quarter; note the street signs
in two languages.

Figure 13-6. A residential
neighbourhood street party.

DOING AS LITTLE AS POSSIBLE

Much of the worst in new development lies in exercising too much control, not too little. It also lies in the direct translation of land use and density zoning ordinances—a two-dimensional process—into physical plans that never ask the fundamental questions: "what is the vision for this place; what kind of place do we want?"—a case of the tail wagging the dog. Bylaws that prohibit "nonconforming" uses inhibit the evolution of diverse and healthy neighborhoods and life on the street. The destruction of old buildings and industrial artifacts in urban renewal areas destroys connections with the past, and the enrichment that history affords to cities. Doing as little as possible is *not* a laissez-faire principle. It implies, rather, that change can be brought about by giving direction, by capitalizing on the opportunities that site or social trends reveal, or by setting a framework within which people can create their own social and physical environments, and where landscapes can flourish on their own with the minimum required investment in energy and intervention. There is a great temptation to impose solutions on places, to dictate how they should be used, and how they should look. But as William Whyte has shown, the most dynamic and successful public places are usually those where people themselves take charge, where design intervention may be no more than providing an overall structure for activity, such as seats that can be moved around at will[13] (Figs. 13-4, 13-5, 13-6). In effect, the approvals process usually suffers from problems of excessive control

13. William H. Whyte, *The Social Life of Small Urban Places* (Washington, D.C.: The Conservation Foundation, 1980).

that inhibits the creative solutions that become possible when essential and clear-cut environmental, social, and planning guidelines and performance criteria provide an appropriate framework for development. This principle also implies that more is achieved, and quite different solutions are available when traditionally separated disciplines such as engineering, the biological sciences, site planning, and the behavioral and social sciences can be brought together.

In summary, doing as little as possible implies four things: an understanding of social and ecological processes; knowing where and how to intervene democratically to create the conditions where change can occur in its own way; bottom-up planning, where people accept and direct change on their own terms, rather than falling victim to change that only benefits others; and finally, having the collective humility to let natural diversity evolve on its own where it will.

To sum up, the policies and regulations that have traditionally been used to control development in the past will need to be rethought to reflect changing public values and the perceived rights of society to a healthy environment. It will be necessary to adopt a holistic planning view that encompasses bioregional influences and environmental values, a recognition of social and natural processes and the interdependence of decision making. The basis for an effective alternative to current practice may well lie in a deeper understanding of how we make places. When the processes of nature, people, economy, and political action are allowed to become part of an organic and evolutionary—as opposed to a fixed—view of the planning and approvals process, the opportunities for regional identity, and consequently an appropriate aesthetic, are enhanced.

14

Carbuncles, Columns, and Pyramids: Lay and Expert Evaluations of Contextual Design Strategies

Linda N. Groat

University of Michigan, Ann Arbor

PROLOGUE TO THE ISSUES: TWO EXAMPLES

The concept of contextual compatibility has in recent years been the focus of highly contentious debates on the merits of various architectural and urban design projects, particularly those of symbolic importance to the public realm. Consider, for example, two projects that were subjected to intense scrutiny and debate within the last decade: the addition to the National Gallery at Trafalgar Square in London and the addition to the Louvre Museum in Paris.

The former project is particularly notable because it so clearly exemplifies the reactions of many nondesigners to projects generally well-regarded in the professional communities. In this case, the Prince of Wales ignited a major controversy by calling into question the competition-winning scheme for the addition to the National Gallery. Not only did he criticize the scheme itself, calling it a "carbuncle on the edge of a much-loved and elegant friend" (Wales, 1984), but he also attacked the architectural profession for ignoring the sentiments of ordinary people. The public, he argued, should not be "made to feel guilty or ignorant if their natural preference is for more traditional designs, for arches and porches, ornament, and soft materials." Thus, he argued passionately for an addition that would comple-

ment the original Gallery by continuing "the concept of columns and domes."

The latter project, the addition to the Louvre, is significant because it highlights the range and complexity of associations that may underlie people's evaluations of contextual design strategies. Designed by the well-known architect I. M. Pei, the addition to the Louvre takes the form of a glass pyramid structure at the center of the grand Cour Napoleon. On the one hand, opponents of the design argued that it was visually and aesthetically incompatible with the style and tradition of the Louvre. On the other hand, supporters of the scheme maintained that the design was not only "pleasingly insubstantial" (Hoelterhoff, 1985), but also symbolically appropriate; they argued that the design represented an appropriate reference to the Egyptian exploits of Napoleon I, who was responsible for opening parts of the museum. In effect, then, the proponents countered their opponents' demand for *visual continuity* with a justification for *associational relevance*.

These examples raise several important questions central to the debate on contextual compatibility, including: 1) are there indeed major and consistent differences among the various constituencies in such public debates with respect to their preferences for actual contextual design strategies? and 2) regardless of stated design preferences, are there major differences in the manner in which contextual compatibility is *conceptualized?*

The purpose of the research reported here was to investigate a broad range of psychological responses involved in the conceptualization of compatibility, especially as relevant to the issues raised by the two examples above. Surprisingly, despite the high profile of such controversies and the increasingly widespread initiation of design review procedures, relatively little research has been conducted on the topic. To this end, the research reported in this chapter investigates how contextual compatibility is viewed from the perspective the major participants in the design review process: design professionals, design review commissioners, and the lay public.

In this light, the following two segments of this chapter each represent a comparative analysis of the perspectives of two groups of this triad.

1. Visual Continuity, Replication, and Hierarchy: The Differing Perspectives of Architects and the Lay Public. This analysis highlights some of the general aesthetic and perceptual principles underlying lay preferences in contextual design strategies. These principles are analyzed with specific reference to the various contextual design strategies advocated by influential architects and critics.

2. Converging Views of Contextual Compatibility: The Conceptualizations of Review Commissioners and the Lay Public. This analysis highlights both the general similarities between commissioner and lay judgments of compatibility as well as the subtle but important differences in the manner in which compatibility is actually conceptualized.

These issues were investigated through a series of research studies conducted by the author over a period of five years. Briefly, the research entailed extensive interviews (of 1–1½ hours in length) with nearly 100 respondents—73 nonarchitects and 24 design review commissioners. The respondents were asked to comment on a set of infill projects that represented a range of contextual design strategies, simulated through color photographs. In addition, in order to incorporate responses to in situ environments, the interviews with nonarchitects were conducted at three sites included among the color photographs. Thus, each lay respondent was asked to comment on the compatibility of a known environment as

well as on a broad array of photographed environments.

VISUAL CONTINUITY, REPLICATION, AND HIERARCHY: THE DIFFERING PERSPECTIVES OF ARCHITECTS AND THE LAY PUBLIC

In order to investigate differences between architects and lay perspectives on contextual compatibility, this research initially sought to: 1) test empirically the extent to which each of various theoretical perspectives on contextual design in the architectural literature is supported by the evaluations of the lay public; and 2) identify actual contextual design strategies that are most preferred by the lay public.

With respect to the first of these objectives, four major theoretical viewpoints were identified and defined as follows.

1. *Architecture as a Historic Document*. The essence of this position is that architecture embodies the history of a civilization, and therefore serves as a record of the evolution of built form. Although this sentiment echoes the arguments expressed over a hundred years ago by William Morris (Morris, 1966), in recent times this point of view is most firmly associated with the Modernist perspective. Thus, visually disparate infill buildings and additions are justified because they represent "the spirit of the times" or because they represent the ongoing stylistic and technological evolution of contemporary architecture.

2. *The Importance of Visual Continuity*. The essence of this perspective is that visual continuity among ensembles of buildings is one of the most important and valued qualities of the urban streetscape. Although earlier in this century Trystan Edwards argued for the primacy of the streetscape as a civic amenity (Edwards, 1924), this plea went largely unheeded until the hegemony of modernism had been effectively challenged. Typically, proponents of this viewpoint are prepared to endorse some degree of replication, particularly of small-scale detail and ornament, in order to achieve apparent visual continuity (e.g., Brolin, 1980).

3. *Deeper Levels of Significance*. The essence

of this third perspective is that contextual compatibility should involve more than superficial visual continuity among buildings: compatibility should suggest deeper symbolic and cultural relationships. Although this viewpoint has been expressed by a number of authors, Graves and Wolf (1980) offer the Banacerraf house addition as one example of this perspective. According to them, the open, fragmented form of the addition creates a transition between the enclosed, self-contained house and the landscape, such that it encourages the viewer to reinterpret both the house and the landscape.

4. *Freedom for the Creative Designer*. Finally the fourth perspective argues that appropriate contextual design is best achieved by leaving the creative architect unconstrained by guidelines or other legislative mandates. This view is illustrated by Cavaglieri's insistence that "Good design is the result of artistic ability. . . . It is difficult, perhaps impossible to establish guidelines to judge what is suitable or unsuitable in historic surroundings." By implication, if this view were upheld by the study data, one would expect to find few, if any, consensual patterns of preference among the respondents.

The overwhelming conclusion from this study is that, of these four major perspectives identified in the architectural literature, only one—the importance of visual continuity—is validated by the interview responses of the nonarchitects. Despite the fact that proponents of the other three perspectives have maintained that visual harmony and blending constitute merely a superficial link between buildings, visual continuity is nevertheless the primary concern of the vast majority of nonarchitects.

In this light, the second objective—identifying specific contextual design strategies preferred by nonarchitects—is a prerequisite for clarifying how visual continuity might best be achieved. In order to pursue this line of inquiry, a conceptual framework was developed for categorizing and analyzing the constituent components of the design strategies represented in the 25 photographs the respondents were asked to evaluate.[1] This analysis of actual design strategies has led to two

---

1. The specifics of this analytical framework have been discussed in detail in other publications and will not be presented here (Groat, 1983; Groat, 1988).

Figure 14-1. East Cambridge Savings Bank addition, East Cambridge, Mass.; Charles G. Hilgenhurst & Associates. (Photo: Patricia Gill.)

complementary conclusions: 1) Contextual design strategies that are *replicative* of, rather than *contrasting* with, nearby design features are generally preferred; and 2) *Facade design* is relatively more important than either site organization or massing as a device for linking new to old.

These conclusions can be easily illustrated by some of the examples actually used in the study. For instance, with respect to conclusion number 1, buildings such as the addition to the East Cambridge Savings Bank (Fig. 14-1) and the Alumni Center at University of Michigan (Fig. 14-2) are two of the most preferred contextual relationships; both represent highly replicative strategies. In contrast, the library at Mt. Mary College, Wauwatosa, Wisconsin (Fig. 14-3) and Enderis Hall at the University of Wisconsin-Milwaukee (Fig. 14-4) were among the least favored contextual rela-

Figure 14-2. The Alumni Center, University of Michigan, Ann Arbor, Mich.; Hugh Newell Jacobsen. (Photo: John Rahaim.)

Figure 14-3. Library, Mt. Mary College, Wauwatosa, Wis.; Pfaller Herbst & Epstein, Inc. (Photo: Linda Groat.)

Figure 14-4. Enderis Hall, University of Wisconsin-Milwaukee; Plunkett Keymar Reginato. (Photo: Linda Groat.)

Figure 14-5. Maryland National Bank, Annapolis; RTKL Associates, Inc. (Photo: courtesy of RTKL Associates, Inc.)

tionships and were both highly contrasting strategies.

This general pattern of preference for relatively more replicative schemes is, however, significantly affected by the manner in which the replicative effect is achieved. This point is best illustrated by comparing the design strategies for the East Cambridge Savings Bank and the Maryland National Bank (Fig. 14-5). Detailed analyses of these schemes reveal that both schemes demonstrate a similar degree of replication. However, whereas the Maryland bank is relatively more replicative in site organization and massing, the Cambridge bank is relatively more replicative in its facade design and is therefore far preferred over the other.

While the general principles identified above—the importance of replication generally and the relative significance of facade design—

seem to underlie the general pattern of responses, unfortunately they do not fully account for the respondents' evaluation of a few specific buildings in the study, particularly the postmodern designs. For example, both the Portland Building (Fig. 14-6) and a private residence in Boston (Fig. 14-7) were viewed as busy and not especially compatible with their contexts, even though their design strategies clearly demonstrated a concern for the elaboration of detail and facade articulation. As a consequence, in the second phase of the research, the data were reanalyzed through more qualitative procedures. Anecdotal comments from respondents in the study were reviewed in tandem with the apparently anomalous data.

This analysis led to the conclusion that the compositional principle of hierarchical ordering

Figure 14-6. Portland Public Services Building, Portland, Ore.; Michael Graves. (Photo: Frances Downing.)

Figure 14-7. Residence, Boston, Mass.; Graham Gund. (Photo: Steve Rosenthal; courtesy of Graham Gund.)

is an equally important device for achieving contextual compatibility. Moreover, in some instances it is more successful than a simply replicative model in so far as the *underlying* principles of the neighboring older buildings are maintained.

To illustrate this point, the Venturi and Rauch addition to the Allen Memorial Museum at Oberlin College serves as a potent example (Fig. 14-8). Many respondents found the use of the checkerboard pattern of the white and rose stone to be both busy and offensive, despite the architects' intention to create a link with the older museum by using the original materials in a new way. In fact, one respondent repeatedly referred to the addition as "Ralston Purina," a reference to the

checkerboard-patterned packaging of that company's product.

Careful analysis of the facade treatment of the new addition, however, suggests that while the use of the white and rose stone is consistent with the older museum, its actual *application* violates the principles of hierarchical ordering evident in the original building—and most premodern buildings for that matter. Hierarchy in any aesthetic composition, including architecture, can be defined as an ordering principle whereby subsections of the artifact maintain their their own compositional order while also being subsumed within the compositional order of the whole. The art

Figure 14-8. Allen Memorial Art Museum addition, Oberlin College, Oberlin, Ohio; Venturi Rauch and Scott Brown. (Photo: Venturi Rauch and Scott Brown.)

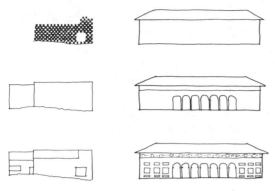

Figure 14-9. Compositional analysis of the Allen Memorial Art museum and addition.

historian and critic Ernest Gombrich (1979) takes this definition further and argues: "[A]ny hierarchical arrangement presupposes two distinct steps, that of *framing* and that of *filling*. The one delimits the field or fields, the other organizes the resultant space" (p. 75).

The presumption is, then, that most premodern facade compositions are largely developed and organized according to this principle of *frame* and *fill*. In other words, major segments (fields) or a facade are defined, these are further subdivided, and each subdivision is "filled" through the articulation of fenestration and ornament. Thus, each subdivision of the facade is ordered both within itself and in relation to the whole. Although this analysis of premodern architectural composition is admittedly simplistic in that it minimizes real variations across the gamut of stylistic movements, it nevertheless presupposes that certain basic principles of composition are maintained regardless of "style," a position consistent with many premodern nineteenth- and early twentieth-century texts (e.g., Robinson, 1908).

Extrapolating from these analyses of composition, it is possible then to compare the hierarchical ordering of the museum and its addition (Fig. 14-9). The right-hand side of the figure represents the compositional hierarchy of the original museum building; the right-hand represents the addition. For the original museum, the first, most visually prominent level of the hierarchy is manifested in the overall massing elements. Next, because there are no obvious secondary massing elements, the second level of visual prominence is articulated by the frieze and arched arcade that effectively subdivide the building into three segments. Fi-

nally, at the last level of hierarchy, the ornament and differentiation of materials serve to elaborate these segments.

In contrast, the Venturi and Rauch addition has inverted the conventional premodern compositional hierarchy of the original museum. Thus, the first, most visually prominent level of hierarchy is manifested in the differentiation of colored stone, a device that in the original museum represents the last, least prominent level of hierarchy. As a consequence, the overall massing of the addition, is relegated to a level of secondary visual importance; the articulation of the building's horizontal and vertical rhythm becomes the least prominent level of hierarchy. In other words, the Venturi and Rauch addition has violated the essential hierarchical principle of frame and fill, which is fundamental to the composition of the original building. And although this scheme may represent one of the more extreme inversions of hierarchical ordering, many contextual design strategies that rely primarily on replication of key features also violate the compositional hierarchy of premodern conventions.

Hierarchical ordering represents, then, a refinement of and complement to the principles of replication. Although replicative design strategies may well be relatively more appropriate than earlier modernist strategies, they may nevertheless fail to establish visual continuity with the local context when the principles of hierarchical composition are substantially violated. Most important, the informed application of hierarchical ordering principles would actually give designers *more* freedom to reinterpret or invent new ways of expressing ornamental detail and facade articulation. In fact, the juxtaposition of various premodernist styles that is so admired in many historic districts is a clear expression of these compositional principles.

CONVERGING VIEWS OF CONTEXTUAL COMPATIBILITY: THE CONCEPTUALIZATIONS OF REVIEW COMMISSIONERS AND THE LAY PUBLIC

With architects and the lay public so often at odds with each other over issues of contextual compatibility, design review commissioners frequently find themselves in a pivotal role, for a number of reasons. First, and most obviously, as decision makers, review board members must weigh the arguments of all sides of a dispute carefully while representing the interests of the entire community. But, just as important in psychological terms, review board members typically share aspects of both the expert architect's perspective and the lay public's orientation. Moreover, this mixed perspective is in many cases accentuated due to the requirement on some boards that design or real estate professionals be appointed to a certain number of seats.

In this light, an important goal of this research study was to elucidate the similarities and differences between review commissioners and the lay public in their perspectives on contextual compatibility. Because the full range of analyses included in the research was quite broad, only four key points will be elaborated here: 1) preferences for contextual design strategies; 2) the conceptualization of contextual compatibility; 3) the relationship between preferred building designs and preferred contextual relationships; and 4) cognitive complexity.

1. Preferences for Contextual Design Strategies. Overall, at an aggregate level, the review commissioners and the lay respondents revealed very similar judgments of the broad range of infill projects they were asked to evaluate. More specifically, in technical terms, the two groups' composite rankings of 25 infill projects were correlated at a statistically significant level. On this basis, it is fair to say that these two groups— 73 nonarchitects and 24 review commissioners— seem to display a common set of judgments about what constitutes an appropriate contextual relationship.

2. The Conceptualization of Contextual Compatibility. Although the lay respondents and review commissioners seem to share similar judgments of compatibility, they nevertheless reveal distinct differences in the manner in which they *conceptualize* the notion of compatibility.

First, the review board members are considerably more likely than the lay respondents to invoke the issue of compatibility in evaluating urban scenes. This important difference emerged in the context of the interview procedure whereby each respondent was asked to select his/her own category system for sorting the urban scenes into distinct groups. Among the review board respondents, 79 percent employed some aspect of the concept "compatibility" as a category system for sorting, whereas only 49 percent of the lay respondents did so. This difference is category usage (which was statistically significant) suggests that contextual compatibility is a relatively more salient concern for the review commissioners' than for the lay respondents, a result that is hardly surprising given the commissioners' far more frequent involvement with the issue.

Second, further analysis of the review board respondents' sorting criteria reveals the tendency for the design-trained members to employ criteria characteristically different from that of their nondesign colleagues. Moreover, among the design-trained group, those that are currently architectural practitioners use sorting criteria that are also somewhat distinct from the design-trained members who currently work in other career roles such as real estate. This suggests, then, that despite the similarity of judgments among these design review members, they nevertheless employ characteristically different criteria by which to make those judgments.

And third, another important difference in the conceptualization of compatibility is revealed in the tendency for the lay respondents to conceive of compatibility in *dichotomous* terms and the design review commissioners to conceive of it in more diverse ways. To be specific, the lay respondents tended to conceptualize the various infill projects as either compatible or not compatible; but while a substantial number of design review members also employed a dichotomous category system, an even greater number conceptualized compatibility as a continuous scale. Additional analyses also reveal that the review commissioners are more willing than laypeople to make extreme judgments (e.g. *highly* compatible or *highly* incompatible). This, of course, is consistent both with the higher degree of ego-involvement on the part of the commissioners (Sherif and Sherif, 1967) and with their greater experience in having to make such judgments.

3. The Relationship between Preferred Building Designs and Preferred Contextual Relationships. Yet another objective of this research was to explore the relationship between the preference judgments people make about individual building designs and their preference judgments of relationships among buildings. In other words, if people like a particular building on its own, are they likely to think it fits in well with its context also?

Various statistical analyses reveal that indeed there is a very high correlation, among both lay respondents and design review commissioners, between their evaluations of individual buildings and their evaluations of those buildings' contextual relationships. In other words, people tend to like buildings that are likely to be viewed as contextually compatible. However, more detailed analyses also reveal that among the design review members, there is a relatively greater tendency to differentiate between the two judgments. Among the three groups of lay respondents (from the three case study sites), such differentiation between the two judgments was found only among a subgroup at one case study site. The conclusion, then, is that lay respondents are much more likely to conflate the two judgments than the review commissioners.

4. Cognitive Complexity. Finally, a fourth difference between the lay and design review respondents is the the tendency among the review commissioners to employ a more complex range of descriptors for analyzing compatibility. More specifically, when asked to identify specific features that either contributed to or detracted from the contextual relationship of particular infill projects, the design review members consistently generated a greater *number* of items. In a similar vein, the review commissioners also tended to employ a *more even distribution* of cited features, whereas the lay respondents tended to support their judgments by referring to a smaller set of feature items.

Moreover, a further differentiation among respondents is the tendency among the design-trained commissioners to refer relatively less frequently to facade design and relatively more frequently to massing features; whereas the nondesign-trained members rely, like the lay respondents, almost exclusively on reference to facade features, the design-trained members are more likely to cite other types of features as well. This suggests, then, that the more "expert" commissioners display any even higher degree of cognitive complexity than their nondesign-trained colleagues.

CONCEPTUALIZATIONS OF COMPATIBILITY AND THE ROLE OF DESIGN REVIEW

The preceding discussion has focused on the differences in perspective—both great and small—among the various constituencies in the design review process. This research has demonstrated that, in general, there are far greater differences between architects and laypeople than between review commissioners and laypeople.

With respect to the comparison of architect and lay evaluations of compatibility, the differences reflect the very same dynamics that were brought to the fore in the Trafalgar Square debate. Not only does this research reveal differences in judgments of compatibility, but also different *bases* for those judgments. Whereas the issue of visual continuity is only one of several possible goals in architects' contextual design strategies, it appears to be the primary goal for most nonarchitects.

This antipathy in value systems is important because it underscores a more general tendency among architects and critics to undervalue certain popular codes in interpreting the environment. But while the values that architectural theorists wish to promote may be important, they will likely be accepted by the lay public *only* if they are used to complement popular environmental values. In the case of the urban streetscape, it may be that the public, on occasion, may apprehend an ensemble of buildings as artifacts that document the evolution of built form or alternatively as devices for reinterpreting cultural and symbolic relationships. However, the evidence of this research would suggest that such interpretations are likely to occur only when they can be understood as *both* supplemental to and complementary to the primary concern for visual continuity.

Second, crucial to the discussion of the differences between design review and lay respondents are the implications that such differences have for the design review process. In this light, the most important observation is that not only do the lay and design review respondents share a similar pattern of judgments, but there is also a very strong consensus among the review board members. This argues well for the validity and feasibility of setting consensual standards and making normative judgments, a position not always accepted in the design professions.

Moreover, while the design review respondents do clearly show a greater sophistication in their conceptualizations of compatibility as well as evidence of greater cognitive complexity typical of "experts," these conceptualizations seem to complement rather than contradict those of the lay respondents. This is particularly evident in the tendency of the review board members to make a clear distinction between judgments of buildings and of contextual relationships; this would suggest that they are not likely to let their particular architectural preferences substantially influence their decisions on committee matters, a necessary and important aspect of their role.

In addition, the preceding observations raise the question of the effect that the committee process may have in encouraging the development of consensus judgments of relationships and minimizing the influence of individual preference for building designs. For example, one review commissioner (an architect), admitted in an informal discussion that his judgments had been substantially modified by his experience on the review commission.

In sum, the exploration of the differences and similarities in the conceptualizations of design professionals, design review board members, and the lay public has revealed many complexities and contradictions that might otherwise not be imagined by the various players in the design review process. By bringing such differences in conceptualizations to light, the participants in design review may be able to promote a more informed debate and thereby insure the kind of design quality that reinforces the shared values of the public realm.

REFERENCES

Brolin, B. 1980. *Architecture in Context.* New York: Van Nostrand Reinhold.

Edwards, A. T. 1924, reprinted 1946. *Good and Bad Manners in Architecture.* London: John Trianti.

Gombrich, E. H. 1979. *The Sense of Order: A Study in the Psychology of Decorative Art.* Ithaca, N.Y.: Cornell University Press.

Graves, M., and G. Wolf. 1980. "Beyond Mere Manners and Cosmetic Compatibility." In *Old and New Architecture: Design Relationship,* ed. J. Biddle, pp. 69–78. Washington D.C.: Preservation Press.

Groat, L. 1983. "Measuring the Fit of New to Old." *Architecture: The AIA Journal.* November: pp. 58–61.

Groat, L. 1988. "Contextual Compatibility in Architecture." In *Environmental Aesthetics: Theory, Research, and Applications,* ed. Jack Nasar, pp. 228–53. Cambridge, England: Cambridge University Press.

Hoelterhoff, M. 1985. "Pei's Pyramid: Revolution in Napoleon's Court." *Wall Street Journal,* April 23.

Morris, W. 1966. "Manifesto of the Society for the Protection of Ancient Buildings." In *William Morris, Artist Writer Socialist,* ed. M. Morris, vol. 1, pp. 109–12. New York: Russell and Russell.

Robinson, J. S. 1908. *Architectural Composition.* New York: D. Van Nostrand Company.

Sherif, M. and Sherif, C. 1967. "Attitude as the Individual's Own Categories." In *Attitude, Ego-Involvement, and Change,* ed. C. Sherif and M. Sherif. New York: John Wiley & Sons.

Wales, HRH The Prince of. 1984. Speech at the Royal Institute of British Architects Gala Evening, Hampton Court.

15
Local Architectural Language and Contextualism

Anthony D. Radford

University of Adelaide, Australia

> *"More and more communities are becoming missionaries of control, often inspired by one form or other of built abuse or by a vision of a future place. Amongst architects, few issues elicit such strong and divergent reactions as those of design control, especially in the realm of aesthetics. Emotions run high, touching on fundamental beliefs we hold as professionals and citizens"* (Rosenthal, 1990).

There is international recognition of the importance of design control and review issues, centered around the intersection of aesthetic preferences, a desire for spatial and temporal continuity, and cultural perceptions of the "meaning" of built form. This chapter speculates on a theoretical framework for design review based on the careful analysis and description of architectural language. It draws from three sources: a discernable movement within the community of those professionally concerned with urban design issues toward accepting a need for greater community control over design of the public realm; a decade of research into formal expression of architectural language as grammars of shapes and designs; and experience of the particular situation in Adelaide, South Australia, a planned city in which local politicians, community groups, and most architects now perceive as having suffered considerably from ineffective design control. The following sections review briefly the concept of architectural language, outline the strategies that have been used by communities to gain control over architectural language, describe the elements of a "shape grammar" as a representation of aspects of architectural language, and describe how a design review process using local architectural language as context might operate.

ARCHITECTURAL LANGUAGE

The definition of "architectural language" adopted here is the presentation of form and formal relationships (both large and small scale) in architectural works and the understandings of people in response to form and formal relationships. The term originated as a metaphor with a spoken or written ("natural") language but (like all metaphors that are adopted in widespread use) has come to be understood as a concept in its own right over and above reference back to natural language. It is an equivalent metaphor to such others as body language, graphic language, and computer language, all of which include elements of form, structure, and meaning. The nuances of expression in body language or graphic language cannot be adequately described in words. Similarly, the meaning in architectural language can only partially be translated to and expressed accurately in words.

The terms of spoken or written language are also used in architectural language. Both the terms *grammar* and *meaning* are applied in architectural contexts, with associated terminology such as *syntax, expression, composition, vocabulary, articulation, coherence,* and so forth. Grammar and syntax are associated with the organization and disposition of form and space and are a focus of study independently of the study of meaning. Many studies of the work of individual architects, urban designers, and landscape architects have emphasized syntactic compositional aspects.

The study of architectural language involves the detailed analysis and expression of architectural elements and the spatial relationships between them. These relationships are usually expressed as "rules," although the role of rules in this context is different from their role within laws and regulations because in any one situation there are usually many rules that can be chosen to be applied. Krier writes of having "a very complex package of rules in mind—the aesthetic operators of architecture," which are "no less complicated than the rules of composition in music" (Krier, 1988, p. 43). Krier does not go on to express these rules, and implies that they are universal rather than drawn from local context. Design theorists such as March, Stiny, and Fleming have explored the expression of architectural language through formal *shape grammars* (see below), which are very specific to a particular corpus or style of design. The *pattern language work* of Alexander (Alexander et al., 1977) begins to map translations between human activities, natural language, and architectural language, although the mappings are very loosely defined. Alexander uses the term "laws" in a similar way, and asks: "what kinds of laws, and at how many different levels, are needed, to create a growing whole in a city or part of a city" (Alexander et al., 1987, p. 19).

A particular architectural language is one with a particular grammar (vocabulary and syntax) and conveys meaning to those who understand the language. It is not possible to carry over the full sense of even a simple word in one natural language (e.g., French) into translation in a second natural language (e.g., English). Similarly, it is not possible to carry over the full sense of one architectural language into another architectural language, for example to conceive of a classical building that conveys the same meaning as a Gothic building.

For design review, the primary point is that the issue of aesthetic design control is not primarily an issue of aesthetics (which can too easily be reduced to an elitist concern to impose personal preferences) but an issue of *language* (which is fundamental to human experience and has meaning, not necessarily in the same way, for the whole population). Development and redevelopment is inevitably controversial because it involves *interfering* with language. An indication of the significance of language to people is provided by letters to the editor about both the appropriateness and the correctness of the use of language in a newspaper. In an architectural language, issues of "correctness" are only likely to arise in special cases such as building restoration.

The secondary point is that if it is not possible to convey the full sense of one language in another language of the same type (e.g., translating from French into English, or by extension from one architectural language into another architectural language), attempts to describe fully an architectural language in a language of another type (e.g., using words) are equally misdirected. Among other implications, this suggests that attempts to formulate design codes expressing architectural language in words will not succeed. They may assist in understanding the language, but they cannot be complete. The question of how architectural languages might be better described in languages of other types is addressed later.

The history of processes of aesthetic design control of development in relation to townscape and urban design can be framed as a sequence of tentative steps toward the expression of architectural language in terms understood by all the players in the development process. The next section will outline such a framing.

STRATEGIES FOR AESTHETIC DESIGN CONTROL

In rough chronology, one might identify the following strategies that have been used to gain community control over architectural language via regulations and procedures. All these approaches, and combinations of them, are currently in use in various places. None directly addresses a description of architectural language.

1. "Hands off," with no overt aesthetic design control. In times and places where there are few building types, few options in materials and construction methods, and a coherent society with shared values and shared interpretations of the "meaning" of building forms, formalized design control is unnecessary. These constraints collectively ensure that buildings tend to belong to a common local architectural language: Italian hill towns, Fijian tribal settlements, Greek island fishing villages are among innumerable examples. When these factors cease to apply and no other constraints are imposed, the resulting development is occasionally serendipitously exciting, but usually merely incoherent.

2. Indirect control through height limits, plot ratios, and so on, originally intended for other purposes. The breakdown in a shared language has led in many communities to controls appropriate for environmental, traffic, and public health control being pressed into service for urban design and aesthetic control. This is particularly the case in existing residential areas, where the preservation of existing block sizes as minimum site areas for dwellings has served to make replacement of existing housing stock (valued because of its consistent local architectural language) economically unattractive. Although having the merit of easy enforceability, such regulations drive redevelopment at higher densities to a neighboring area without such controls.

3. Urban design guidelines, emphasizing the description of acceptable forms of new building design. These specify the character and style of proposed developments, expressed as built form characteristics that "approved" buildings should display. A typical and quite good example, from Northern Ireland, is:

> The design guide sets out basic concepts which should be respected and employed, and indicates architectural styles and elevational features which are considered to be appropriate. Buildings of a design or possessing features which are significantly at variance with the advice given in the design guide are unlikely to be given planning permission (Department of the Environment for Northern Ireland, no date).

Although they begin to address issues of architectural language and can be useful if treated seriously by developers, guidelines produced by development control authorities tend to be written in general terms as an elementary text book on urban design. They also tend to take the form of a "wish list" of isolated features rather than providing a coherent description of, or constraints on, architectural language. They have engendered a negative reaction from many architects who believe that their professional expertise places them above the need to look at such things.

The most successful applications of design guidelines appear to have been in new developments rather than existing urban areas. They have formed a basis for many housing and shopping developments in the United States (e.g., Boles, 1989), including such celebrated examples as Seaside (Mohney and Easterling, 1991; Dixon, 1989; Delafons, 1990). The City of Gardens project in Pasadena, California (Wall, 1990), is particularly interesting in that it involved the development of new planning ordinances that included a requirement for following and demonstrating a particular process in the development of building form. The concentration on process rather than characteristics is typical of the writing and research on shape grammars within the architectural language paradigm (see below). The interest in design guidelines among design and planning professionals is a very significant indicator of changing attitudes.

4. "Expert" panels, emphasizing the existence of "informed opinion" that is able to make judgments on the positive and negative townscape effects of proposed developments. The degree to which the work of expert panels is directly related to architectural language varies. Where the panel's role is to advise on the application of preexisting design guidelines, they have a description (however weakly expressed) of architectural language characteristics with which to work. Where the panel's role is not so constrained, there may be no expressed context of architectural language to guide their work. In a review of methods used in the United States to control the design of buildings, Delafons observes:

> "The review process works best where there are Design Guidelines to which both the developer or architect and the Review body can refer. But this is not always the case. In some cities, major projects, or all schemes in a designated area, have to be referred to the Review Board or Architectural Commission with no prior knowledge of what that body is looking for. The results of this process are generally unpredictable, arbitrary, incoherent, in-

consistent, and unsatisfactory for all concerned" (Delafons, 1990, p. 66).

The "expertise" of an "expert panel" is not usually seen to lie in the professional ability of panel members to understand and work with representations of architectural language. Commonly, membership is made up of expert designers rather than expert interpreters. While design and interpretation are linked and much of the expretise common, the need for the deliberations of a panel to be transparent and decisions consistent demands a theoretical foundation that can be understood by members, applicants, and the community.

Expert panels for every project are a major undertaking. If they are not asked to consider every project, the judgment of which projects should be referred to the panel itself requires a theoretical foundation.

5. Protection of the existing townscape through the extensive identification and protection of "contributory buildings" in that townscape. Dissatisfaction with the effect on townscape of recent development, and a lack of confidence in the effectiveness of urban design guidelines as an instrument in achieving better results, contributes to a desire to give what exists and is perceived to be of value direct rather than indirect protection. This approach discourages the degradation of existing townscape by listing and protecting individual buildings (and sometimes whole precincts) that are considered significant in establishing the character of the place; for example:

> Development in areas of designated townscape character shall conserve the contributory items which comprise the townscape. Contributory items shall be retained according to the street location to the depth specified (City of Adelaide Plan Review Townscape Proposal, 1991).

Contributory buildings tend to get confused in the public mind with local heritage buildings (also called listed buildings or register buildings), with an assumption that the protection of individual buildings of individual heritage value will protect the urban design quality of the whole. In terms of architectural language, identifying and protecting buildings that are considered to contribute to townscape allows the continuance of an existing architectural language. The criteria of choice is

often controversial: is it that the relevant building be simply old, or one of many similar buildings in the neighborhood, or of high design quality?

These various approaches to aesthetic design control do not address the primary issue of architectural languages as one of the many language types that play a central role in human experience. To do so, one needs to be able to better understand and describe architectural languages. The next section addresses this issue.

ARCHITECTURAL LANGUAGE AND GRAMMARS OF SHAPES AND DESIGNS

The most extensive body of work so far on representing architectural languages has concerned itself in representing specific architectural and other spatial grammars. Following the argument above that architectural languages cannot be adequately described using words, I shall use a closer translation into a graphic language and adopt the *shape grammar* formalism for describing a grammar for houses in my own residential area of Adelaide, South Australia.

Shape grammars are concerned with the description of form via a grammar—analogous to a grammar in natural (human) languages—that expresses the way a design can be derived through the application of rules that operate on parts of the design. A good introduction to the field is provided by March and Stiny (1985) and a formal description by Stiny (1981). For this section, the essential concepts are those of shape rules, derivations, and families of designs.

1. Shape rules take the form "Shape A becomes Shape B," such that if shape A is present in a design it can be (but usually does not have to be) replaced by shape B. A shape can be any physical part of a design. These shape rules can express basic compositional massing or minor decorative details. An illustrative set of shape rules is shown in Figure 15-1 for a grammar describing the composition of an Adelaide suburban house typical of those built around the turn of the century. This set is incomplete, but shows the nature of the formalism and how the shape rules can be interpreted in the generation of many different designs. Rule 1 states that the starting point for placing an Adelaide four-roomed house on a suburban lot is

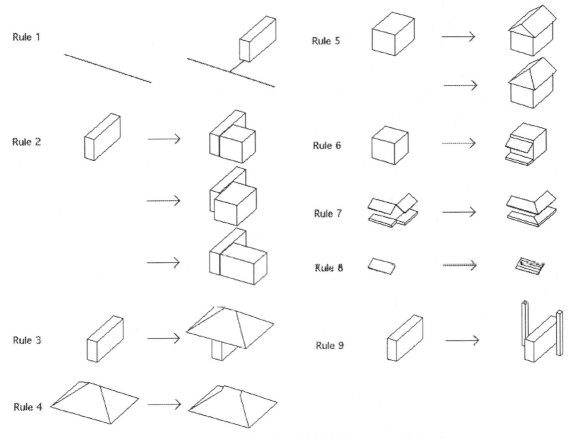

Figure 15-1. Illustrative rules for the composition of an Adelaide four-room suburban house.

to locate an entrance door and hallway at some setback from the street frontage. Rule 2 states that if a hallway exists in the design, then square or oblong rooms can be placed beside the hall. This rule must be applied four times, each time in one of three ways, and controls the basic massing of the house. Rules 3, 4, and 5 provide for a pitched roof to be located over this mass. Rule 6 states that any outside wall of a room may have a verandah added to the outside, rule 7 that if there are verandahs on two adjoining walls then they should join, and rule 8 that this verandah roof may be curved ("bullnosed") instead of straight. Finally, rule 9 states that a chimney should rise on the line of the dividing wall between the rooms on each side of the hallway.

2. A design can be said to be *derived* by the sequential application of shape rules. Thus an Adelaide four-roomed house can be derived by applying in turn the rules described and a derivation sequence showing the generation of one such house is illustrated in Figure 15-2. Here some of the alter-

natives for the massing of the bulk and wings of the house are shown, with a single derivation line elaborating one of these compositions. Choosing between alternative rules results in different derivations from an earlier state of the design.

3. If all possible rules were applied in all possible ways the result would be a *set or family* of associated but different designs. A large number of designs are possible using the rules of even the simple grammar illustrated in Figure 15-1, and many of these are evident in houses in the inner suburbs of Adelaide. In Figure 15-3 some of the designs generated from the grammar are arranged as a street.

This grammar encompass the interior as well as exterior of the structure, reflecting a relationship between the facade and the body of the building. The expression of this relationship provides a basis for considering other forms of internal planning that will result in comparable external form. One can also speculate on deriving a grammar for a residential area in which the starting point

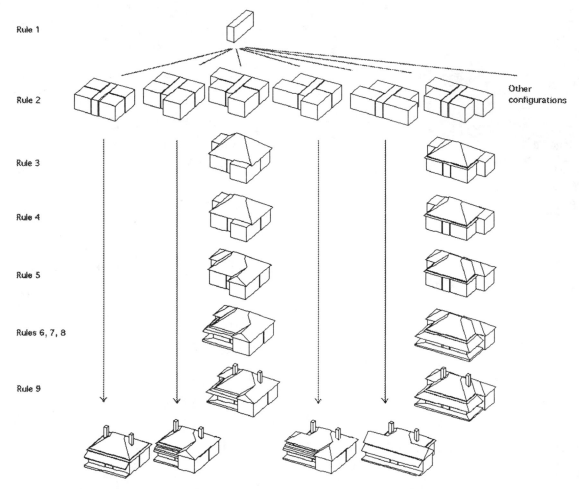

Figure 15-2. The derivation of some house designs using the rules in Figure 15-1. Two derivations are shown with intermediate stages. The configurations of rooms which result from the application of Rule 2 can each result in many different house designs, although only one is shown here.

is not the central corridor of a house, as here, but the street. A grammar can also encompass materials as well as shape, a significant aspect of local architectural language in many areas.

Although these rules can be used directly in the design of "reproduction" traditional houses, their more interesting and extensive role is as a basis for dialogue in the discussion of how such rules can be extended and modified in the creation of new designs, both for extensions to existing buildings and for new buildings. Figure 15-3 shows a "block" outline of a building proposal where a corner site, the garden of an original house, has been subdivided. The rules provide a basis for discussing appropriate forms for this new building, which may not necessarily follow the rules but should be shown to relate to them.

A much more extensive example where concepts of grammars have been applied to urban areas is provided by *A Pattern Book for Shadyside* (Flemming, 1985). This includes a grammar for generating house designs in the Queen Anne style typical of the Shadyside neighborhood of Pittsburgh, Pennsylvania. The work describes a sequence of compositional steps that, if followed, ensure the production of a house design that matches the style of those houses already in the area. This grammar is complete enough for designs to be generated within a computer program, the human designer choosing which shape rules are to be applied or rejected in the particular design (Woodbury, 1990). Other well-known examples of shape grammars include those that generate designs within the style of certain Palladian villas (Stiny and Mitchell,

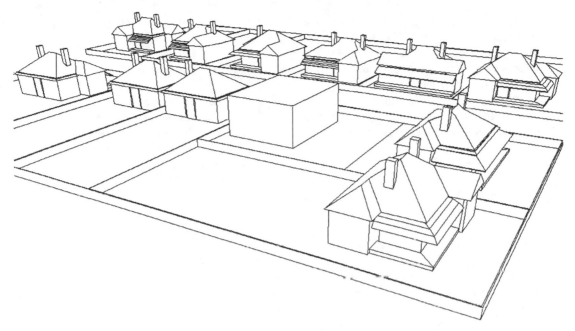

Figure 15-3. Subdivision of a suburban block. The rules of the grammar provide a basis for discourse about the detailed form of a new house development in the location of the rectangular block.

1978), Frank Lloyd Wright's Prairie Houses (Koning and Eisenberg, 1981), and Moghul gardens (Stiny and Mitchell, 1980).

The representation of aspects of an architectural language in a shape grammar is itself a translation to another type of language. Like all translations, this involves interpretation. The grammar for an Adelaide house described above is my interpretation at the end of the twentieth century of expressions in a language in common use at the beginning of the century. There is nothing intrinsically "right" or "wrong" about this interpretation, and it will in any case be subject to interpretation by others. In this respect the rules of grammar are similar to the rules of law. Snodgrass (1991) cites Gadamer on judicial judgments. These demonstrate that rules in law need to be interpreted and reinterpreted in accordance with each particular context and conditions. Law is only fully understood when it comes to be applied, and application is inseparably connected with interpretation and judgment. The same situation will apply here; although a grammar is expressed, there will inevitably be variation in the interpretation of that grammar. Its value is as a basis for dialogue and description that can assist in taking architectural language from the realm of personal opinion to the realm of community opinion.

A grammatical description needed as a context for design review would rarely need the degree of completeness demonstrated in most of the shape grammar literature, but would be similarly process- rather than product-based. Its possible role in the definition of context-dependent architectural language descriptions is described below.

DESIGN REVIEW IN THE CONTEXT OF ARCHITECTURAL LANGUAGE

The approach will be described here in the form of an operational hypothesis based on certain assumptions. The postulated assumptions are:

1. The relevant issue is entirely the design and protection of the public space. What happens "in private," out of sight, is irrelevant. (This assumption is itself contentious; it invites architectural criticism of "facadism," but here it is postulated that it is up to individual designers to establish the relationship between facade and the body of the building. The assumption may also be simplistic in not giving enough significance to the relationship between what a building is used for and how it is perceived.)

172   Anthony D. Radford

In this view, what is most important to the community is the design of the street, with the buildings as secondary, and not vice versa.

2. The most successful way to guide urban design control is one in which the community can feel it "owns" the result, with most members of the community believing that they have had the chance to be involved, have a stake in the success of the result, and in which some do not feel personally disadvantaged while others have escaped disadvantage or have gained.

3. It is possible to characterize key aspects of a local architectural language as a "grammar" of design, represented as a process rather than as a catalog of features. Such descriptions of architectural language could be tightly bound, determining in fine detail the form of any development within the language, or loosely bound, allowing wide variety of forms within guiding parameters. They would be developed by professionals with extensive consultation with the local community, independently of any development proposals. The area of "meaning" and "symbolism" in relation to architectural language is very much still a subject of research; however, I believe that working with our limited existing knowledge will result in more successful results than previous approaches.

4. Design skill and ability can be manifested within any such grammar, and designs that fit within the given grammar should be automatically acceptable.

5. There are no negative connotations of "reproduction" in this context. A building may be worth preserving for historical reasons (it was occupied by a famous person; it was the location of some significant event; it represents a significant construction form or place in architectural history; it is part of a significant historic precinct of old buildings) but not prima facie for urban design reasons *if* the proposed replacement is as good or better in urban design terms. (This assumption is also contentious. There is a view that age itself is important, and that the replacement of an "old" building by a reproduction that is apparently identical when seen from the outside is not a satisfactory outcome.)

6. Grammar formulation and interpretation will change with time, and any grammar description will require periodic revisions to reflect community values.

7. There should always be a "way out," a way of building that represents a new vision or approach if it is of high enough quality even if it requires a special extension to the grammar.

8. There should be no disadvantage in owning a contributory building. The redevelopment of other buildings in the precinct should reach the same standard as redevelopment of contributory buildings; in the long run, *all* buildings should be contributory buildings.

As hypothesized here, the emphasis is on community "ownership" of such design characterizations, coupled with a clarity of expression that permits self-certification by designers and an "open end" that allows, through a design review panel, individual developments beyond the normal boundaries of the characterization providing it is of high quality. The local context would be important. In some precincts it might be appropriate that the grammar be defined very closely, while in others a much more open characterization would be called for. In principle, the model can apply to both existing and new developments. It is not concerned exclusively with the protection of precincts considered of present urban design value, but extends to all areas. It is the community's interpretation of the grammar that matters, not any intrinsic grammar for the situation. The characterization of the grammar will change over time, as will the degree of freedom in its interpretation that is allowed.

This approach does represent a form of mandatory guidelines, in the sense that developers would be expected to follow them, either as they are constituted at the time or as an extension to them via the design review panel. In his review of aesthetic control in the U.S., Delafons comments: " 'mandatory guidelines' . . . expresses what I deduce to be the essence of some of the most successful city planning regimes in America and, in terms of aesthetic control, it may point a way forward for the UK" (Delafons, 1990, p. 37).

This approach could be implemented by a process of self-categorization of the relationship between a design and the language and self-certification of designs within the language. The following outline is not a complete description of such a process, but merely some possibilities that may be exhibited in such a description.

1. Design clearly *within* the grammar would require self-certification by those authorized to do so. Presumably under this model designers could lose their authorization, based on their work. Designs by others would be reviewed with respect to the language. (There is clearly a question raised here about the relation between a designer "authorized" in these narrow terms and an "architect.")
2. Design possibly *outside* the grammar would require submission to an expert panel. There would be an expectation of the highest quality if a design is outside a presently constituted local language, but it would not be automatically rejected. "Highest quality" would be assessed by peer review and by reference to the designer's previous work. Allowing such development is a necessary part of allowing development and change in the interpretation and expression of architectural language, in the same way as natural (written and spoken) languages develop and change. In reviewing these cases, design review panels would consider both the particular instance and any resulting suggestion for modifying the local language description in a general way.
3. Redevelopment of "contributory buildings" would perhaps always require submission to the expert panel, but would not be a priori rejected because it is a "contributory item."
4. Redevelopment of heritage buildings would not, in general, be allowed. These are by definition under this scheme buildings that are significant *because* they are original, and no reproduction or new building, however good, would replace that quality. If they are significant for the community, it seems reasonable that the community should contribute toward any cost for their preservation.

CONCLUSION

Any proposal for design review and control is controversial. It is linked to questions of community power versus private power (rights) and the status of designers (particularly professional ar-

chitects) as agents for society rather than acting solely as agents furthering the interests of individual developers. The proposal espoused here for a major role for local architectural language and grammar is intended to provide the necessary basis for dialogue between the players in the development process in a way that allows a common public base of criteria but will not preclude the "brilliant alternative," the unanticipated design. I have argued that these issues are not peripheral ones of personal aesthetic preference, but fundamental ones of language and community understanding of language.

ACKNOWLEDGMENTS

I thank David Week for many discussions on architectural language and for the example of his built work. I also thank Stephen Loo for reviewing the first draft of this chapter. Responsibility for interpreting their work and comments is, of course, my own.

REFERENCES

Alexander, C., S. Ishikawa, and M. Silverstein. 1977. *A Pattern Language: Towns, Buildings, Construction*. New York and Oxford: Oxford University Press.

Alexander, C., H. Neis, A. Anninou, and I. King. 1987. *A New Theory of Urban Design*. New York and Oxford: Oxford University Press.

City of Adelaide. 1991. *Plan Review Townscape Proposal*. Adelaide: Corporation of the City of Adelaide.

City of Adelaide. 1988. *Urban Design Guidelines*. Adelaide: Corporation of the City of Adelaide.

Flemming, U. 1985. *A Pattern Book for Shadyside*. Pittsburgh: Department of Architecture, Carnegie-Mellon University.

Delafons, J. 1990. *Aesthetic Control: A Report on Methods Used in the USA to Control the Design of Buildings*. Berkeley: Institute of Urban and Regional Development, University of California.

Department of Environment and Planning. 1990. *2020 Vision: Issues for Adelaide*. Adelaide: South Australian Government Department of Environment and Planning.

Department of the Environment for Northern Ireland.

No date. *Antrim Coast and Glens: Area of Outstanding Natural Beauty Design Guide*.

Dixon, J. M. 1989. Seaside Ascetic. *Progressive Architecture* 8:59–67.

Koning, H., and J. Eisenberg. 1981. "The Language of the Prairie: Frank Lloyd Wright's Prairie Houses." *Environment and Planning B* 8:295.

Krier, R. 1988. *Architectural Composition*. New York: Rizzoli.

March, L., and G. Stiny. 1985. "Spatial Systems in Architecture and Design: Some History and Logic." *Environment and Planning B*, 12:31–53.

Mohney, D., and K. Easterling. 1991. *Seaside: Making a Town in America*. New York: Princeton Architectural Press.

Rosenthal, A. 1990. "From the Editor." *Architecture California*. 12(1):2.

Schön, D. A. 1983. *The Reflective Practitioner: How Professionals Think in Action*. New York: Basic Books.

Snodgrass, A. 1991. "Hermeneutics and the Application of Design Rules." *Gadamer: Action and Reason, a Two-Day Conference on the Application of the Hermeneutic Philosophy of Hans-Georg Gadamer within the Human Sciences*, pp. 1–11. Sydney: University of Sydney Department of Architecture.

Stiny, G. 1980. "Introduction to Shape and Shape Grammars." *Environment and Planning B*. 7:343–51.

Stiny, G., and W. J. Mitchell. 1978. "The Palladian Grammar" *Environment and Planning B*, 5:5–18.

Stiny, G. and W. J. Mitchell. 1980. "The Grammar of Paradise: On the Generation of Moghul Gardens." *Environment and Planning B*, 7:209–26.

Wall, P. 1990. "A City of Gardens: The Challenges of Implementation." *Architecture California*. 12(1):45–50.

Woodbury, R. F. 1990. " 'Realities' of Design." In *Reality and Virtual Reality*, ed G. Goldman and M. S. Zdepski. Newark: Association for Computer-Aided Design in Architecture, New Jersey Institute of Technology.

16
Disciplinary Society and the Myth of Aesthetic Justice

Patrick J. Pouler

Architect, Santa Barbara, California

ARCHITECTURE AND THE POLITICS OF SPACE

Architectural design review is a social practice and as such cannot avoid being part of a complex network of power structures and relationships. The fact that it impacts upon the production of architecture and the built environment clearly indicates the political implications of aesthetic control. Space is neither innocent nor neutral: it is an instrument of the political. More than a simple container, architecture is a place that shapes beings; it has a performative impact on whoever inhabits it: it works on its occupants. At the micro level; space prohibits, decides what may occur, lays down the law, implies a certain order, commands and locates bodies. At a societal scale, space incorporates social action. Control over space is thus a fundamental and all-persuasive source of power. Buildings formalize the various relations and guarantee the performance demanded by authority. Power is structured by architecture and architecture celebrates and monumentalizes the structural networks of power.

Since space is essentially a political domain, the manipulation of space is an important requirement in securing and perpetuating existing social hierarchies. As Henri Lefebvre has articulated in *The Production of Space*, "Ideological and political hegemony in any society depends upon the ability to control the material context of personal and social experience" (Lefebvre, [1974], 1991, p. 227). Thus, space can ultimately be conceived as a social morphology, a system of containers of political power: institutions are materialized in the form of government centers and capital hills.

The critique that follows is an attempt to situate design review within this larger domain of a social morphology. One must analyze institutions from the standpoint of power relations that are often rooted in the social nexus. Consequently, my analysis operates on several different, although intimately connected levels, in addition to that of the formal. These can be identified as the psychological, the political, and the economic. Any meaningful critique of the contemporary institution of aesthetic review boards is difficult without confronting and deciphering such diverse contexts. In looking at urban morphology as part of the dynamic calculus of power, one must often stray from the dominant and pristine paths of a naive formalism and traverse some of the messy byways of a committed interpretative critique. I believe that only in this way can one begin the deconstructive enterprise of exposing and undermining the ideological web of relations between power and architecture.

This interpretive exercise is diagnostic in approach rather than prescriptive. The methodology I have adopted structures the argument in terms of the antagonism of strategies whereby architectural design review is institutionalized within the matrix of contemporary society. It is organized in two parts. The initial section of this chapter attempts to articulate and examine the social objectives of architectural review with a focus upon the desperate desire to revive a myth of community within the framework of a radically discontinuous culture. The second part critiques the ideological mechanisms that the design review apparatus utilizes in order to legitimate and perpetuate its practices. Here, the argument considers the authoritative strategies employed, in the name of justice and tradition, that serve the psychological need to mask repressive social conditions. Throughout the text, specific examples of the practice and theory of architectural design review are cited as a means to facilitate a critical diagnosis of the ideology of aesthetic control. These, for the most part, come from the city of Santa Barbara, in Southern California, a city with a severely self-conscious image and a long and influential tradition of design review.

THE MYTH OF COMMUNITY: THE OBJECTIVES OF ARCHITECTURAL REVIEW

What has been lost, and what architecture mourns for, is the community. Contemporary towns and cities are seldom like the places where people lived and worked even a generation ago. Our culture is no longer grounded; many of the conditions necessary to establish and nurture a community do not exist. This is evident not only in the decay and erosion of the infrastructure, housing stocks, public spaces, and buildings that once provided for communal integration, but is also apparent in an individual and collective alienation.

We simply no longer live in a continuous society. Long-enduring conceptions such as time and space have been fractured across the globe. Temporal horizons have shortened to the point where it seems that the present is all there is. The pace and scope of change, the extreme dynamism and instability of institutions as well as of values and beliefs is the stark reality of the present. The industrialization of war has assured the future of arms manufacturers, with their monopoly of the means of violence, as the dominant agent within the world market. Increasingly, inequalities between the rich and the poor, the educated and the illiterate, the privileged and the disempowered, represent the success of the logic of late capitalism, a success perpetuated and expanded through the technologies of communication: the global impact of the word. Finally, unprecedented ecological dangers continually lurk on the horizon while we willfully ignore those directly confronting us.

In the domestic realm, the traditional extended family is virtually an anachronism. Indeed, notions such as family and neighborhood or the church have not maintained any sense of the authority they once carried. What has replaced these unifying elements of the social fabric is division, exclusion, segregation, and separation. The modern democratized self differs from participants in traditional culture in that a social identity is missing: one can assume any role or take any point of view. Lost is the membership in social groups in which the individual identifies herself or himself and is likewise identified by others.

Traditional monumental space at one time offered each member of the community a sense of that membership. Today's monuments, however, have lost value and intelligibility due to their commodity character: old monuments are overtaken by new signs with even higher exchange values. These icons of contemporary monumentality constitute the collective mirror of our culture; however, the built-in obsolescence of postmodern monuments only generates fractured and fragmented reflections of an imagined community. The faceted surfaces of the carnival mirror simply multiply this representation in an endless, ever-changing, and ultimately incoherent fashion.

As the microcosm of community, the failure of the traditional generators of collective identity trumpets the failure of any sense of meaningful community. This has left a psychological vacuum that desperately demands to be filled with something immutable. This something assumes the *myth of community* and has become the objective of many social organizations including the architectural review establishment.

As a product of the context of postmodern, disciplinary society, contemporary architects and planners have often taken on the ideological responsibility of re-forming a community through its architecture. This is a potentially dangerous endeavor, for the reification of culture can only result in an *illusion* of community. The myth of community differs from an authentic community in the way in which exhausted ideals are artificially resurrected in order to elicit unity from the chaos of a society desperate for security and stability. Here, the invocation of myth supersedes concrete and productive social activity: the image attempts to overcome the reality. In this sense, architecture is the perfect medium by which to perpetuate the dominant power structures. Facades act as masks that conceal the discontinuous and heterogeneous elements of society, the deformed and the mal-formed. However, painting on buildings, as Lefebvre has noted, simply "dissolves conflicts into a general transparency, into a one dimensional present" (Lefebvre, [1974], 1991, p. 145). The volatile reality most certainly remains; ready to explode as we witnessed in Los Angeles in the spring of 1992.

In the following sections I will attempt to outline and critique what I consider some of the basic theoretical objectives of design review, all of which to varying degrees aims at that elusive target, the phenomena of community in the postmodern context.

Protecting and Preserving the Illusion

The Santa Barbara Ordinance on architectural design review is a document that mirrors the image that the city has carefully formulated for itself. This image, however, is maintained by an objective that is essentially negative. The focus here is not upon inspiring creative change but in avoiding loss. The reflection is ultimately that of a fear of the passage of time. Consequently, what often is evoked is a new pathos of preservation: the laws and guidelines are meant to "protect and preserve" and "prevent poor quality" of design. The architecture is to "maintain the character" of the existing, and "ensure compatibility" with the neighborhood. This fundamental decree to protect and preserve aims at maintaining the existing formal, political, and economic organization of the city. Thus, the architecture perpetuates the status quo, its power structures and social morphology: everything compatible and in its place. Following a pragmatic (if perhaps contradictory) logic, our

cities now struggle to control the economic and political modes of operation that have determined the urban context since at least the industrial revolution. This erosion in the faith of capitalism as a genuine philosophy of community may seldom be made outright, nor with revolutionary zeal, but it certainly reflects one of its basic internal contradictions. Unfortunately, the method in which this crisis is addressed is derived from the existing institutions of our society. Rather than confronting our complex and often paradoxical condition, we merely construct barriers intent upon protecting anything that still suggests an imagined old order, or simply establish controls that prevent the "poor" design of the new. The speculators still enjoy outrageous short-term profits with the same myopic investment programs and strategies that provide pathetically little for the community. What happens behind the facades of power depends little upon style and all upon economics.

Review boards often assume the task of controlling this monster of speculation, or at least masking its effects with an acceptable illusion. The assumption that the owner or builder will inherently construct something ephemeral, cheap, or ugly unless forced to do otherwise by law reflects the enormous suspicion that exists within our culture. The controls imposed upon architectural form and surface attempt to protect the face of our cities from the juggernaut of greed and speculation. From a psychological perspective we fear the self-destruction of our towns and cities but cannot identify the disruptive force because we are identical with it. So we pretend so as to avoid this realization and in the process surround ourselves with phantasms of the familiar, of another time and place; within the secure framework of a stage-set, self-conscious environment. Although some of the resulting places are executed in a fashion more authentic than even the original sources, on closer investigation, they not only reveal a mute and dumb iconography, but also mononomadic inhabitants. The triumph of surface over depth; of the superficial over the difficult and substantial; of the easily consumed and charming culturescape over an architecture of a differential counterspace, is a resounding victory for the dominant political economy and a loss to the individual and community. Often, all that remains of any sense of a working, thriving, communing society is the memory that comprises the myth of community: a pleasing illusion, a day dream to a pre-industrial utopian existence: the nostalgia for lost common values.

Without a community based on *praxis;* that is; action and social interaction, any architectural production simply contributes to the maintenance of a monolithic yet fragmented public domain. The architecture may easily provide the appropriate facade for a chimerical community but certainly cannot alone deliver the substance.

Morphological Delusions: Harmony as Community

Together with the erosion of the traditional forces that established and maintained a sense of community—that is, the ethical—we are today increasingly experiencing the impact of the aesthetic within the public realm. This combination of politics and aesthetics is, of course, not a unique occurrence in history; however, its elevation above ethics is responsible for a number of dubious episodes. Before looking at the effects of the aestheticization of politics let us first consider the concept of harmony within the domain of the city. For, perhaps, the ideal of "harmony" is invoked more forcefully than any other objective in design review texts. The following citation from a Santa Barbara ordinance captures something of the significance attached to the concept: there "shall be harmony of material, color, and composition . . . there shall be a harmonious relationship with existing and proposed developments, allowing for similarity of style if warranted but avoiding excessive variety and monotonous repetition" (Santa Barbara County, 1974). How are we to define this term and what does it mean to use it in the context we do?

A genealogy of the concept of harmony within Western philosophy can be traced back to Pythagoras and his followers. It is believed that the Pythagoreans were the first to advance the study of mathematics. For them, all things were numbers; that is, everything in the universe was held to be constituted by various harmonious proportions. Harmony, however, was a "blend or composition of contraries" (Aristotle, *De Anima*). The contraries were the principles of things, and the reconciliation of opposites constituted the theory of har-

mony. This was neither an aesthetic nor epistemological concept in antiquity. Not only were all things numbers, but all numbers were virtues—not mere quantities, they had qualities as well. Consequently, to the ancients mathematical inquiry was an active, ethical pursuit designed to purify the soul of man.

This view of harmony as a composition of contraries was maintained in essential form by Plato and Aristotle, was dominant during Christian scholasticism, and was revived during the Italian Renaissance by Cusanus, Ficino, and others. It was Kantian aesthetics that first introduced a *harmonistic* interpretation to the concept of harmony. Immanual Kant's severe formalism seeks almost violently to arrange and compose every detail of a work of art or architecture. Lost is the dynamic equilibrium that recognizes the tensions that are essential to a harmonious product. Harmony thus assumed a political strategy, in the name of classicism, to smooth over discontinuities, to homogenize, and to normalize. As an ideological imposition upon culture, the intent to formalize societal relations, to impose harmony from the outside, is a sometimes violent and unilateral action against form, and consequently, against the productive dynamic of community.

This desire to synthesize a harmonious man-made environment is of course an ancient story of the micro-macro dialectic that surfaces throughout the history of architectural theory. What is different, however, in its present configuration, is an unbalanced faith in the formal over the political. What has become important is not the community as a political entity but a sign that proclaims harmony: an architectural billboard that persuades us to buy into the community-thing. The harmonistic objective is to create a material illusion of community. The passive yet alluring sign substitutes for creative action. It functions to legitimate culture as the guarantee of mass values. The architecture, its style and order fills the vacuum resulting from the disappearance of a legitimate political community. Style and aesthetics replaces politics and ethics. Style, Theodor Adorno writes, "represents a promise in every work of art" (Adorno, [1944], 1972, p. 130). It relies upon its similarity with other works and as such assumes a surrogate identity. When imitation becomes absolute, however, as in reconstructions and design board formulas, the architecture ceases to be anything but style—

a medium too easily manipulated to the ends of the social hierarchy.

It is apparent that our contemporary conception of harmony is seriously impoverished and no longer communicates any meaningful design criteria. Likewise, objectives such as compatibility and continuity are simply ideological forms of the words *conformity* and *restraint* and are deeply entangled within the networks of disciplinary society. If indeed, architecture has any voice, perhaps we should look to an alternative conception of harmony. Rather than equalizing and disempowering all that is different, we could embrace its ancient meaning and intention. As Adorno has observed, there is no harmony without dissonance: dissonance is not a foreign element, but is in fact, the truth about harmony (Adorno, [1970], 1984, p. 160). Harmonistic logic is ultimately incoherent if the objective remains that of smoothing over those discontinuous and ambiguous architectural fragments of surprise and delight. In addition to precluding the creation of new dissident forms our towns and cities are rapidly losing those existing voices of architectural discord that often gave significance to the environment.

The Myth of Community as *Gesamptkunstwerke*

Increasingly, the ideals of harmony invite ideological abuse. Indeed, it has been suggested that the aesthetic is the very paradigm of the ideological. Ever since the Enlightenment, aesthetic questions have occupied a crucial place in the philosophical hierarchy. In the epistemological domain, aesthetics emerges as a kind of prothesis to reason: art can reveal a truth inaccessible to purely rational thought. For Kant, this pseudo-knowledge of the third critique takes its place along with pure reason and practical reason in the triad of truth. Indeed, the critique of judgment, in Kant's own words, is the means of combining the two parts of philosophy (epistemology and ethics) into a whole (Kant, 1951, pp. 12–170). Curiously, with such a move, the aesthetic assumes an overtly political nature. The aesthetic experience is a form of intersubjectivity; the beautiful pleases universally and expresses a shared humanity. It creates spontaneous agreement. It is a *sensus communis*. More importantly, the sublime, as a humiliating power, also decenters the

subject by the awesome awareness of our finitude within the unbounded universe.

Both of these concepts provide a consoling fantasy that the world is uniquely ours, that nature conforms essentially to human understanding. To confront the power of nature is the ultimate aesthetic experience, one that necessarily forms a universal subjectivity, a common sense. The imitation of nature, in art, was thus to assume a heightened status as a social endeavor that attempted to capture the awesome qualities of the world. Much of German philosophy from Kant to nineteenth-century Romanticism maintained the fantasy of creating the total work of art, the *Gesamptkunstwerke*. This of course, was Richard Wagner's objective and was in many ways the official program of German national socialism. Dr. Goebbels, Hitler's propaganda minister, captures this aestheticization of politics when he writes: "Politics, too, is perhaps an art, if not the highest and most all-embracing there is. Art and artists are not only there to unite; their far more important task is to create a form, to expel the ill trends and make room for the healthy to develop" (Reimann, 1977, p. 171). One must not forget the powerful political impact of the spectacles created by Albert Speer and his followers. These productions perhaps came closest to achieving the ideological dream of the total work of art. They also critically depended upon the power and authority of scenographic architectural form as an aesthetic agent of fascism.

The dream of the city as a work of art embraces the same ideology. The effort to produce a collective artwork, to fuse a community through formalism, is indeed still part of our contemporary psyche. The design and development of theme towns throughout the country are contemporary examples of this aestheticization of politics. The problem, of course, centers upon the danger of the misinterpretation of culture as form, of community as an artificial, material construct, of something simply to be produced and consumed and not as a social production of human relations. The fascist mythologies of cultural identity, collective memory, and the locality of place are often uncritically embraced as objectives to be pursed in the *construction of tradition*, in the desire to form a community through an Herculean aesthetic undertaking that depends too much on form and too little on content. This is the fallacy of vulgar environmental determinism embraced by conservatives and progressives alike.

REVIEW BOARDS AND THE CRISIS OF AUTHORITY

"Because we are used to unconditional authorities we have come to *need* unconditional authorities."

In this aphorism, Friedrich Nietzsche exposes the reciprocal relationship between tradition and the desire for security. Our continued psychological need for authority is a product of our political conditioning and thus is rarely subject to critical reflection. In contemporary society the apparatus of bureaucratic government, with its trust in "expert" systems, has assumed this authoritarian role. To a certain degree, the architect or design professional occupies the position of aesthetic arbitrator whose authority rests upon the same traditional hierarchy we have both taken for granted and come to depend upon. The institution of design review, however, reflects the administrative character of postmodernity. This dominant aspect of our culture depends substantially upon the power of the norm, which is ideologically related to our juridical mindset.

Indispensable to the strategy and hegemony of disciplinary society is the establishment of norms. According to Herbert Marcuse, a normal individual "lives his repression 'freely' as his own life: he desires what he is supposed to desire; his gratifications are profitable to him and to others; he is reasonably . . . happy" (Marcuse, [1955], 1966, p. 46). The restrictions imposed upon the individual's libido appear rational and are internalized: "the societal authority is absorbed into the conscience and unconscious of the individual and works as his own desire, morality and fulfillment" (Marcuse, [1955], 1966, p. 46). Oedipus teaches us to desire our own repression by obediently following the commands of the norm. Normative order is a modality of power that hides behind its mundane anonymity. It functions by continuous regulation and correction, which are the operative tactics of discipline: "such a power has to qualify, measure, appraise, and hierarchize, rather than display itself in its murderous splendor" (Foucault, 1978, p. 144). In many respects, design control is a direct product of the culture of normal-

ization; a result of the good intention to feverishly embrace, yet dominate an increasingly fragile environment. This exclusionary methodology can readily be identified in the administration of design review, which relies so heavily upon normative guidelines. The aim is to eliminate or exile meaningful difference; to unite scattered differential spatial fragments by force into a homogeneous and ultimately disempowered norm.

Aesthetic controls on architectural production are invariably dependent upon the legal authority of codes, rules, and regulations, which tend to reduce options to a fixed number of alternatives. Such limited choices are evident at each progressive scale of decision making; for example, form and massing, style, fenestration, materials, color, and details. The regulations, in effect, establish a formula intent upon molding identical places, whereby all the variables are controlled within subsets of a severely limited number. The serial monotony resulting from design based upon the formulas of review boards tends to reduce buildings to masks (stressing the signifier—i.e., style—over the signified) and empties space of the meaning that is achieved through diversity and the genuinely historical. The products of such control tend toward a homogeneity dependent upon surfaces, screens, and stylistic clichés. In the process, the architecture becomes neither a decorated shed nor a duck but a sign that promotes the desired image of the dominant political economy. It is a politics of distraction, an anathema where the perpetuation of control mechanisms remain hidden behind so many superficial variations on a theme.

The opening section of this chapter locates the position of architecture within the networks of power relations and attempts to explain how the control of aesthetic production is neither objective nor innocent. That part of my argument is an exposition of what I consider the important objectives of design review, made either as outright declarations or concealed within the margins of the text. The following sections will explore what I call the machinery of review boards: the strategy and tactics employed in order to achieve the desired result. Not surprisingly, the *appeal to authority* constitutes the primary strategic movement. In the case of design review, the judicial and the historical sound the voice of a necessary authority.

Aesthetic Justice and the
Rhetoric of Consensus

There are several models from which design review legitimates its existence as aesthetic arbitrator. The most important is that of the juridical. Just as disciplinary society depends upon juridical examples for the control of deviation and the assurance of the norm, so too do we encounter in the aesthetic realm a reliance upon the concept of justice together with all of its administrative and institutional apparatuses. Design review boards often assume a legal status and follow pseudo-juridical procedures and practices. Perhaps, since architects usually comprise the dominant contingent of such panels they welcome this privileged role. Here they occupy the other side of the architectural inquisition; no longer the student justifying a design at the final review, but a juror seated comfortably in the position of authority. What is more revealing in this circumstance is precisely the need to establish a basis of authority that can confidently dispense with the "serious business" of aesthetic justice.

In order to understand the meaning of a notion such as aesthetic justice we must first consider our contemporary conception of justice itself. The philosopher Alasdair MacIntyre has characterized postmodern society as a culture "not of consensus, but of division and conflict" (MacIntyre, 1984, p. 2). This inability to achieve a traditional consensus regarding critical issues is certainly apparent when one considers the meaning of justice. As a result, one discovers many different and often incompatible conceptions of justice. Indeed, some are logically incommensurable. Rival arguments appear to have no common rationality and result in pure assertion and counter assertion: a clash of antagonistic wills. The practice of design review must recognize the social dilemma of competing conceptualizations not only of justice but of the ideology of aesthetics itself. From what criteria are we to judge and evaluate the artistic merit of a project? Is an appeal to the weight of consensus still valid?

Previous sections of this chapter have considered the ideologies of harmony, style, and the "total work of art." These theoretical strategies are inherently connected to the traditional notion of consensus and its attempt to establish a self-authorization. However, consensus as a contemporary juridical model is flawed due to its inability to achieve any sense of coherent agreement between rival opinions. This impasse manifests itself in a sort of bureaucratic individualism that hides behind a *rhetoric of consensus*.

The rhetoric declares that rules must be followed for the public welfare of the community, however each individual determines that, in their particular case, an exclusion should be granted. Attend any public review board meeting and you may encounter a strange and irrational logic where one individual is utterly convinced that his or her neighbor should not be allowed the same opportunity that he or she already enjoys. Scenarios such as these are often encountered: "Although my house may block a neighbor's view, your addition cannot block mine," "We moved here five years ago, but now the city should limit new growth," or "Although I live in a ranch house, your house must be Spanish in style." Sometimes, the arguments, criticisms, and pleas reach a nearly paranoic level, especially when groups of neighbors "unite" in order to block someone else's project. Such meetings can create an almost lynch-mob atmosphere of surreal accusations and denials, reflecting the deeper fear and anxiety of alienated individuals' attempts to substantiate their being in a groundless consensus of paranoia. For a moment, perhaps, neighbors together engage an imagined common enemy; their motives and actions, however, inherently follow the same logic of fascism that depends upon the abdication of the individual to bring about an illusionary condition of security and well being for all. Such a perverse consensus is a product of manipulation. Is not the consciousness of the *sensus communis* an apology of what already exists? The contemporary notion of consensus has simply assumed the status of commodity; that is, an instrument of alienation and the very opposite of community (Kolb, 1990, p. 37). Indeed, money has become the real community and architectural review boards have often become assimilated within its matrix. In this case aesthetic justice assumes an economic role: nobody shall have an unfair advantage nor impact negatively upon the full economic potential of neighboring properties. Indeed, they must contribute to the increase in property values.

Given the right political and economic circumstances a juridical claim of fairness and objectivity can quickly change to rhetoric. In the case of Santa Barbara, the moralistic ideals of the board members were readily sacrificed when a joint venture for a large downtown shopping mall was pushed through the city bureaucracy. This resulted in the approval of an architecture grossly violating the most specific guidelines regarding scale and massing. The scheme, of course, incorporated the appropriate *paseo* topology with plenty of the usual formula elements such as blind arcades and inaccessible towers. The morphological reality, on the other hand, monstrously imposes its consumer body upon the humble context so much desired and protected by the landmarks committee with its renowned community members. The subsequent increase in tax revenues and rental income generated by the development more than explains the momentary lapse of design judgment on the part of the review board. Thus, the most comprehensive and complicated urban design intervention ever undertaken in the city's history, essentially proceeded outside the constraints of even a rhetorical community consensus, was forced upon (and in a number of cases, displaced) the existing social and economic context.

The Return to History

"They had taken out such a good insurance policy that when their house burned down, they were able to build another one older than the first." (Jean Baudrillard)

In such an utterly uncontinuous society the logic of postmodernity has increasingly turned toward history as a source both for authority and security. The impulse to preserve the past is an impulse to preserve the self (Huwison, 1987). A society invents tradition in order to ground a shaken identity in a rapidly transforming world. The volatile and ephemeral nature of our existence, the instantaneity and disposability of our culture, the erosion of consensus and estrangement from identity, all contribute to the desire to create a collective image of society. Such a desperate operation, however, is problematic and exposes a deeper psychological social condition.

In many ways, the postmodern return to history resembles a fetishistic psychology. According to

Freud, a fetish is an object that serves as a substitute for a castrated penis; a substitute that covers up a perceived lack. Fetishism is a refusal of loss: the fetish object blocks or displaces this traumatic discovery of loss. By nature, a fetish is also preoccupied with surface appearances that conceal a deeper anxiety, a more profound sense of loss. The desire to return to the past, to the security of an imagined world, not only reveals a nostalgic ideology of history but also assumes history as a substitute for authority much desired considering the uncertainties of the postmodern condition. In architecture, the myth of history is translated into material form. Postmodern architecture, especially that promoted by review boards, displays many of the tendencies of a fetishistic mentality: historical styles are revived as a defense against the realities of the contemporary; style is inherently concerned with an image, in the surface quality of the architecture, in facades, masks, and decorated sheds (what is seen dominates what is known); and buildings and plazas—that is, form and space—substitute for a legitimate phenomenology of place that once provided for the ontological needs of individuals and groups.

This fetish of history is further complicated when history becomes simply a source for arbitrary arrangements from the past: the forms and signs of a dislocated historical construct masquerading in a profoundly different time and place. Such a timeless image cannot overcome the subsequent reduction of content. A loss of temporality translates into a loss of depth. A return to the myth of history, to a sort of imagined idealism, writes the philosopher Paul De Man is to resort to "a fascination with false images that mimic the presumed attributes of authenticity when it is in fact just the hollow mask with which a frustrated, defeated consciousness tries to cover-up its own negativity" (De Man, 1980, p. 345).

How is it that our search for the authentic is so preoccupied with reviving tradition? Modernity attempted to liquidate history through constant innovation and a persistent and utopian vision of the future. The history of modern architecture certainly reflects this attitude, while the polemics of the various avant-garde movements represent an extreme example of an antihistorical position. Today we look upon those ideal projects from the early part of the century with a certain amount of skepticism. Much has been written about the failure of modernism, from Robert Venturi to Colin Rowe, from Leon Krier to the Prince of Wales. The problem with all of these critiques, however, is their severely limited scope of reference: the contextualists have all consciously avoided confronting the context: that is, the economic, political, and cultural forces that determine the material realities of the built environment. The danger is that a complex historical understanding is reduced to a series of formal observations that displace an intelligible interaction between time and space. The resulting theoretical move toward tradition via style is unfortunately little more than a strategy of nostalgia, at once a compensation for an illusionary childhood and a denial of reality: "To see other periods as mirrors of our own is to turn history into narcissism; to see other styles as open to our own is to turn history into a dream" (Forster, [1985], 1989, p. 17). To demand a continuity with the past is to pretend there is some immanent purpose, a chimera of stability in an ephemeral culture. This is pretending so as to avoid the real historical conditions of the political economy: retreat from politics into psychology, the imaginary resolution to a real contradiction.

Santa Barbara once again is an informative case to consider in terms of the architectural realization of a nostalgic ideology. The city is in many ways a lost fantasy of a world that never existed. Until the earthquake in 1925, Santa Barbara was in many respects a typical midsize American town. Historic photographs reveal a style in the commercial district that could easily be mistaken as that of a midwestern, Victorian-inspired architecture. Similarly, perspective maps in the form of aerial views indicate surprisingly little Hispanic influence. Of course, things changed dramatically after the earthquake, with the implementation of a board of architectural review. This provided the opportunity for the cultural elite to invent and promote a specific identity, one the city is famous for today: that of the Hispanic, genteel myth of old California. Within a month of the disaster, the board approved the designs of over a hundred projects, virtually all in the Spanish style. During the complete restoration process, nearly two thousand building proposals were received and critiqued (Starr, 1990, p. 288). This same review apparatus remains today, however, in a considerably more restrictive version. What were the motivations behind the creation of

such a self-conscious identity and how is that need fulfilled today? The bourgeois and cultural elite desires the soothing comfort of the architectural cliché, the simulation of a staged reality that is ultimately based upon absence: that which has eroded away or had never existed in the first place. This was clearly a reaction to modernism, an alternative vision to the exploding capitalist experiment in Los Angeles, and established the model for the architecture of the postmodern future— the society of simulation.

Architecture and the Society of Simulation

An architectural manifestation of a society of simulation, which Santa Barbara so transparently represents, is the historical reconstruction. As a formal strategy this is often the product of the institution of design review. Architecture acts as an advertisement for the status quo by reestablishing a historical image with the reconstruction of buildings from the past. That which had previously been annihilated becomes an object of adoration. This is clearly an exercise in the re-creation of an image of an image, where the simulacrum has replaced a vital and purposeful representation of culture. This is also a phenomenon encountered across the globe, from the deserts of Iraq where Saddam Hussein is rebuilding Babylon (reportedly, including the mythical tower of Babel) to the idyllic shores of Southern California, where in Santa Barbara, any number of structures from its past have been creatively reconstructed.

Before considering these architectural examples it is important first to outline what is meant by the triumph of the simulacrum and how this philosophical observation impacts formal thought. A simulacra, according to the schema of French philosopher Jean Baudrillard, is a reproduction of an object or event, an "image of an image." In Simulations, he generates a historical sketch of the various orders or stages of simulacra appearing in modernity (Baudrillard, 1983, pp. 83–104). In the first stage (during the Renaissance), the counterfeit assumed the paradigmatic model of representation: art imitates nature. During the Industrial Revolution, a condition arose where objects can be mechanically produced in series, as exact replicas of one another; this constitutes the order of industrial simulacrum. In the contemporary order, simulation devours representation. Models and codes (as signs) take precedence over things. Now the dominant principle is digital. Everything has been reduced to a binary structure whose opposing forces "cancel out each other's differences, and serve to maintain a self-regulating, self-same, self reproducing system" (Kellner, 1989, p. 81). Within this binary schema all radical change is ruled out. Responses are simply structured as either yes or no. Advertising is now the prototypical medium: individuals are forced to respond to precoded messages, options are programmed and choices are predetermined. As the triumph of the sign over the referent, advertising is also the "triumph of superficial form, the smallest common denominator of all significations, the zero degree of meaning, the triumph of entropy over all possible tropes" (Baudrillard, 1981, p. 133). Signifiers are attached to commodities seemingly at random. Qualities are attributed irrespective of their function or material utility.

The resulting image of an image is impoverished of content beyond that of a preprogrammed and prepackaged set of slogans or commercial trademarks. Thus, cultural production increasingly focuses upon that ever-so-thin screen that serves as the neutral surface whereby any pleasant cinema effect can be projected. Curiously, for many reconstruction projects a simple sign of a building is not enough to achieve the desired effect. In the case of Santa Barbara the reification process turns inward: one must know that the walls are truly constructed in adobe, to the most minute detail of eighteenth-century technology. The objective is to replicate these ancient buildings with such an exactitude that the difference between the original and the copy becomes almost impossible to detect. Indeed, origins are put in doubt because the *imitations become real*. The incredible contradiction, however, is nakedly revealed (yet evidently goes unnoticed) when cement is added to the adobe bricks and reinforcing bars are doweled and cemented into the walls. Everything, of course, is plastered over in the end, which conceals this paradoxical and disturbing internal image.

Within this fantasy context we no longer need meaning. History has been disciplined by the charming pseudo-historical that is more easily consumed. Not only has the pseudo-historical re-placed a relevant historical consciousness, but the postmodern return to history is actually a profoundly ahistorical movement. In addition to disregarding the actualities of context and the necessities of the present, this strategy also radically trivializes the specificity of the past. Such a return to history, writes the critic Hal Foster, seems more to be a liberation from history, a collapse of history, a "morbid attempt to compensate for loss via the resurrection of archaic images and forms" (Foster, [1985], 1989, p. 16).

The Commodification of History

"Where the dream is at its most exalted . . . the commodity is closest at hand" (Adorno, 1981, pp. 91–92). The famous critique of the culture industry published in 1944 by Adorno and Horkheimer still maintains its relevance today. Their critique presents a totalizing picture of society that reflects the ruthless unity of the culture industry. Monopoly capitalism is the eternal return of the commodity. Everything remains within the matrix of its order; including even our dreams and fantasies.

The commodity, according to Marx, is a concrete abstraction, divorced from its materiality, from its use, from productive activity, and from the need that it satisfies. Space has become a commodity through the marketing and speculative development of history and tradition. To an alarming degree, cultural life is consumed by the logic of exchange and accumulation of capital. Two such industries of spatial consumption that are relevant to this discussion center around leisure and tourism; both possess an aesthetic exchange value that is realized through architecture.

Theme towns such as Nantucket, Santa Fe, or Santa Barbara operate with the same logic as Disneyland. Each is a reified dreamworld, a materialized fantasy turned commodity. The Andalusian images incorporated in the architecture of Santa Barbara reflect this transformative process. Even one of the city's main streets is named after the native Chumash word for a mirage: *Anacapa* means a pleasing delusion, a dream of escape from laborious daily reality. Those who were instrumental in the invention of Santa Barbara—in "creating a new Spain"—clearly understood the potential power of their vision. This radical experiment from the turn of the century was an early and influential example of a postmodern conceptualization of history and culture which today we find ourselves completely engulfed in.

Culture is treated as so many ready-made styles at the service of a heritage industry intent upon plastering over social differences with the creation of an appearance of a normal community. History is viewed as an endless reserve of equal events available for speculative development. However, as with fashion, our freedom to choose is limited to a choice among the same. Fashion is the truth of cultural consumption—be it architecture or automobiles. The ideology of fashion answers both the avant-garde need to innovate and the necessity that nothing shall change: its mode of operation is the recycling of styles. Paradoxically, even the concept of permanence can be incorporated into fashion's program, as can readily be seen in any architectural restoration or reconstruction project. As Hal Foster writes, "the corrosive effects of time are disavowed by illusion to canonical sources" (Foster, [1985], 1989, p. 124). The canonical sources, are, of course, style, the authority of which is intentionally utilized to manufacture duration. However, as long as duration is projected as a commodity and becomes intentional, if architecture "exorcises what it deems ephemeral by resorting to pure impregnable forms or even to such intangibles as universal human values," then "it works against itself, shortening rather than prolonging the life of the work." Simply stated, "they perish the more quickly, the more directly they aim at duration" (Adorno, [1970], 1984, p. 254). This is more than simply a theoretical observation by Adorno; perhaps it reveals a psychological response one experiences when confronting a historicist facade: a sense of dislocation and not continuity with tradition. What one knows infinitely intersects with the phenomenological event. Thus, even when we perceive a thick wall pretending to be masonry behind plaster we know it is hollow and experience the wall as empty and not solid and stable, not protective and secure. In effect, it assumes a heightened ephemeral character exactly because the wall pretends to be something else, to escape time and space, to become a surrogate history dependent upon concealing the lack that is essential to its being. Here the commodity character is most ap-

parent. The architecture becomes divorced from the emotional and physical need to provide protection from the elements. Once again the form is surely correct, just as the miniature Piazza San Marco at Epcot Center is accurate to the smallest detail. The inherent lack, however, consumes any sense of the genuine. Thus, we experience both examples in terms of the negative, from what is missing, not from what is present.

CONCLUSION

"We live in societies whose aim is not simply to combat radical ideas—but to wipe them from living memory: to bring about an amnesiac condition in which it would be as though such notions had never existed, placing them beyond our very powers of conception" (Eagleton, 1990, p. 7).

The role of architectural production within the contemporary context of disciplinary society is problematic. After our awakening from the nightmare of modernity we find ourselves inhabiting a radically discontinuous world and are caught behind the powerful momentum of nihilism. The institution of architecture has reacted to this condition in a number of ways both theoretically and practically. Perhaps the most dominant and extensive movement quietly unfolding behind the noisy and often trivial discourse on deconstruction is that of design review. In this chapter my argument has been that aesthetic decision making is ultimately not founded upon objective or mutual standards of judgment, nor in consensus, but simply reverts back to those in control, the same forces that determine much of the public realm; the political, capitalist, and cultural elite. Those groups outside of the dominant power matrices—the disenfranchised and marginal—are characteristically excluded from the important decision-making processes. Furthermore, the trends toward homogeneity, toward the violent elimination of difference through control, of regionalism and nationalism are all trends toward domination. The pressing need to discover or fabricate a security of fundamental truths betrays either a myopic reversion to the images of an imaginary past, or, considerably more dangerous, the invocation of tradition, collective memory, local or national identity, ultimately—like fascism—divides rather than unites. In architecture, repetition has defeated uniqueness and the ephemeral masquerades as stability. Authentic difference has been replaced by differential signs that are not the democratic signifiers that they may claim to be (Foster, [1985], 1989, p. 29). Political justice is not a matter of consensus, but involves the respect for boundaries and difference rather than the violent destruction of otherness. The manifest repetition imposed from the outside by agencies such as architectural review boards—the grid of similarity—serves as a form of aesthetic sanction that counters innovation and creative thought. Finally, as Lyotard and others have articulated, *without difference there is no meaning*.

Form itself is impoverished of content. However, intention does not equal content. What a culture puts into the signs determines their meaning. Any attempt to construct a community through its architecture is, at best, a fantasy of escape. It could also be, however, the reflection of a nihilistic cynicism that has already made the apocalyptic declaration that the world cannot be other than it already is.

Nietzsche defined nihilism as the historical devaluing of transcendental values self-imposed by metaphysical thinking. His completed nihilism, summed up in the brief statement *God is dead*, speaks of the destining of two millennia of Western philosophy. Nietzsche's revaluing, however, represents an affirmative stand against the flow of nihilistic thought in that it is a *creative* enterprise simultaneous with the dismantling of ideological constructs. The task of contemporary criticism is, however, even more fundamental. Rather than searching to recover a lost identity of architecture, and return to a mythical time where art fulfilled consolatory functions, perhaps we should simply choose *not* to ignore the condition. For as Adorno clearly understood, to overcome nihilism we must first recognize it: "consummate negativity, once squarely faced, delineates the mirror-image of its opposite" (Adorno, [1951], 1978, p. 247).

REFERENCES

Adorno, T. A. [1944] 1972. *The Dialectic of Enlightenment*, trans. J. Cumming. London: Verso.

——— [1951] 1978. *Minima Moralia*. trans. E.F.N. Jephcott. London: Verso.

——— [1970] 1984. *Aesthetic Theory*. trans. C. Lenhardt. London: Routledge and Kegan Paul.

——— 1981. *In Search of Wagner*, trans. R. Livingstone. London: New Left Books.

Baudrillard, J. 1981. *Simulacres et simulation*, Paris: Editions Galilee.

——— 1983. *Simulations*. New York: Semiotext.

De Man, P. 1980. "Criticism and Crisis." In *Aesthetics Today*. ed. M. Philipson. New York: New American Library.

Eagleton, T. 1990. *The Ideology of the Aesthetic*. Oxford: Basil Blackwell.

Foster, H. 1989. *Recodings: Art, Spectacle, Cultural Politics*. Seattle: Bay Press.

Foucault, M. 1978. *The History of Sexuality*, vol. 1. New York: Pantheon.

Hewison, R. 1987. *The Heritage Industry*. London.

Kant, I 1951. *The Critique of Judgement*, trans. J. H. Bernard. New York: Hafner.

Kellner, D. 1989. *J. Baudrillard: From Marxism to Postmodernism and Beyond*. Stanford, Calif.: Stanford University Press.

Kolb, D. 1990. *Postmodern Sophistications: Philosophy, Architecture and Tradition*. Chicago: University of Chicago.

Lefebvre, H. [1974] 1991. *The Production of Space*, trans. D. Nicholson-Smith. Oxford: Basil Blackwell.

MacIntyre, A. 1984. *After Virtue: A Study in Moral Theory*. University of Notre Dame Press.

Marcuse, H. [1955] 1966. *Eros and Civilization: A Philosophical Inquiry into Freud*. Boston: Beacon Press.

Reimann, V. 1977. *The Man Who Created Hitler*. London: W. Kimber.

Starr, K. 1990. *Material Dreams: Southern California Through the 1920's*. Oxford: Oxford University Press.

17
Private Design Review in Edge City

David J. Baab

Planning Consultant, Irvine, California

If the aesthetics of the physical environment are to be controlled by design review, who should be responsible—government or private organizations?

In many communities, government agencies control the aesthetics of the physical environment as an extension of zoning enforcement. Government professionals working through an appointed commission, or independently by administrative action, review private development for compliance with aesthetic criteria, in addition to compliance with the designated land use, building height, square footage, setbacks, parking capacity, landscape adequacy, and life safety features.

In many other communities a powerful alternative exists: private design review, the aesthetic control of the physical environment outside the framework of government, by private agreements, typically through community associations.

In an age of increasing suspicion of government intervention in daily life, many American communities continue to embrace private design review as a legitimate alternative to public design review. Compared to many government agencies, residents and property owners who engage in private design review often may have more intimate first-hand knowledge of the actual social-physical environment, may be more personally vested in the results of their decisions, and may be more cognizant and supportive of community values.

More important, if residents live in a community with private design review voluntarily supporting the values inherent in the process, then private design review can also empower residents to take greater responsibility and control over their neighborhoods. It can make residents feel as if their neighborhood belongs to them, not to a remote, special-interest, government agency.

This chapter examines the fundamentals of private design review. It describes details of the process through case studies set in "edge city," defined as the newer districts of urban regions, in which private design review has become very popular in controlling the aesthetics of the physical environment. It discusses the characteristics of a successful design review process, and ends with a prescription for a much-needed role for public design review.

BACKGROUND

Two private agreements form the foundation for private design review: *conditions to land sales contracts,* which control first-generation development (the transition from uninhabited land to urban development); and *conditions, covenants, and restrictions* (typically called CC&Rs or deed restrictions in some localities), which control subsequent changes to property.

Conditions to land sales contracts are private agreements between the land developer and land buyers. They mandate the aesthetics of the physical form of the first generation of development through specific *design guidelines* and a defined *design review process.*

Design guidelines are illustrated principles that promote certain values, articulating a prescribed aesthetic vision for a district: "appropriate" and "inappropriate" aesthetic approaches to site organization, architecture, landscape design, lighting, and signs. Typically, the design guidelines exceed the minimum development standards enforced by government agencies. For example, design guidelines may specify a particular variety of shade tree for parking lots, while the local jurisdiction's development standards may only specify a minimum number of trees.

The intent of these first-generation design guidelines is to establish an identity for a geographic area as idealized by the developer. Often the intent is to create a coherent character, similar to older neighborhoods that evolved slowly over time, shaped by topography, available technology, and culturally dominant building-landscape traditions.

The goal of many design guidelines is not to sacrifice design creativity, but to set parameters to challenge designers to consider their buildings to be primarily a part of a physical context, rather than primarily a part of their personal portfolio: a piece of the physical-social fabric, rather than the most up-to-date example of their body of work.

The *design review process* implements the values inherent in the design guidelines. For first-generation development, the developer's in-house architects or consultants use design guidelines to review and approve plans for new development. The intent is to produce buildings that demonstrate the principles in the guidelines, setting a benchmark for future construction.

Over time, as more buildings are constructed that begin to define the intended character of the district and as more precedent-setting decisions are made, the design guidelines and the design review process evolve, incorporating previously unforeseen shifts in values and changes in technologies, such as new attitudes toward energy/water use and new types of building materials.

Conditions, Covenants, and Restrictions (CC&Rs) are private agreements between the land developer, the initial land buyers, and future land buyers. CC&Rs control the aesthetics of the physical changes to the first-generation development. They are written by the land developer, called the "Declarant," recorded with the deed, and stay attached to the land through subsequent ownership for a specific term, typically twenty to fifty years.

As with conditions to land sales contracts, CC&Rs also prescribe the physical form of development through design guidelines and a design review process.

In residential communities, the CC&Rs establish a private community association governed by an elected board of directors that appoints a volunteer group of property owners and residents as an architectural committee. This committee reviews the aesthetics of proposed physical changes, using an abbreviated version of the original design guidelines.

A property management company generally organizes the process to ensure fairness and consistency. Frequently in larger associations, a consulting architect will assist the committee in reviewing plans and giving professional advice. However, unlike many situations in public design review, in private design review the final decision is typically made directly by residents, not by staff.

In business districts, the declarant of the CC&Rs (the land developer) generally reviews construction plans using in-house architects or consultants. The declarant typically has a vested interest in maintaining quality, since if the quality of the physical environment declines, the declarant suffers directly from a loss in the economic value of both the developed and undeveloped properties owned in the district, and indirectly from a loss in credibility and a decline in reputation.

Throughout the term of the CC&Rs, the design guidelines and design review process can be amended by agreement by the declarant and/or a prescribed percentage of the property owners. At the end of the term, the CC&Rs can either be extended or abandoned.

EXCLUSIONARY NATURE OF PRIVATE DESIGN REVIEW

In addition to the basic objections to both public and private design review, that freedom of expression is being restrained and that a certain idealized physical form might be frozen in time, private design review is more objectionable to some individuals because it is exclusionary, in the sense that communities with CC&Rs are not meant to appeal to everybody. The values reflected in many CC&Rs—such as harmony, compatibility, and privacy—are not universal values.

This statement does not imply that CC&Rs are exclusionary in that they restrict access, as minimum lot sizes restrict access by poor people to an affluent community, or a maximum number of dwelling units restricts access by young people to a no-growth community.

In the past, when CC&Rs were a tool to discriminate against race and religion, CC&Rs clearly did restrict access. Today, however, people from many income levels, family sizes, and ethnic backgrounds live in communities with CC&Rs, as can be quickly discovered when looking beyond the manicured appearance of the physical environment to the high numbers of apartments and town houses that are often distributed among the single-family homes, the low-income housing that is designed to blend in with market-rate housing, the numerous homes occupied by extended families and unrelated roommates who share housing costs to live in the community, and the wide range of language and dress in the schools and grocery stores.

Although CC&Rs are exclusionary in that they do not have universal appeal, similar comments can also be made about unpopular government policies that apply academically fashionable planning concepts unilaterally on residents, such as urban renewal in the 1960s or biodiversity in the 1990s. To many government professionals who agree with the values being promoted, these policies seem reasonable: the public good is being protected. To residents who disagree with the values, the policies seem exclusionary: the values of a powerful government agency are simply being imposed on residents.

In reality, exclusionary CC&Rs may be easier to avoid than exclusionary government policies. Residents usually can manage not to live in areas governed by CC&Rs. Alternatives do exist, whereas avoiding jurisdictions with exclusionary government policies is much more difficult given the quixotic nature of advocacy planning trends, from mandated freeway construction in the 1950s to mandated citizen participation programs in the 1960s to mandated energy regulations in the 1970s

to mandated Neo-Traditional urban design in the 1980s.

Communities with exclusionary CC&Rs can provide a needed balance in an urban region. They can complement communities without CC&Rs, by providing a place for individuals of all income levels, family sizes, and ethnic backgrounds who want to volunteer to restrict their personal freedom, in return for limits on the actions of their neighbors, to establish a place that reflects shared community values.

WHY PRIVATE?

The public sector is often blessed with highly capable and committed professionals. Yet in many communities today, the prevailing system of governing the use of land is fragmented. Specialization by function is all too common. Government professionals frequently act as if their area of expertise is most important, whether it be flood control, traffic engineering, endangered species protection, air quality, housing policy, maintenance, or crime prevention.

Too often this functional approach to governance leads to conflicting demands, overshadowing an intimate understanding of geographic areas by government professionals. The system seems to reward government professionals more for their technical knowledge in a functional area than for their personal experience living in the community.

Although elected officials live in the same community as their constituents, in many cases government professionals do not reside in the community they regulate. The result can be the adoption by some government professionals of second-hand, stereotyped impressions of the community, leading to a lack of understanding, respect, and/or support of the values held by its residents. Instead, the perceived values of future residents, or the values of hand-picked, like-minded elected officials, may be imposed by administrative action.

The impact on design review is that values promoted in public design review may not be the values held by residents and property owners. Instead, they may be values held by a few government professionals. The danger is that public resources may be wasted, because the values inherent in the design review policies are unsupported by residents; or that radical physical changes to the community may occur, causing the displacement of current residents. Or the impact is that the parties involved in public design review may not have a vested interest in the outcome. If private design review leads to negative results, property owners suffer economically though declining property values, and residents suffer socially through a deteriorating quality of life. If public design review leads to negative results, government professionals may merely need to seek positions in other cities or departments. To many regulators, loyalty to the profession is frequently dearer than loyalty to residents and property owners.

In communities where government professionals are cognizant and supportive of the values held by residents, where they have first-hand knowledge of the actual social/physical environment, and where they are personally vested in the results of their decisions, public design review can be effective in protecting and enhancing the aesthetics of the physical environment, as in many historic districts, scenic areas, and downtown development zones. Yet in other communities, private design review may be more effective than public design review. Compared to many government agencies, residents and property owners who engage in private design review often may have more intimate first-hand knowledge of the actual social/physical environment, may be more personally vested in the results of their decisions, and may be more cognizant and supportive of community values.

More importantly, if residents live in a community with private design review voluntarily supporting the values inherent in the process, then private design review can also empower residents to take greater responsibility and control over their neighborhoods. It can make residents feel as if their neighborhood belongs to them, not to a remote, special-interest, government agency.

CC&Rs can give property owners a powerful tool to protect their personal investment, and residents a powerful tool to protect their quality of life. In return for limiting personal freedom, participants can restrict the actions of their neighbors. Individual property rights become subordinate to community values. Since the 1960s, such an approach to community building and protection has become very popular with the general public, as measured by the increasing numbers of new communities built with CC&Rs and private community associations (*Economist*, 1992) and by the preservation of homeowner equity in depressed real estate markets (Gaines, 1992).

The popularity is not limited to new neighborhoods. Mature neighborhoods are also forming voluntary associations to protect and enhance their existing quality of life. As of 1992, over 3400 community associations existed in Orange County alone, a growing metropolitan area with over two million residents in Southern California (Mouchard, 1992).

CASE STUDY: WOODBRIDGE

Woodbridge is a planned community of 25,000 residents on 1700 acres in Orange County, Southern California, within the city limits of Irvine, part of edge city. "Edge city" is new term, coined by Joel Garreau in his 1991 book, *Edge City: Life on the New Frontier,* to describe the newer districts of an urban region, typically mislabeled "suburbs." Unlike older districts that developed around mercantile seaports or industrial railroad centers, edge city is developing around postindustrial freeways and airports.

With the decline of rail transport and the rise of trucking and air freight, edge city is emerging as the economic engine of contemporary urban regions, often supplying the majority of jobs, housing, shopping, and leisure-time activities in an urban region. Although lacking sufficient academic study, edge city is slowly assuming a greater social role, as inner-city residents turn to edge city to search for positive examples for protecting and enhancing their quality of life (Rowe, 1992).

Since 1980, Southern California has grown into an enormous edge city-state, with over fourteen million living on a broad coastal plain and several inland valleys, connected by a network of freeways, airports, and electronic communication. Orange County is one of the several metropolitan areas that form Southern California's urban region. Other areas include West Los Angeles, South-Central Los Angeles, the San Gabriel Valley, the Downtown Los Angeles/Hollywood/East L.A. area, the San Fernando Valley, the LAX/South Bay/Long Beach area, Ventura County, the High Desert, the Inland Empire, and the Coachella Valley. In forty years Orange County has grown from an agricultural community to a bedroom community to an edge city business community, with 2.3 million residents, 1.2 million jobs, and no central city.

Irvine is one of the thirty-one cities in Orange County. With 110,000 residents living in planned communities, 100,000 employees working in planned business districts, and over 8800 acres of permanent open space protected by urban limits lines, Irvine is considered by many observers to be one of the most successful new towns in the country.

In the 1950s, the land upon which Irvine is built was undeveloped. It consisted of grazing land, vegetable fields, and citrus groves; part of the historic 100,000-acre Irvine Ranch owned by the Irvine Company. Urban development in Orange County had leap-frogged over the property since the Irvine Company elected to continue farming, not to engage in land development. In the 1960s, land development was forced on the Irvine Company by new federal regulations. Rather than extending unplanned urbanization over the ranch, the Irvine Company decided to develop its property as a series of the master-planned communities. The centerpiece of the plan was the new town of Irvine, designed by William Pereira, to be built in conjunction with a new campus of the University of California.

The cornerstones of the Irvine new town plan were:

- Establishment of distinctive neighborhoods or "villages" with strong identities, to give residents a sense of place within the Southern California urban region;
- Balance of development and open space, with an extensive park/greenbelt program;
- Balance of land uses, with diverse residential neighborhoods, business districts, cultural centers, shopping, religious, and institutional activities;
- Maintenance of a high quality of life through sensitive planning and ongoing care.

Incorporated in 1971, the new City of Irvine adopted these principles as the foundation for the state-mandated "general plan." In the last twenty years, the Irvine plan has become one model of successful community building, attracting the worldwide attention of planners and developers involved with other new towns, as well as inner-city neighborhoods.

Built between the mid-1970s and late 1980s, Woodbridge is one of the newer and larger villages in Irvine. With entitlement granted by the City of Irvine, the Irvine Company conceived of the plan, built the major infrastructure, controlled the aesthetics of the initial development through an internal design review process, and established a private homeowners association to care for the infrastructure and to control the aesthetics of future development.

The physical plan of Woodbridge reflects many of the principles in Kevin Lynch's book *The Image of the City*. Its 1700-acre superblock is bounded by a wide greenbelt, with limited access points. Within the superblock is a loop street that collects and distributes traffic, knitting the village together as a circular spine. This street also functions as a landmark: a tree-lined boulevard lined with town homes designed to appear as large estates with front lawns.

Bisecting the square are twin east-west parkways that define an "Activity Corridor." Restaurants, shopping centers, professional office buildings, lighted ball fields, churches, senior housing, day-care centers, and two high schools are located in the corridor, conveniently near the residential neighborhoods, without becoming disturbances to the quiet, truck-free environment. With nearby higher-density apartments, the Activity Corridor forms the setting for a future urban rail line now being planned for central Orange County.

Bisecting the superblock north to south are twin lakes (Fig. 17-1) serving as orientation landmarks and the setting for lakefront swimming complexes and tennis clubs. Bike trails connect the lake with adjacent residential streets and over thirty private neighborhood parks.

In the geographic center of Woodbridge is the primary shopping center, Woodbridge Village Center, designed to face the north lake; and the primary public park, the future Woodbridge Community Park, facing the south lake, linked to the residential areas by pedestrian bridges.

Maintenance of the lakes, private parks, bike trails, and street trees is the responsibility of the Woodbridge Village Association, a private community association established by the CC&Rs. The organization is a nonprofit corporation con-

Figure 17-1. Lakefront development at Woodbridge Village.

trolled by a board of directors elected by the owners of the 9500 homes in the community. A sixty-member, on-site staff manages day-to-day operations: maintenance, recreation programs, educational classes, excursions, and organized social events, such as the Fourth of July Fireworks display. Security is not provided, except for protection of association property from vandalism. Landscape services are provided by forty gardeners working under contract.

Each Woodbridge homeowner is obliged to join the Woodbridge Village Association, to pay monthly dues, and to abide by the policies in CC&Rs, including design review. Consistent with the CC&Rs, all exterior changes to dwellings in Woodbridge must be reviewed and approved by the Woodbridge Village Association's architectural committee, a group of six residents appointed by the board. The committee may include architects and other design professionals who live in the neighborhood, as well as individuals who are deeply concerned about the appearance of the community but have no formal training in design.

Homeowners submit plans to the Woodbridge Village Association staff, who guide the plans through the design review process, leading to approval or rejection by the committee based on conformance with the design guidelines, with the right of appeal to the board of directors. Typical projects include room additions, patio covers, spas, replacement windows, landscaping, and exterior color changes. More common today are major remodelings, in which one-story homes are converted into two-story homes, because of the high land value in relation to construction costs. For these major projects, the committee uses professional assistance.

In the eighteen years of existence, the Woodbridge Village Association design review process has become much more elaborate, including on-site reviews, photography, and video taping. As community values have changed, the CC&R design guidelines have also been amended. For example, in the 1970s, almost all new Woodbridge homes reflected a Sea Ranch aesthetic, with the generous use of wood shakes, heavy wood trim, and earth tones. In the 1980s, new Woodbridge homes reflected a lighter, crisper style, with a greater use of white trim and painted horizontal siding (a "Seaside" aesthetic). Woodbridge residents in the older parts of the village worked with the architectural committee to develop an alternative color palette, so that residents had a framework in which to repaint their homes from dark earth tones to lighter colors.

The Woodbridge model of community planning has been adopted by newer neighborhoods in Southern California, particularly in the Inland Empire. These neighborhoods adopt both Woodbridge's physical plan, with identifiable boundaries, strong landmarks, organizing spines, and a hierarchy of streets; and Woodbridge's management plan, with CC&Rs establishing a community association to maintain amenities and to control the aesthetics of physical changes.

Even in older inner-city neighborhoods, features of the Woodbridge model have been introduced or retained, from using barricades to control through traffic in Berkeley, to having private associations care for the physical environment in both wealthy neighborhoods of St. Louis and more modest neighborhoods of South-Central Los Angeles (Sipchen, 1992).

Although the recent "Neo-Traditional" planning model from the 1980s has advocated residential communities with a tighter mix of land uses and a less rigid street hierarchy than Woodbridge, it still adheres to the basic management principles of Woodbridge, that a local entity is necessary to maintain the community amenities and to monitor physical changes: the community association and the town architect.

CASE STUDY: IRVINE SPECTRUM

Irvine Spectrum is a 2600-acre planned business district in Irvine, strategically located at the confluence of the two major freeways in Southern California. Over 200,000 cars pass through the district each day, as well as every Amtrak and Metrolink commuter train traveling between San Diego and Los Angeles. With over ten million square feet of office, industrial, medical, institutional, research, and retail space developed since 1977, Irvine Spectrum is also part of edge city.

As with Woodbridge, Irvine Spectrum was developed by the Irvine Company, after entitlement by the City of Irvine. Unlike Woodbridge, which was a continuation of residential planned community principles, Spectrum is a deliberate attempt by the Irvine Company to remake the concept of the research/industrial park.

The predecessor to Irvine Spectrum is the Irvine Business Complex, located about seven miles distant, at the opposite end of Irvine, centered around the Orange County Airport. When the Irvine Company began development of the Irvine Business Complex, the airport was a quiet commuter facility. In the 1960s, defense-related companies bought large tracts of land for industrial uses. With the recognition of the airport area's increasing popularity, the Irvine Company began more aggressive land sales programs, marketing the airport area to potential land buyers as the Irvine Industrial Complex.

To protect the nearby residential villages also under construction, the company adopted CC&Rs to control industrial development. The goal of the CC&Rs was to establish a top-quality industrial park: highly landscaped, with generous setbacks, and limited signage. Control of building architecture was limited. A high-quality image was preferred, but even metal "Butler" buildings were technically permitted by the CC&Rs.

By the mid-1970s much of the airport area was built out. To satisfy the demand for industrial users, the Irvine Company initiated a new industrial park, called Irvine Industrial Complex-East, planned as a duplicate of the airport area, now renamed Irvine Industrial Complex-West, with low-rise warehouses and manufacturing buildings in a landscaped setting with strict controls on signs and limited controls on building architecture.

Then in 1980 the airport area began to change. Landowners petitioned the City of Irvine to revise the zoning regulations to permit new uses, renaming the area the Irvine Business Complex. In the next ten years, numerous one-story, tilt-slab warehouse buildings less than twenty years old were pulled down, replaced by new midrise office buildings, luxury apartment complexes, restaurants, and retail centers, built to satisfy new market demands fueled by three unrelated events:

- *Airline deregulation,* changed the role of the Orange County Airport from a commuter airport to a regional airport. Nonstop flights to the emerging hubs such as Denver, Dallas–Fort Worth, and Chicago made the area more attractive to national businesses.

- *Banking deregulation and tax law changes,* spurred commercial construction. New financial institutions entered the real estate development market, dramatically increasing the amount of available capital, and

- *California Proposition 13,* intensified the competition between local jurisdictions for new development to increase sales tax and hotel tax revenue to replace residential property taxes. Entitlement for revenue-generating, nonresidential development became easier.

Overnight a low-rise industrial park became a "boomer" edge-city business district. The CC&Rs adopted for industrial users ensured a minimum level of quality for the redevelopment activity, but as the buildings became taller and the activities more varied, the area became less harmonious: more a collection of individualistic projects than a single, coherent place.

To satisfy a demand for a more unified business district, the Irvine Company, now under new ownership, redefined the role of Irvine Industrial Complex-East, then ten years old. A new name, Irvine Spectrum, was adopted. Stricter design guidelines were written to control landscape and building appearance, and a more detailed private design review process was initiated, administered by a new department at the Irvine Company, Urban Planning and Design, a group of registered architects headed by Roger M. Seitz, FAIA.

A new architectural approach was taken to establish a sense of place and timelessness, actively opposing "trendy" design: such as the postmodernism of the late 1970s, deconstructivism of the mid-1980s, and historicism of the late 1980s. It also actively opposed the tendency by architects and developers to design stand-alone buildings that compete for attention by striving to be "unique."

The preferred building appearance was crisp and simple, using wall planes, structure, and fenestration as theme elements, with emphasis on building entries (Fig. 17-2). An evergreen canopy street tree program defined the landscape setting. Individual landscape expression was encouraged in the interior of the site. The site's perimeter was required to conform to the overall landscape structural framework of the district. On key streets, the landscape was installed well before individual site development, establishing a strong sense of place before the buildings arrived.

The result was a distinctive "Greenfields" edge city business district of white buildings in an evergreen setting, adjacent to two of the busiest freeways in Southern California.

As in Woodbridge, a private association is responsible for maintaining the street landscaping, ensuring that trees and shrubs are trimmed to create a highly manicured appearance. Funding comes from mandatory assessments levied on property owners.

As in Woodbridge, each property owner is required to abide by the policies in CC&Rs, including design review. Consistent with the CC&Rs, all new construction must be reviewed by the Irvine Company. Unlike Woodbridge, the aesthetic control of physical changes to existing buildings is not the responsibility of an architectural committee. Instead, the Irvine Company, as the declarant of the CC&Rs, reviews plans with assistance from a consulting architect. Typical projects include building additions, signs, communication equipment, landscape upgrades, and exterior color changes.

In the seven years of existence, both the first-generation design review process and the ongoing design review process in Irvine Spectrum have become simplified, as more land buyers, real estate brokers, facility managers, sign designers, landscape architects, and building architects have become more familiar with the intent of the design guidelines, and as more buildings are constructed that demonstrate the design guidelines.

Irvine Spectrum has proven to be very successful in appealing to businesses that desire a consistent, well-maintained environment in which property values are retained, especially to firms with a long-term economic outlook, such as Japanese-based organizations.

SUCCESS AT PRIVATE DESIGN REVIEW

From examining the experience in Woodbridge and Irvine Spectrum, the success of private design review depends on four characteristics:

Figure 17-2. Example of an industrial project constructed under guidelines for Irvine Spectrum industrial park.

1. An *effective legal structure* is needed to ensure that participation in the design review process is mandatory, not voluntary. The conditions to the land sales contract need to be binding, and the policies in the CC&Rs need to be enforceable.

2. *Design guidelines* need to be concise and well illustrated, firmly stating the intended vision of the neighborhood, while also allowing flexibility to address unforeseen changes in values and technology.

3. *Design reviewers* must possess a combination of skills, including (a) intimate knowledge of the design review district: the existing streets and buildings, the fundamental planning principles, the design review history, and the values of residents and property owners; (b) skill to clearly articulate the vision of the community to the designer, while not discouraging creativity, and without redesigning the project; (c) ability to read plans, with personal experience (or professional assistance) in architectural design, landscape architecture, site planning, and urban design, including practical experience in designing and constructing projects; and (d) talent to quickly recognize the designer's intent and not be persuaded by graphic style or oral eloquence, including the talent to recognize which pieces of information are missing from the presentation—information that can have a dramatic impact on the project's ultimate appearance, such as lighting, mechanical equipment, colors, fences, and signs.

4. *Strong support* by residents and property owners for the values inherent in the design guidelines. Residents must believe that the existing neighborhood is a better place in which to live because of the design review process: control over the actions of neighbors outweighs restrictions on personal activities.

Successful design review is difficult when the process is voluntary; when the guidelines are ambiguous, subject to the personal interpretation of reviewers; when the reviewers are unfamiliar with the community, cannot articulate design review goals without redesigning submitted projects, cannot read plans, are overly influenced by the graphic or oral skill of the presenter, or are easily swayed by the opinions of the individual on the design review board with the dominant personality; or when the decisions of the design review board are inconsistent with the values of the residents and property owners, such as when design review is used as a personal or political weapon.

A RECOMMENDATION

In recent years, many American communities have entered into public design review, leading to many success stories where the aesthetics of the physical environment have been protected and improved. Older residential neighborhoods have been protected from new development that may have destroyed the existing character. Downtowns have been redeveloped into first-class office districts.

Unfortunately, in too many American communities, a powerful opponent to improving the aesthetics of the physical environment has appeared: the direct actions by government itself.

Many single-purpose government agencies seem to ignore the negative impact their actions have on the aesthetic (and functional) quality of the physical environment:

- Capital planning policies that require new civic centers, high schools, and post offices to be designed as single-use enclaves, isolated from their communities.
- Street standards that require new local streets to be a minimum of 36 feet wide, for the ease of maneuvering oversized trash trucks and firefighting equipment.
- Public works standards that require sidewalks to be built adjacent to curbs to eliminate government-maintained street trees.

The result is a community where the direct action by government agencies weakens civic pride by creating places with inaccessible public facilities, dysfunctional streets, and token sidewalks. Today in many communities with private design review, unsightly physical features—such as graffiti, billboards, chain-link fences, weeds,

and overgrown landscaping—are now only found on public property.

Public design review should focus first on reviewing government actions that influence the aesthetics of the physical environment: the planning, design, and management of government facilities, including public streets. Then after demonstrating more sensitivity to the aesthetic impact of public projects, government agencies might be more credible at regulating the aesthetic impact of private projects.

In the meantime, private design review may be more effective than public design review. Compared to many government agencies, residents and property owners who engage in private design review often may have more intimate firsthand knowledge of the actual social/physical environment, may be more personally vested in the results of their decisions, and may be more cognizant and supportive of community values.

Perhaps the most worthwhile approach to design review is a partnership between the public sector controlling the aesthetics of public projects and the private sector controlling the aesthetics of private projects (Baab, DeSelm, 1990). Rather than being condemned or ignored, private design review should be encouraged by government agencies as a way for residents and property owners to become empowered to improve their quality of life and property values without the need for government intervention.

REFERENCES

Baab, David, and DeSelm, David. 1990. "Design Review: Public or Private Responsibility?" *Architecture California*, August 12, p. 55.

Gaines, James P. 1992. "Home Sales in Master-Planned Communities." *Urban Land*, June.

"Government by the Nice, for the Nice." 1992. *Economist*, July 25, p. 25.

Mouchard, Andre. 1992. "A Homeowner's Challenge." *Orange County Register*, May 3, p. B1.

Rowe, Jeff. 1992. "Out of the Ashes: An Irvine in LA?: Overseers of City's Rebuilding View OC Community as a Model." *Orange County Register*, June 17, p. A1.

Sipchen, Bob. 1992. "Barricades Define Isle of Peace in L.A." *Los Angeles Times, Orange County Edition*, August 11, p. A20.

18
Battery Park City: An American Dream of Urbanism

Francis P. Russell

University of Cincinnati

The process of creating design guidelines brings into play important existential questions about how we view ourselves as a culture through our architecture and urban form. In some cases, design guidelines are the perpetuation of existing misunderstood value systems or, worse yet, the unwitting perfection of ideologies that are reluctantly understood to be disdainful. The results are comfortable and supportive of the existing socioeconomic conditions, but contain an underlying crisis of meaning, experience, and culture. With this perspective we will examine Battery Park City in Manhattan, which was formulated according to a comprehensive set of design guidelines governing both its urban morphology and architectural expression. Of particular concern is the resultant urban morphology and architectural iconography as it reflects the underlying ideology of the design guidelines themselves. Battery Park City is relevant because of its comprehensive planned structure within one of the world's most well-defined cities, as well as its manifest ideology, created during this "moment of late consumer or multination capitalism," as Frederick Jameson labels the end of the twentieth century (Jameson, 1983, 125).

Battery Park City is a $4-billion mixed-use development on 92 acres of landfill in the Hudson River adjacent to the west side of Lower Manhattan. The landfill is a product of the early 1970s excavation for the foundations of the nearby World Trade Center towers and other buildings. Proposals had been made for the planning of this site as early as 1969; the current proposal was formulated during 1979–85 by Alexander Cooper Associates (Cooper Eckstut). This proposal called for structuring the new urban morphology on a grid system, with land parcelization as is typically found in Manhattan. In addition to the master plan of the development, Alexander Cooper formulated specific guidelines to determine building siting and massing, and a detailed set of restrictions on architectural qualities that determine colors, materials, and facade articulation. As promulgated by the designers, Battery Park City was to recreate and extend Manhattan across a narrow strip of landfill. In analyzing this plan, its guidelines, and built form we are able to understand its ideology and observe how it operates as a reflection of our current culture.

THE MASTER PLAN AND ITS URBAN MORPHOLOGY

Prior to its annexation and landfill, the Battery Park City site was part of the Hudson River pierhead. While this landfill is certainly the largest single expansion of Manhattan in recent years, it represents only a continuation of the expansion process that began shortly after the settlement of the city. Because Manhattan is an urban island, the quality of the relationship of the urban fabric with the edge takes on a special meaning. Until the 1940s, the Manhattan waterfront was devoted to the service of maritime industry with an active pierhead. The edge of Manhattan was defined by the nature of activities along the river as well as the river itself. While the port defined the edge of the city, both physically and functionally, the core of Manhattan grew up around the spine of Broadway, where retail, commercial, banking, and legislative functions congealed to constitute "downtown." Manhattan's development up to the mid-twentieth century had been driven primarily by a tendency to turn away from the river toward the interior of the island and the "civilizing" activities of culture. When the necessity of open space became apparent, New Yorkers proceeded, with the help of Frederick Law Olmsted, to fabricate their own version of "nature" in the 500-acre Central Park. Only after World II did new pressures of land speculation and urban density force a reconsideration of the waterfront as habitable space. In 1947, Paul and Perceival Goodman wrote of Manhattan, "By taking advantage for the first time, of its rivers hitherto, almost prevented by commerce and industry—it can become a city of neighborhoods wonderful to live in, as leisurely and comfortable as it is busy and exciting." (Goodman, 1960, 227). But as the port activities of the waterfront declined under the encroachment of rail and road, the edge of Manhattan was redefined by the east- and westside highways, and the Goodman's vision was abandoned.

Noncommercial Manhattan developments have typically initiated ambivalent responses to the waterfront. The highrise housing of Tudor City on the East River oriented its views away from the river and its industrial structures along the waterfront. But in the 1940s the United Nations chose a site on the river where it replaced a stockyard. Perhaps the most positive response to the river was Riverside Park, modeled by Olmsted, which avoided the Westside Highway and moved directly to the water's edge. The park itself became a transparent buffer that replaced the function of the previous working edge of Manhattan.

The first major proposal for building to the waterfront was described in a 1966 proposal for Lower Manhattan in a linear city of low-rise, high-

Figure 18-1. Rendering of 1969 Battery Park City Plan.

density fabric by Wallace-McHarg, Wittlesey and Conklin. This proposal covered the waterfront from the Brooklyn Bridge on the east to Canal Street on the west. Office and housing towers on stepped section plinths with courtyards were to constitute whole blocks on the waterfront. These blocks were disengaged from the pattern of the inner-core fabric, blocking many vistas from the center core to the rivers. All of the buildings, except for the towers, were six to eight floors and bordered by a continuous promenade along the rivers. When the Battery Park City landfill was suggested, a new study was undertaken by Harrison and Abramovitz, Johnson and Burgee, Conklin and Rossant in 1969 (Fig. 18-1). Similarly, this was a "megastructure" scheme that designated north and south waterfront housing groups, or "pods," on either side of a retail and recreational area across from the World Trade Center, with three interconnected office towers at the southern end of the development.

The current proposal, developed in 1979 by Alexander Cooper Associates (Cooper Eckstut), differs from the previous proposals in choosing to reemphasize the "street" by extending the Broadway grid over the site. The development is zoned into two residential areas at the north and south, bracketing a commercial center situated across from the World Trade Center (Fig. 18-2). The six-million-square-foot commercial center consists of three 50-story office towers and a cluster of low structures at their base. The residential areas are organized on small east-west cross

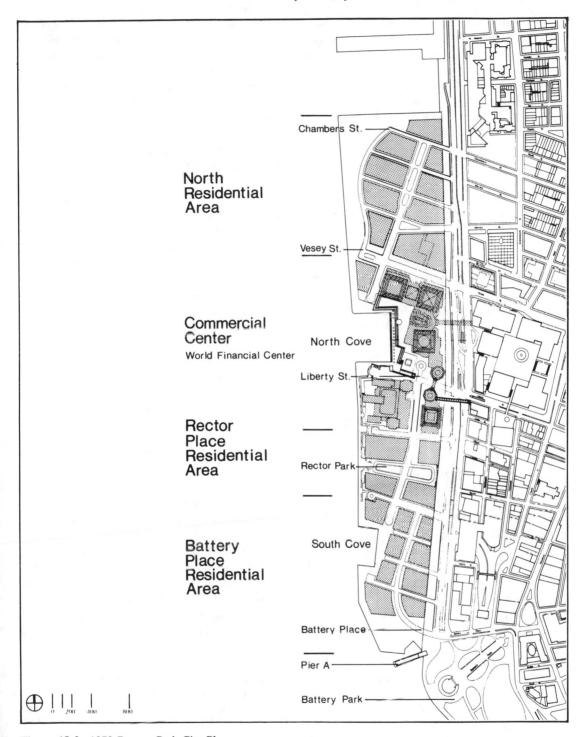

North
Residential
Area

Commercial
Center
World Financial Center

Rector
Place
Residential
Area

Battery
Place
Residential
Area

Chambers St.

Vesey St.

North Cove

Liberty St.

Rector Park

South Cove

Battery Place

Pier A

Battery Park

Figure 18-2. 1979 Battery Park City Plan.

streets originating from the Broadway grid and a few major north-south avenues. Each residential area has special open spaces, such as Rector Place, South Cove, and Battery Place on the south, and North End Avenue and Chambers Park on the north, and is ringed along the river by a 1.2 mile esplanade running the length of the development to Battery Park.

A relationship to "edge" marks most clearly the heritage against which new developments on Manhattan's waterfront can be viewed. Accordingly, we can understand the novelty of Battery Park City relative to the historical attitudes about development of the Manhattan waterfront. At no point in Manhattan is the street grid extended to the water, either over or under the existing roadway barriers, though the experience of the river in an esplanade and a park has been used successfully in Riverside Park, Carl Schurz Park on the Upper East Side, and elsewhere. Where building has moved to the river, it occurs as an "overlook" condition without direct access to the water, for example, Sutton Place and Brooklyn Heights. Traditional modernist methods of building to the water have advocated a puncturing of the edge with megastructures, such as Paul Rudolf's proposal for a media center and Davis Brody's Waterside Apartments built in 1974. This later built project is a semisuccessful creation in which the megastructure projects as an object-island into the East River.

The Block and Street morphology of the Battery Park City plan clearly has much more in common with Manhattan than previous modernist waterfront proposals. However, this proposed "extension" of the city's urban fabric is distinctly apart from that from which it is derived. Though extended from Broadway the Battery Park City street grid is dissimilar to the rest of the city's block structure. The Manhattan grid is composed of rectangular blocks that provide an orienting structure within the city. Rectangular blocks in the east-west direction, combined with the narrowness of Manhattan Island, tend to direct views in either direction from the core to the waterfronts. Even though the river is largely inaccessible, this view mechanism also provides orientation. Battery Park City's mostly square blocks may create a disorienting factor within the new district (Schwarting, 1981, 36).

Additionally, the divisive position of West Street at the east side of the new district functions to isolate the area. While the scale of this road is smaller than the previously planned Westway proposal (a six-lane highway along Manhattan's west side), it still poses an insurmountable barrier between Battery Park City and the core of Lower Manhattan. Despite the intentions of Battery Park City's planners to extend the fabric of the city, the 275-foot width and high-speed vehicular activity of West Street prevent an experiential unification of the new development with the city. Because of this, Battery Park City will remain a separated and autonomous part of Lower Manhattan. A more effective approach to integrating Battery Park City with the rest of the city would have considered not only the basic grid structure of the city, but more importantly the existing relationships between districts in Lower Manhattan. "Generally the districts relate to areas with distinctive character and place and often relate to the formal morphology of Manhattan, their name alone provides a degree of awareness." In addition, "it would appear that Lower Manhattan . . . has a very complex morphology which, if ordered, is more latent than actual, or more implicit than explicit" (Schwarting, 1975, 5). Districts in this area would have an adjacency, which is somewhat amorphous, created by areas of overlap and buffers operating as transition zones. This is the organic nature of the urban fabric.

Battery Park City does not participate in these mechanics, primarily because of West Street. The boundary condition will be too severe to permit overlap. So that while the extension of the grid, though distorted, carries with it a conceptual idea of the continuation of the urban fabric, this is not reinforced by the perceptual unification of the parts that manifests itself in the urban fabric of Lower Manhattan. In its ambivalent response to the basic existing edge conditions of Manhattan the new morphology of Battery Park City does not adhere to the inherent urban structure of its context. The designer's initial response of extending the grid to reassert the primacy of the street is a logical extension of the urban fabric, but an essentially superficial one. This is a theme that carries through the development, in its determining design guidelines, and its underlying ideology.

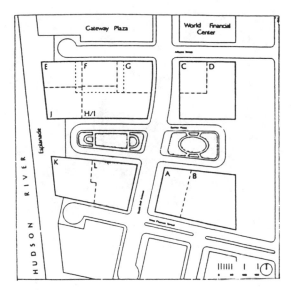

Figure 18-3, Rector Place Plan.

Figure 18-4. Proposed Rector Place model viewed from the Hudson River.

Figure 18-5. Proposed Rector Place model viewed from the south.

DESIGN GUIDELINES AND ARCHITECTURAL FORM

The development at Battery Park City represents a public-private partnership on a scale unprecedented in New York. Because of the proposed participation of numerous parties, Coopers Eckstut enacted a far-reaching set of planning and design guidelines for the development. The bulk of these guidelines were created for the residential areas north and south of the commercial center. This analysis of design guidelines and architectural form will focus on the south residential area, Rector Place in particular (Fig. 18-3), as this is the first completed district, and the first to reflect the final product of the design guidelines.

The established development guidelines for the south residential area are as follows. Massing is largely composed of 6- to 9-story buildings with taller buildings interspersed at the ends of Rector Place (Figs. 18-4, 18-5). A series of towers along West Street steps up from 250 to 400 feet. All massing maintains strong street walls. Rector Place is massed with two 25-story buildings at both west and east ends with a 25-story building across from a 44-story building on the south. In the middle on the north side is a 15-story apartment building situated across from a low 9-story building. Height of street walls are dictated as 60–85 feet on the west and 110–35 feet to the

east of South End Avenue. Land allocation is dominated by residential use, except on the ground floors, where retail and professional office use are preferred on all north-south avenues. Restaurants and community facilities are sited adjacent to large open spaces.

In addition to guidelines governing the project at the scale of the massing, land use, and so on, another set of guidelines dictated specific architectural details of each building as follows. Buildings should be made of brick with a two- or three-story stone base; metal and glass curtain walls and concrete are prohibited. Special articulation is required at lobby entrances, polished stone is discouraged. Brick walls should be constructed with standard $2\frac{1}{4}'' \times 8''$ bricks with intermediate expression lines of stone at 75–85 feet on the facade to reduce the scale of the streetwall. Different color brick tones are required for adjacent or opposite development parcels. Reflective glass in the windows is prohibited, with variation in the window size encouraged. Masonry colors must be within a range of warm earth tones, contrasting colors are discouraged. "Sensitive arrangements of colors and materials are desired for decorative purposes in special locations." Colors of metal elements, window frames, railings and fences are to be a "parklike" black or dark green. Rooftops and bulkheads of buildings should be designed to create special and interesting effects with terraces and setbacks recommended. Articulated roof lines or parapets should be major decorative features made of stone or masonry. Expression lines marked by changes of color, texture, materials, or fenestration are required at 75–85 feet. Pedestrian arcades are required on north-south avenues to provide weather protection and access to retail and commercial facilities. Balconies may not occur within ten feet of a corner nor below the sixth floor. Relief of scale is encouraged on the stone bases of the buildings through changes in type, height, and pattern of the stonework to visually distinguish two different buildings and "thereby avoid excessively large massing on the streets." Roofs of parking structures must be landscaped and all roofs should be designed with consideration to the views from above. All exterior lighting will be the same type of lamp commonly used in New York City parks. Other guidelines restrict signage, fencing, canopies, and exhausts, and so forth (Cooper, Eckstut, 1985).

These guidelines, set forth in the May 1985 Master Plan for Battery Place, are those that governed the design of the Rector Place residential area and other residential areas when built. The recently completed Rector Place is part of the southern residential district, located just south of the commercial center and the preexisting Gateway Plaza. As intended, the existing massing of the eight buildings along Rector Park follows the massing guidelines. All of the buildings have unique qualities, but they also have, necessarily, the same types of features—stone bases, expression lines and cornices, honorific articulation of entry, and a picturesque massing of the upper floors and bulkheads. Some buildings are highly articulated while others meet the minimum requirements of the guidelines. For example, the building on site H/I (Fig. 18-6) at the northwest corner of South End Avenue, by Charles Moore,

Figure 18-6. Initial Architectural Proposal for Parcel H/I.

is perhaps overdesigned for a "developer's condominium," with multiple cornice lines, balconies, and a distinctively framed arched opening midway up the facade. Conversely, the building across Rector Park on site L and A by Bond, Ryder, James is plainly articulated on the upper stories with dominant brick panels extruded from a stone surface. Most of the detailing, with cornices, arched openings, rustication, and the like, is based on traditional models of masonry construction, even though all surfaces are veneered. This detailing in the construction of the stone bases, with the use of carved panels and varied textured, colored, and sized coursing gives the illusion of bearing wall joinery. Bulkhead design on the buildings range from a semiconstructivist treatment in James Polshek's corner tower, a recycled Art Deco expression across the park in the top of Ulrick Franzen's building, and a traditional heavy cornice on Charles Moore's building.

Distinctive design in these buildings, ranging from picturesque massing to detailing of the stonework, is an attempt to use a stylized architectural vocabulary to denote a distinctive identity intended to contribute to a feeling of "place." Every detail, as structured by the guidelines, is successful at reducing the scale of fairly massive buildings to the level of the pedestrian and at attempting to lend the buildings and space some intimacy. In summary, the entire complex is apparently successful at bringing together the best aspects of Manhattan's urban fabric. Attractive brick and limestone buildings, a plentitude of landscaping in street trees and pocket parks, and a beautiful waterfront esplanade complemented by a luxurious yacht club are all set within the New York gridiron structure. This adoring view of Manhattan is intact down to the reproduced Central Park lampposts and prewar cast-iron benches.

It would be interesting at this point to return to the design guidelines with a closer examination of their origins and implications. Battery Park City is conceived, in its morphology of grid extension and articulation of building mass, to be a continuation of Manhattan's urban fabric. What the master planners sought was a way to reproduce the essence of the best qualities of "New Yorkness" in its physical—if not exactly its social—form.

The formulation of the development control guidelines applied to Battery Park City have their roots in the early 1970s. Alexander Cooper, together with a team of planners for the city of New York, worked on a project that resulted in a new Zoning for Housing Quality, enacted in 1975. The study brought to fruition the efforts to promote and protect integral urban form that gained impetus in the 1960s with the theories of Jane Jacobs. At the root of these motivations was the notion that the city is wonderful and that it operates in a complex and miraculous way. The object was to study the city, understand how the best aspects of it worked, and then distill this into a usable formula. According to Cooper, "The challenge was to define and then quantify quality." The group ended by establishing those goals common to neighborhoods, and good urbanity in general: security, stability, maintenance, privacy, scale, variety on a city scale with homogeneity on a neighborhood scale, vitality, convenience, and identity. These were the tools with which planners could start "providing the basis for genuine and original architectural expression growing out of valid needs and aspirations" (Reiss and Kwartler, 1974, p. 4). And this was the ideological foundation promulgated by the Battery Park City master planners and their guidelines.

The guidelines are a distillation of the morphological and iconographic conditions that make the traditional, prewar, block of New York successful. Cooper Eckstut catalogued those conditions

Figure 18-7. Photo of architectural precedent included with design guidelines document.

from the cornices down to the fence railing and presented them in a formula for what the residential areas of Battery Park City should look like. In support of the guidelines they went so far as to include photographs of the nicer residential districts of Park and Fifth Avenues, the rooftops of Central Park West and others (Fig. 18-7). In the conception of Battery Park City, Cooper Eckstut has achieved the intent of the goals defined in 1975. The existing and projected built environment does achieve scale, variety and homogeneity, vitality, and identity. The spaces of Battery Park City are pleasant. The perceptual elements of the existing space are functioning well. The semiological aspects of the architectural language in the built projects work on a superficial level of apparent variety. The predominant stylistic tendency of borrowing historical styles is not immediately disturbing even where precedents are literally apparent, such as Chanin's Century Towers in the work of Franzen, the McGraw-Hill building adapted by the Gruzen Partnership's first proposal for parcel D, Conklin-Rossant's duplication of the Dakota in the unbuilt first proposal for parcel C, and references to McKim, Mead and White's 999 Fifth Avenue by Charles Moore (Marpillero, 1984, 21).

IDEOLOGY

Ideology can be seen as a certain set of representations and beliefs—religious, moral, political, and aesthetic, which refer to nature, society, and to life and activities of men in relation to nature and society. Ideology has the social function of managing the overall structure of society by inducing men to accept in their consciousness the place and role assigned to them by this structure (Gandelsonas, 1973, 94).

The desire to control the urban development of large areas is essentially utopian. New forms are continually engineered to improve the environment of city dwellers, if not to propose a perfect society in themselves. The intent, or ideology, of these "perfections" is manifest in the form of the improvement and is of considerable impact to the occupants. The presence of ideologies is revealed in either latent or active form, each perfection adopting its own critical posture toward all others that preceded it. Clearly, to understand the true ideological foundation of this controlled urban development, we must look beyond the well-intentioned stated notions of the designers.

The ideology of Battery Park city as manifest in its design guidelines and built form is complex. The development of Battery Park City in both urban morphology and architectural expression postulates a pervasive disaffection with modernist notions of making urban form and architectural context. An essentially historicist attitude toward making architectural expression dominates the articulation guidelines of Battery Park City, and a contextual approach is adopted in recurrent reference to Manhattan's morphology and iconography. This thinking reveals a romantic view of the mature urban context and its cultural richness that describes the uniqueness and essential fragility of the complex framework of urbanity.

At the same time, despite the antimodernist derivations from context and historical precedent, the form and guidelines of Battery Park City retain an inherent modernist attitude toward urban planning. In the tradition of the planning theory of the 1950s and 1960s the designers of Battery Park City have relied on a highly rational "systems approach" to defining and then "quantifying quality." It is the rational approach to contextual and historicist applications through design guidelines that results in an ideological conflict. In formal terms this approach creates, at best, a "scientific picturesqueness." Unfortunately, the street and block morphology and the prewar iconography, as recommended by the plan and guidelines, are mechanically derived from the New York context without benefit of its inherent cultural framework. Contextualist urban designers understand that the

character of Manhattan is difficult to formulate and in cases of redevelopment is far more easily destroyed than recreated, as in recent proposals for Times Square (Hiss, 1990, 94). More importantly they know the essential qualities of "place" and context to be the history of the city and the nature of the people that occupy it. The architectural form of Battery Park City has been rendered without true insight into the nature and form of the city, much as the new urban morphology has been structured without understanding the complex district identities of Manhattan.

Further inconsistencies are evident. The mechanical derivation of design guidelines stems from positive humanistic concerns, but its misapplication results in serious consequences. According to Jencks, today's notions of reinserting meaningful signs and symbols into architecture was a by-product of the response to the negative semiosis of late modern architecture (Jencks, 1980, 110). Yet the methodology proposed in the design guidelines to carry this out was still essentially modernist: to intellectually dissect, and then reconstruct, a "system" of meaningful architectural form. This same rational system of thought that, in late modernism, insisted that truthfulness of form was to be reflective of the inherent function of the building, now accepts the notion that the mechanical derivation and production of meaningful iconography through design guidelines is an acceptable functional activity for an architect. As Geoffrey Broadbent would say, "According to these, the creation of meaning is seen as functionalism" (Broadbent, 1980, 120).

However we understand the following discordance. While the creation of meaning is a functional goal, the meaning attempted at Battery Park City (historical "New Yorkness") is unacceptable because it represents neither the true character of the new urban form nor its contemporary culture. Subsequently true modernists will reject this attempt though today, in the postmodern culture, we accept what they would not: that there necessarily exists a close relationship of sign behavior to "substitution," as Umberto Eco put it (Eco, 1976, 6–7). The resultant architectural form of the guideline process at Battery Park City, the Rector Place Residential District in particular, displays rather clearly the "substitution" of a misappropriated language.

This is important in ideological terms, but also

for the "making of place." "Things . . . tell . . . about their own making, historical circumstances under which they were made, and if they are *real* things, they also reveal truth" (Norberg-Schulz, 1979, 187). The structural nature of the design guidelines is present in the architecture, even if the sought after qualities of "New Yorkness" are lost. It is the visibility of the design controls within the "unauthentic" architectural form that causes our identification of the "place" to be "untruthful." This condition causes deeper problems, particularly alienation, in which "man's loss of identification with . . . his environment . . . loss of place [causes] things [to] become mere objects of consumption which are thrown away after use" (Norberg-Schulz, 1979, 168).

It is just this urban alienation that the notion of the progressive master plan and architectural guidelines are designed to prevent. The reactionary response of postmodern planners, which attempts to recreate a known successful precedent, is not in itself dislikeable, but it is naive. It cannot succeed at making a place because of its own inherent limits. This method is not able to create new forms, but only to recombine environments, many of those without their necessary cultural structure. The "quantification of quality" is in itself a contradiction in terms. At best, it results, through design guidelines, in the uniformity of quality control.

In retrospect, we can see that the designers and the Battery Park City Authority do clarify early on that restrictive development guidelines, however eschewed by the developers themselves, would ensure a consistently high quality of environment, attractive to investors and consumers alike. Once developers became comfortable with the idea that guidelines would help them, they worked closely with the planning officials. Battery Park City represents the best of the political hybrid system, typical of New York, in which massive development projects are initiated and sometimes carried out through a colossal marriage of corporatism and public policy making, such as Westway, Lincoln West, and the Times Square Redevelopment Plan (Savitch, 1988, 59). The detailed guidelines are the ersatz legal manifestation of a corporate desire. Overarching this is the pervasive attitude that, indeed, above all else, the "city is a machine for wealth creation" (Hall, 1988, 343). Here it is difficult to avoid the Marx-

ian critiques of planning popular in the 1970s. "Planning is an historically specific and socially necessary response to the self-disorganizing tendencies of privatized capitalist social and property relations as they appear in urban space" (Hall, 1988, 337). The design guidelines for Battery Park City have more to do with protecting developers from themselves than anything else.

It is possible to recognize another sinister yet successful ideology from within this analysis. As the ends justify the means, so the misappropriation of form in functional terms represents clearly three themes: the reinforcement of the urban symbols of the status quo, the vehicle for the driving economic pragmatism that makes New York what it is, and the structure for the protection of the economic system that will keep it working. Some would argue that the pursuit of profit *is* the "nature" of Manhattan. Notwithstanding, as Norberg-Schulz puts it, "the socio-economical conditions are like a picture frame, they offer a certain 'space' for life to take place, but do not determine its existential meaning" (Norberg-Schulz, 1979, 1).

MEANING

Economic pragmatism is the predominant theme typical of what Peter Hall terms "the Rousification of America" (Hall, 1988, 357). In the case of Battery Park City, the image being sold is "New Yorkness" with an economic and legal framework erected to support it. Most disturbingly, the result is more than the intentions of the developers, it is what the consumers demand.

> Wholly preoccupied with reproduction, with the creation of urbane disguises . . . the Ersatz Main Street of Disneyland . . . the phony historic festivity of a Rouse Marketplace . . . this elaborate apparatus is at pains to assert its ties to the kind of city life it is in the process of obliterating . . . an architecture of deception which, in its happy-faced familiarity, constantly distances itself from the most fundamental realities. The architecture of this city is almost purely semiotic, playing the game of grafted signification, theme park building (Sorkin, 1992, xiv)

It is the design guidelines that structure this urban illusion. Within a standard spatial structure and urban morphology, the architectural expres-

Figure 18-8. View of Rector Place looking northwest toward Parcel H/I.

sion functions over a rigid syntax to produce a required varied semantic. The overall image is structured to create a "New York" environment. Individual buildings are designed to create a limited diversity. Images of turn-of-the-century Beaux-Arts work sit next to Art Deco or picturesque chateaux in relative pluralism, but a pluralism that is only "a willy-nilly juxtapositioning akin to the variety of media images that we can see on television" (Sorkin, 1985).

Controlled development and design guidelines have created a crisis of meaning in the architecture and urban structure of Battery Park City. Perhaps the strong contextualist approach to creating new urban and architectural form is to blame. Through the guidelines, the individual designers are required to look at prewar New York for models of appropriate architectural expression. They have accommodated the guidelines by creating "recombinant" architectural expressions that are not creative acts of interpretation and translation, but are directly borrowed from an established precedent (Fig. 18-8). This becomes both a confirmation of the designer's restraints in creating original form and contemporary culture's comfort with relying on known "cultural alibis" (Norberg-Schultz, 1979, 169).

As a prime component of the crisis of meaning the design guidelines' reliance on historical precedent is an important issue and one endemic to the controversy of postmodern architecture. On the one side, it is clear that some reference to precedent is necessary as the precondition of any common understanding of architectural meaning. On the other side, we find that nontransformative recall of historical architectural form is more effective in undermining the desired meaning than in promoting it. According to Colquhoun, we are standing today, on one side of the "chasm" of twentieth-century modernism, where, when we recall historical form, "we tend to express its most general and trivial connotations; it is merely the 'pastness' of the past that is evoked" (Colquhoun, 1984, 38). Theorists claim that historicism is appropriate in appealing to society's collective memory. In the context of Battery Park City, this tendency is more exploitive than accommodating as it taps "the semantic potential of *heteroglossia,* the ragbag collection of historical quotations" (Boyer, 1990, 126).

Without the meaningful expression of referent historical form, we are left with another problem. The architectural signification of recombinant form is not only chaotic, but it is directed toward "nonmeaning" in a very specific way. This product is "kitsch," which according to Leon Krier, "leaves us today either with shambles and detritus or with arrogant caricatures and illusions of culture, but in most cases with kitsch. Kitsch might be described as an amorphous compilation of confused codes. . . . It is truly the most violent indication of the profound alienation which lies at the basis of industrial production" (Krier, 1978, 57). To a large degree, this is exactly what design guidelines are intended to prevent.

EXPERIENCE

As design controls have contributed to the crisis of meaning, they have also created a crisis of experience. The nature of the design guidelines at Battery Park City has confined the experience of the architecture and urban structure to a series of "images." Each building is expressed, largely, through a basic structural framework as a two-dimensional architectural image. Each urban space is a volumetric and visual composition that recalls other Manhattan spaces. All of this relies on references to architecture and urban form other than itself. The processing of these images is the seminal experience of the viewer, more so even than the spatial experience of blocks and streets or open public spaces. In this case, the phenomenological understanding of built form is overridden by a cognitive "reading" in which one experience depends on another for legitimacy. What spatial reality that exists is transformed into images. Frederick Jameson asserts that this is one of the extremely negative aspects of postmodern culture (Jameson, 1983, 125). The result is a topological understanding of "place" and space. Piaget views this process, not so much negative as naive, in the same way that he proposes that children perceive space, without the critical judgment necessary to define a three-dimensional environment nor the relative understanding of how to interact with it (Arnheim, 1966, 187). However, it is clear that in the same way that children interact with and represent the world with wildly disproportionate elements, so the architectural design guidelines

of Battery Park City have disporportionally loaded the majority of the experience of "place" on the manipulation of what has become imagery. This implies the relative unimportance of spatial qualities in the experience of public places. This is not altogether surprising in its appeal to a contemporary culture for whom the experience of "place" is typically derived from the flat screen of a television.

CULTURE

Every aspect of this analysis of development control in Battery Park City has been constituting a description of a perceived crisis of culture. As urbanism manifests the ideology of the culture that produced it, so Battery Park City tells us about the current culture of consumption and its accompanying social disintegration. At their most fundamental level in Battery Park City, design guidelines are implemented to create a product and to ensure "quality control" during its manufacture. It represents refined methods in the production of "place" by postindustrial culture. The effort to create a more humane built environment through design controls has clearly been coopted by political and economic forces. But the result is not contrary to what the users need and expect. The shaping of the means of making "place" by the directives of marketing forces has come to be expected by contemporary society. The Battery Park City Authority should more accurately call itself the "Urban Experience Development Corporation," as Tony Hiss humorously describes the capitalism of place-making (Hiss, 1990, 99). This tendency manifests itself in the commodification of the urban experience through a production system of development control. The fabrication of consumable images of "New Yorkness" through the control of architectural and urban expression is compatible with the targeted group of users. In spatial and social terms, the experience sought has less to do with New York and more to do with preconceived ideas of what New York is or should be. This "post-modern culture can be said to be about the weaving of ever more elaborate fabrics of simulation, about successive displacements of 'authentic' signifiers" (Sorkin, 1992, 229). The urban experiences at Battery Park City are removed further and further from reality to a fictitious world highly controlled, not only in physical form, but in cultural content.

Social disintegration ensues. Development control has ensured a district, which despite the social pluralism of most other areas of Manhattan, is very homogeneous in makeup. This simulated environment appeals to those interested in an urban experience that has been "sanitized for your protection (as the phrase goes), wholesome, undangerous, and 7/8th's real size" (Hall, 1988, 347). The physical isolation of Battery Park City from the rest of Lower Manhattan, its uniformity of appeal, and its economic exclusivity all work to remove its occupants from any meaningful contact with the adjacent authentic urban experience. This can only be seen as intended and expedited by the development controls. Ultimately, the development mechanism and resultant form originate from the response to undesirable urban conditions in social form. "If the dualities of wealth and poverty create stressful discrepancies, what better way to sidestep these inequities than by connecting the civic and symbolic traditions of New York's architectural heritage to fictional recreations" (Boyer, 1992, 194). One wonders, as Christine Boyer has asked, whether it is ethical to expend public funds and utilize public policy making in development controls for the purpose of creating and sustaining what is ostensibly a private district. What greater inequity to inflict with urban design than the privatization of public space.

CONCLUSION

Battery Park City's Rector Place is a hollow image of New York's iconography. Attention to basic perceptual issues, key to making a livable urban environment, has been sustained. But Battery Park City is somehow unrelated to what it is trying to be. What has been characterized as the essence of New York life—"the anxiety and exhilaration of urban living"—will never exist here. Battery Park City will remain a "perfected," isolated environment outside of the city that it calls itself a part of. If this is the intention of the design controls, then we can call this a success. Unfortunately, it is also a manifestation of the worst aspect of our culture.

The American Dream, which was previously

embodied in two-acre suburban homestead, now returns to the city. Urbanism, in this case New York, has now been idealized, and the appropriate forms have been harnessed to propagate this image. The underlying motivations that will govern life in Battery Park City will not be so different from those found in suburbia, though they will now operate within a coopted morphology. While the new tenants of Battery Park City, a part of a homogeneous group of upwardly mobile aspiring urbanites, are interested in having the form of the city, they are less interested in the actual urban existence. Theirs is an urban life "purified," as Richard Sennet would say, of all of those undesirable elements that lurk in the sometimes psychotic urban environment[1] (Sennet, 1970). Unfortunately, these are inseparable from the "exhilarating" aspects of urban life. Existence in Battery Park City will be very pleasant, but it will never constitute the same kind of rich urban milieu that makes Manhattan what it is.

REFERENCES

Alexander Cooper and Associates. 1979. *Battery Park City: Draft Summary Report and 1979 Master Plan*. New York: Battery Park City Authority.

Arnheim, Rudolf. 1966. *Art and Visual Perception: A Psychology of the Creative Eye*. Berkeley: University of California Press.

Boyer, M. Christine. 1992. "Cities for Sale: Merchandising History at South Street Seaport." In *Variations on a Theme Park: The New American City and the End of Public Space,* ed. Michael Sorkin, pp. 181–204. New York: Noonday Press.

Broadbent, Geoffrey. 1980. "The Deep Structures of Architecture." In *Signs, Symbols, and Architecture,* ed. Geoffrey Broadbent, Richard Bunt, and Charles Jencks, pp. 119–68. Bath, England: Pitman Press.

Colquhoun, Alan. 1984. "Three Kinds of Historicism." *Oppositions* 84, no. 26: 29–39

Cooper Eckstut and Associates. 1985. *Battery Place Residential Area Design Guidelines*. New York: Battery Park City Authority.

Gandelsonas, Mario, and Diana Agrest. 1973. "Semiot-

---

1. Disturbingly, the original intentions of the New York Planning Authorities to provide Battery Park City with low-, moderate-, and high-income housing in equal thirds was abandoned. Currently, all 14,000 residential units are expected to be luxury apartments.

ics and Architecture: Ideological Consumption or Theoretical Work." *Oppositions* 73, no. 1: 93–100

Goodman, Paul, and Percival Goodman. 1960. *Communitas: Means of Livelihood and Ways of Life*. New York: Vintage.

Hall, Peter. 1988. *Cities of Tomorrow: An Intellectual History of Urban Planning and Design in the Twentieth Century*. Oxford: Basil Blackwell.

Hiss, Tony. 1990. *The Experience of Place*. New York: Knopf.

Jacobs, Jane. 1961. *The Death and Life of Great American Cities*. New York: Random House.

Jameson, Frederick. 1983. "Postmodernism and Consumer Society." In *The Anti-Aesthetic, Essays on Postmodern Culture*, ed. Hal Foster, pp. 111–25 Port Townsend, Wash.: Bay Press.

Jencks, Charles. 1980. "The Architectural Sign." In *Signs, Symbols, and Architecture*, ed. Geoffrey Broadbent, Richard Bunt, and Charles Jencks, pp. 71–118. Bath, England: Pitman Press.

Krier, Leon. 1978. "The Consumption of Culture." *Oppositions* 78, no. 14: 55–59

Marpillero, Sandro. 1984. "Rinascenza e Illusione: Battery Park City ed Altre Storie." *Casabella*. 48, no. 507: 16–30

Norberg-Schulz, Christian. 1979. *Genius Loci: Towards a Phenomenology of Architecture*. New York: Rizzoli.

Reiss, C., and M. Kwartler. 1974. "Housing Quality Program Puts Human Scale into Residential Zoning, New York City Develops Guidelines for Builders." *Planner's Notebook* 4, no. 6: 1–10

Savitch, H. V. 1988. *Post-Industrial Cities: Politics and Planning in New York, Paris and London*. Princeton, N.J.: Princeton University Press.

Schwarting, J. M. 1981. "Battery Park City Will Rise." *Progressive Architecture* 62, no. 2: 32, 36, 40

———. 1975. *Broome Street Study*. Washington, D.C.: National Endowment for the Arts.

Sennet, Richard. 1970. *The Uses of Disorder: Personal Identity and City Life*. New York: Random House.

Sorkin, Michael. 1992. "Introduction: Variations on a Theme Park." In *Variations on a Theme Park: The New American City and the End of Public Space*, ed. Michael Sorkin, pp. xi–xv. New York: Noonday Press.

Urban Design Council of the City of New York. 1975. *Zoning for Housing Quality*. New York: City of New York.

Epilogue

Witold Rybczynski

University of Pennsylvania

The old American struggle between gentility and individual liberty has reappeared in the guise of something called "design review," which centers on the idea that the public should exercise some sort of independent, external control over the appearance of buildings, and that the public good requires some sacrifice of private expression. In other words, just as there are building codes, fire codes, and public health codes, there ought to be architectural codes.

Public influence over aesthetic matters in architecture is hardly new; most municipalities already have some sort of jurisdiction in this area. Architectural committees assess building designs before they are built, ordinances require the use of selected materials (or prohibit the use of others), and some municipalities even publish guidelines that provide designers with general lists of do's and don'ts. But full-fledged design review goes much further than that and can involve strict control over every aspect of the external appearance of a building, including colors, roof pitches and overhangs, window shapes, architectural ornament, and even construction techniques.

Not surprisingly, design review is controversial. On one side of the argument are municipal officials, city planners, and neighborhood groups, who tend to support the idea. So do most ordinary citizens, for whom design review is attractive, whether it serves actively to promote the traditional style in a historic district or merely to inhibit the often bizarre and unharmonious designs of some contemporary architects. On the other side are the architects themselves, most of whom, understandably, don't like the idea of curbs on what they consider their creative prerogative. In a recent informal survey of practitioners carried out by the American Institute of Architects and the University of Cincinnati, about half the respondents characterized design review as petty, expensive, and basically ineffective.

Whatever else one can say about design review, it is certainly not ineffective. Four recent museum extension projects by prominent architects illustrate this point. An addition by Gwathmey Siegel & Associates to Frank Lloyd Wright's Guggenheim Museum was the subject of intense public scrutiny that undoubtedly affected the final outcome, unhappily in the eyes of many critics. Moshe Safdie's proposed addition to the Montreal Museum of Fine Art was the result of a public review process that demanded that the architect significantly alter his design to preserve a 1905 apartment building on the site. Michael Graves's addition to the Whitney Museum in New York was also the result of public controversy, so much so that after many iterations, the design was finally shelved. And Romaldo Guirgola's design for a large expansion of Louis Kahn's Kimbell Art Museum in Fort Worth, Texas, was also ultimately abandoned as the result of widespread negative public reaction.

Design review is shaping up to be one of the hottest architectural issues of the nineties, and one might well ask why. What has happened to incite this public muscle-flexing in an arena that has traditionally been left to the experts. To begin with, design review is precisely a reflection of a public disaffection with the idea of expertise, a disaffection that is generalized and hardly restricted to the architectural profession—teachers, lawyers, doctors, and politicians have all come in for the same sort of treatment and the same calls for public control. In the case of architects, the lack of confidence is exacerbated by the profession's current low credibility. After all, what is the public to make of the sea change that architecture underwent in the seventies? One year it was urban renewal, high-rise housing, and stripped-down modernism, the next year, with hardly any explanation, these were replaced by enthusiastic historic preservation and historicist postmodernism.

Another reason for the popularity of design review is the public's realization that there is no longer a consensus in the architectural profession about what constitutes good design. Architecture is currently characterized by a variety of schools: modernism, postmodernism, regionalism, neotraditionalism, classicism, and deconstructivism. The differences between them are conceptual as well as stylistic; it is not merely a question of a building's appearance, but also of how it takes its place in urban surroundings. Increasingly, new buildings are anticipated not with excitement but with trepidation: "What on earth will they do next?" In this context, design review is welcomed as a tool to assure a minimum compatibility between the new and the old.

Critics of design review, particularly of design review that attempts to promote a neotraditional architecture or urbanism, often characterize it as "nostalgic." This is not inaccurate. Nostalgia is defined as a "bittersweet longing for things, persons, or situations of the past," and an awareness of—and an attachment to—the past is a hallmark of contemporary American culture. Just as there are periods when change is eagerly sought (one

thinks of the 1920s, for example) there are times of retrenchment and reflection. The current epoch is certainly more closely allied to the latter than the former, and it is no coincidence that modern design review so often originates in the context of historical preservation. Two things need to be said about the current manifestation of nostalgia: it is deeply felt and should not be facilely dismissed, but it is also unlikely to be permanent.

Perhaps the most powerful reason for the rise of design review arises from a condition within the practice of building itself: the enormous multiplicity of choice that technology has provided the builder. Cities in the past were homogeneous because building materials and techniques were limited. Even when architectural styles changed, load-bearing masonry provided an inflexible discipline within which designers were obliged to work. Today, technology has opened the door to a bewildering array of materials, techniques, and applications. It is now possible to say, without much exaggeration, that anything that can be drawn (or plotted on a computer) can be built.

The thought of unlimited choice was once exciting. Today the realization seems to be slowly dawning on us that there is such a thing as too much choice. Just as the availability of too much rich food has proved an mixed blessing and has produced a widespread awareness of the need for controlling our input of sugar, fats, and protein, so also the rich diet of architectural extravagance has bloated our cities with too much diversity, too many thrills. Since the present variety of architectural views promotes rather than curbs excessive and self-promoting design, it is hardly surprising that design review has emerged as a disciplinary vehicle.

Historic experiences of design review in cities as disparate as Siena, Jerusalem, Berlin, and Washington, D.C., suggest that public discipline of building design does not necessarily inhibit the creativity of architects—far from it. What it does have the potential to achieve, on the other hand, is a greater quality in the urban environment as a whole. Less emphasis on the soloist and more on ensemble playing will not be a bad thing.

Index